COCKSCOMB B.. .IN

WILDLIFE ....RY

Its History, ...Fauna
for Visitors, Teac.. and Scientists

Katherine M. Emmons, Robert H. Horwich,
James Kamstra, Ernesto Saqui,
James Beveridge, Timothy McCarthy,
Jan Meerman, Scott C. Silver, Ignacio Pop,
Fred Koontz, Emiliano Pop, Hermelindo Saqui,
Linde Ostro, Pedro Pixabaj, Dorothy Beveridge,
and Judy Lumb

Illustrated by
Paula Marie DeGiorgis, Terry Lawson Dunn,
Amy Piel, Edward Boles, James Kamstra,
James Beveridge, Katherine M. Emmons,
Robert H. Horwich, Charles Koontz,
Robin Brockett, Osmany Salas,
and Judy Lumb

 A Joint Publication

Gays Mills, WI

Producciones de la Hamaca
Caye Caulker, BELIZE
and
Orang-utan Press
Gays Mills, Wisconsin, USA

Sponsors

Belize Audubon Society
P.O. Box 1001, 12 Fort Street, Belize City

The Belize Audubon Society is a non-profit, non-government membership organization dedicated to the promotion of the sustainable use and preservation of our natural resources in order to maintain a balance between people and the environment.

COCKSCOMB BASIN WILDLIFE SANCTUARY
P.O. Box 90, Dangriga, BELIZE

The Cockscomb Basin Wildlife Sanctuary is dedicated to the conservation and protection of its natural resources. By protecting the Cockscomb Basin, we protect precious renewable resources, habitat for many plants and animals and enhance stability of a healthy ecosystem.

Community Conservation Consultants
RD 1, Box 96, Gays Mills, WI 54631

The mission of Community Conservation Consultants is to catalyze, foster and encourage the involvement of local communities in the conservation process.

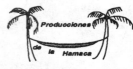

Producciones de la Hamaca
Caye Caulker, BELIZE

Producciones de la Hamaca is dedicated to:
- Celebration and documentation of Belize's rich, diverse cultural heritage,
- Protection and sustainable use of Belize's remarkable natural resources,
- Inspired, creative expression of Belize's spiritual depth.

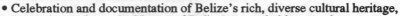

Quick Reference

Copyright © 1996   Belize Audubon Society
All rights reserved under International Copyright Conventions.

Published for the Belize Audubon Society by *Producciones de la Hamaca,*
Caye Caulker, Belize and Orang-utan Press, Gays Mills, Wisconsin,
USA

Printed in Belize by the Angelus Press, Ltd.

Library of Congress Catalog Card No. 95-072397

ISBN   0-9637982-2-7

Photographs used with permission from:
Belize Audubon Society files — pages 18, 19, 21 (top left)
Alan Rabinowitz — page 74
Carnegie Institute — page 78

Preface

Cockscomb Basin Wildlife Sanctuary: Its History, Flora and Fauna for Visitors, Teachers and Scientists is the joint, volunteer effort of many people, authors, photographers, artists, and others. Those of us who have spent time in this wonderful place have become enchanted by it and we would like to share the magic with others, Belizean visitors, the visitors who come from other countries to explore Belize, teachers who bring groups of students, and scientists who long to uncover the secrets of the forest. Thus, this book is intended to be a guidebook for the general visitor and a reference book for teachers and scientists. It is a compromise between a complete scientific treatise and a general guidebook. It is our hope that these detailed descriptions will be of interest to the general visitor and valuable both for environmental education and as a starting point for future research.

The contributors to this book include local Mayans who comprise the Sanctuary staff, other Belize Audubon Society staff and volunteers, Belizean scientists working in the Cockscomb Basin, and scientists from abroad who have worked in the Cockscomb. You can read about each of the contributors in the section entitled "About the Contributors."

Most chapters have multiple authors. Where the text was merged, all authors have been indicated at the beginning of the chapter. Where separate sections were written by one person, the authors are indicated on the individual sections. Illustrators and authors are identified in the Contributor Index.

The book is divided into three parts. Part I includes the history and descriptions of the flora and fauna of the Cockscomb Basin Wildlife Sanctuary (CBWS). Here you can read the history of Maya Center, the nearby Mayan village, and how the CBWS came to be established. You will find descriptions of many of the animals and plants that inhabit the Cockscomb Basin, including a detailed report of the successful reintroduction of black howler monkeys into the Cockscomb Basin. Checklists of mammals, amphibians, reptiles, and birds appear in the back of the book.

Part II is a guide for teachers bringing students to the CBWS, providing practical advice on how to make your visit enjoyable and educational at the same time, along with many ideas for activities. A glossary of biological and conservation concepts, along with the detailed information in Part I, provide a ready reference for anyone interested in environmental education.

Part III includes practical information for the visitor. It gives directions to the Sanctuary, details on how to make reservations, and describes the services available. Trail guides with maps and a guide to the identification of tracks are included to help you enjoy your visit.

A Quick Reference with a different logo for each chapter is shown on the right edge of the page. The Quick Reference Index is on the first page and inside the back cover. Since Part II has a black strip, the three parts are visible from the outside edge of the book.

We are very grateful to Mrs. Lydia Waight, Secretary of the Belize Audubon Society, who has helped with this book in many ways — providing historical photographs, making files available, providing detailed information, and proofreading with her eagle eyes. The many hours devoted by all the contributors on a volunteer basis is a tribute to their love of the Cockscomb Basin and desire to help with its development. All proceeds from sales of the book will go to support the CBWS. We hope you enjoy reading this book and, especially, visiting the CBWS.

Judy Lumb, Editor

CONTENTS

PART II   Environmental Education

PART III   Practical Information

Foreword

It is with great pleasure and satisfaction that I introduce this excellent book on the Cockscomb Basin Wildlife Sanctuary. Despite the passing of more than a decade since I first set foot in the Cockscomb Basin, my memories of that day are as vivid as if it had happened yesterday.

While surveying jaguars in Belize during the last months of 1982, I made my way by motorcycle to the village of Maya Center. I was told that if I wanted to find jaguars, I should follow the narrow dirt road that led west from the village into the dense forest of the Maya Mountains. A timber operation was in full swing as I drove along the deeply rutted skidder tracks that penetrated far into the Cockscomb Basin. What I saw in those first few miles impressed me deeply. Despite all the activity in the area, jaguar tracks were everywhere.

I drove my little Honda further and further into the Basin until I crested a rise at the top of a long, steep hill. Just as I came over the top, a jaguar stepped out from the forest into my path. He turned his head and looked at me as if I were just another in a long line of inexplicable intrusions and then continued on his way, disappearing into the forest on the opposite side. I got off the bike and stood in front of the dense wall of green where the jaguar had entered the forest. It was in that moment that the seed was planted, a seed that was to take root and become the focus of my life over the next few years.

In the years that have followed since I left Belize, I have worked and traveled in many parts of the world. But I can never remember more than a month going by that I did not reflect back on the people, the animals and the mystique of the Cockscomb Basin.

The fact that the authors of this book, as well as other visitors to the Cockscomb, have become completely enchanted by the Cockscomb is no surprise to me, for I, too, was one of its victims, even as I stood among the jungle-eating machinery of the timber camp. Yet, despite almost instantly realizing the beauty and richness of the Cockscomb when I first set foot there, it is only in retrospect that I can appreciate the uniqueness of the Cockscomb on a global scale.

In today's world of growing human population and increased pressures on the remaining natural habitats and resources, there is an increasingly strident cry that areas such as the Cockscomb should not be "closed" as national parks or sanctuaries, but should instead be utilized and managed by the local people for wildlife, small-scale agriculture and forest products. Others, like myself, are of the firm belief that the protection of areas as parks or sanctuaries is the only way to conserve some of the world's exceptional beauty and wildlife species for the future. Amidst such controversy, the Cockscomb Basin Wildlife Sanctuary stands as an exceptional example of a protected area and a management scheme that not only works, but benefits and is highly valued by the local people.

When I initiated efforts to protect the Cockscomb Basin, it was not for jaguars alone that I labored. I had already seen how the destruction of habitat and the unsustainable use of forest resources was decimating many of the wild areas in Belize and was leaving the forest around many local villages quiet and empty. I believed in my heart that if we could protect the Cockscomb, the local people and all Belizeans would realize what a treasure they had saved. The truth is that I never expected such a change in thinking to occur as quickly as it has. My admiration goes out to the local Mayan communities around the Cockscomb Basin Wildlife Sanctuary and to the Belizean people as a whole for their foresight and commitment.

I would like to congratulate all of the authors and illustrators for their time and effort in putting together this fine piece of work. This book is a valuable addition to the natural history literature of Belize and the Central American region. I would also like to congratulate and give my heartfelt thanks to the Government of Belize and to all those Mayan families who have helped give Cockscomb to the future generations of the world. Finally, to the jaguars who have passed on since I walked among them in the forest, you are in my heart always and you have made my heart full.

Alan Rabinowitz
Wildlife Conservation Society
Bronx, New York

PART I

Cockscomb Basin Wildlife Sanctuary

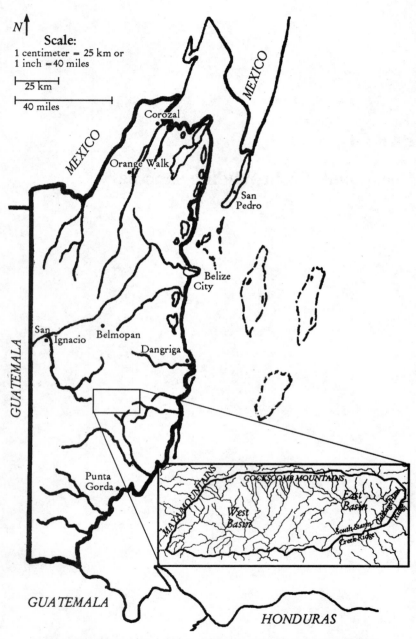

Map of Belize showing the Cockscomb Basin in relation to river systems, district towns (•) and Belize City (○)

CHAPTER 1
The Cockscomb Basin
James Kamstra

The Cockscomb Basin Wildlife Sanctuary (CBWS) is now an established and well-known part of the Belizean landscape. The area received its name from the Cockscomb Range in the Maya Mountains, a spectacular series of peaks that resembles the comb of a proud rooster. Victoria Peak is the highest of these mountains and the second highest point in Belize.

Geography
The Cockscomb Basin Wildlife Sanctuary comprises an area of about 400 km^2 on the eastern slope of the Maya Mountains in southern Belize. It contains the headwater areas for two rivers, the second highest mountain in the country and an excellent representation of the flora and fauna which typify this portion of Central America. One finds tropical humid forest at different elevations and several successional stages, upland pine forest and shrubby floodplain vegetation.

The Sanctuary is 36 kilometers east to west, and 14 north to south. Elevation ranges from a low of about 50 meters above sea level along the lower South Stann Creek to a high of 1120 m at the crest of Victoria Peak. From its easternmost point on Cabbage Haul Ridge, the reserve is only 15 km from the Caribbean Sea. The only way into Cockscomb is via the CBWS Access Road which begins at the village of Maya Center on the Southern Highway. Driving in on this narrow dirt forest road can be intriguing. Luxuriant walls of vegetation line the roadway where colorful birds often zoom from one side to the other. It pays to keep alert for you never know what larger animals might cross in front of you. Potholes and mud puddles may also add to the adventure, especially after prolonged spells of wet weather. The road is periodically graded to ensure regular passage, however.

The Cockscomb Basin has been aptly named. "Cockscomb" derives from the range of mountains on the northern fringe of the reserve which looks like a rooster's comb when seen from the east, especially from the sea. Topographically the area is dish shaped; low in the middle and surrounded by prominent ridges or low mountains on all sides. If one stands at the top of Cabbage Haul Ridge and looks west from there, the relatively level lowlands sprawl out against a backdrop of the Cockscomb Mountains, with South Stann Creek Ridge looming off to the far left and the Outlier to the right.

1

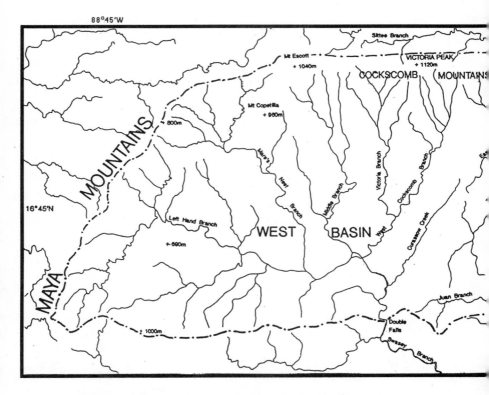

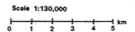 **Approximate Boundaries of the Cockscomb Basin**

Scale 1:130,000

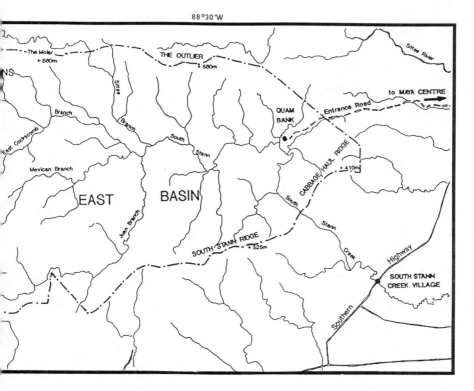

88°30'W

The Molar
+ 580m

THE OUTLIER
+ 580m

Sittee River

to MAYA CENTRE

Entrance Road

QUAM
BANK

CABBAGE HAUL RIDGE
+ 410m

Sittee

Branch

Branch

South

Stann

East Cockscomb

Mexican Branch

EAST

BASIN

Juan Branch

South

SOUTH STANN RIDGE
+ 525m

Stann

Creek

Highway

SOUTH STANN
CREEK VILLAGE

Southern

The Cockscomb Basin

Victoria Peak

There are actually two basins, each occupying approximately half of the Sanctuary, which are separated by a low ridge which forms a watershed divide. On the east side lies the upper watershed of South Stann Creek (East Basin). Immediately to the west, the West Basin feeds the Swasey Branch which joins up with Bladen Branch to form Monkey River downstream of the Sanctuary. The better known South Stann Creek Basin is lower in elevation (mostly below 200 meters) and comparatively level. By contrast, the West Basin is much more irregular topographically and difficult to access since no roads lead there. It is rimmed by higher and steeper boundaries: the Cockscomb Range to the north and the main divide of the Maya Mountains to the west. The West Basin truly is the domain of the jaguar for it is rarely visited by humans.

Cockscomb Basin is laced with literally hundreds of mostly unnamed streams and creeks. Both basins exhibit intricate dendritic patterns of feeder streams. South Stann Creek meanders across its fairly broad floodplain forming occasional oxbow ponds. Most of the river is shallow, no more than a meter in depth. At some river bends, however, holes up to 6 m deep have formed which are important sites for larger fish and other aquatic animals. Snook Eddy is one such site. South Stann Creek flows east, out of the basin through a prominent gap between two ridges. From there it flows across a very flat coastal plain towards the Caribbean Sea.

Although the West Basin occupies a similar-sized drainage basin, Swasey Branch carries a larger volume of water than South Stann Creek, indicative of higher rainfall in the western part of the reserve. Since the terrain is more undulating, the creeks are faster flowing with numerous rapids and small waterfalls present with fewer oxbows or floodplain habitat. The 20% of the West Basin that lies below 200 meters elevation is relatively level. The rest consists of broken terrain, steep creek valleys, irregularly scattered hills and ridges between streams. Drainage divides along prominent high ridges which form natural boundaries to the north, west and south sides. The Swasey Branch flows out of the basin through a spectacular 300 meter deep gorge where the river cuts through a section of the Maya Mountains. Here one also finds Double Falls, Cockscomb's most impressive waterfall.

Geology

The Cockscomb Basin is geologically part of the Maya Mountains, an isolated mountain range that dominates the southern half of Belize and marginally extends into Guatemala. Being among the oldest surface rocks in Central America, the Maya Mountains are essentially an uplifted block of Paleozoic sediments known as the Santa Rosa group. These were formed during the Pennsylvanian and early Permian periods about 250 to 300 million years ago. Rocks of the Santa Rosa group consist of sand-based and clay-based materials subjected to low grade metamorphism. In the Cockscomb area these consist primarily of quartzites and sandstones.

During their formation, the Maya Mountains rose through a period of active folding and faulting. Pressure that built up within the earth's crust caused warping and uplifting of the surface rock layers. This produced large regional fault lines aligned along a northeast to southwest axis through the basin. Presently the Maya Mountains are geologically inactive, especially in comparison to higher mountainous areas of Central America known for their volcanoes and earthquakes. Only minor tremors have been reported from Cockscomb.

The Cockscomb Basin itself is a distinct geological feature. The lower portion of the basin is a major granite intrusion that upthrusted among the older Santa Rosa rocks about 200 million years ago. A hundred million years later, all but the highest parts of the Maya Mountains were covered by the sea, at which time a limestone cap was deposited. Today extensive areas of Cretaceous limestone with impressive karst formations can be found on the north, south and west sides of the range, but not on the eastern slopes where Cockscomb is situated.

Presently, erosion and deposition continue to change the geological face of the Cockscomb, that is, the action of water is eating away at the landscape in some areas and depositing materials in others. Occasional landslides slump down steep mountain slopes and fast flowing creeks continue to scour out their beds. The heavy forest cover greatly retards this erosional process, but not altogether. Sediment deposition occurs on the lower floodplains where the speed of flowing water declines. Here oxbow ponds form along lower stretches of South Stann Creek and Swasey Branch.

Climate

Situated at 16° 45' north latitude, the Cockscomb Basin lies within the outer tropical belt and enjoys a greater range of seasonal temperatures than the inner tropical belt (less than 13°). The average annual temperature is about 25° C. The coolest months are November to February while the warmest are April to June. Average monthly temperatures range only 5° C between the warmest and coolest months, however.

There are four seasons, alternately wet and dry, though not of equal length. The main dry season (generally February to May) varies in length and intensity from year to year. The main wet season often begins with a deluge in June that may last for days. At times like these, the rain fills the numerous creeks which funnel into the South Stann Creek and Swasey Branch. Before long the rivers overflow their banks and rise over adjacent floodplains. Trees are knocked over in the process and sometimes new channels are formed. The mauger season, also called the "minidry," occurs in August or September, before the winter rainy season from October through January.

Two weather stations give specific climatic data on Cockscomb, a longterm climatic station on Cabbage Haul Lookout (about 400 m elevation), which the Belize Forest Department has operated since 1965, and a weather station at the CBWS Headquarters. But these two stations can only give us part of the weather picture. With the extent and elevation range of the Cockscomb Basin, climatic conditions are not uniform throughout. At higher elevations, the temperature is cooler and wetter. The greater flow carried by the Swasey Branch, compared to South Stann Creek with a similar drainage basin, implies that precipitation is considerably greater in the higher western half of the reserve. Average annual precipitation is about 270 cm at Cabbage Haul Lookout but is likely at least 30% more along the upper slopes of the Maya Mountains.

The Cockscomb Mountains form a prominent landmark, rising abruptly from the basin floor, and hence, have an influence upon their own climate. Many days during the dry season, the sky may be clear blue except for a puff of white cloud hugging the upper portion of Victoria Peak. The elfin woodland on top is likely trapping moisture from these clouds at a time of year when there is little atmospheric water elsewhere. Wetter and cloudier microclimatic conditions influence the vegetation here.

Prevailing easterly winds move warm moist air from the Caribbean Sea over the eastern slope of the Maya Mountains, providing abundant rainfall. This would explain the greater rainfall in the West Basin than in the East Basin. In the Chiquibul Forest which lies on the leeward side of the Maya Mountains immediately to the west of the Cockscomb Basin, rainfall is noticeably less.

Situated in the northern portion of the Caribbean Basin, Belize lies in the hurricane zone. Although rather infrequent in any one locality, when a hurricane strikes, its impacts are felt for decades. This is true in both human terms as well as for nature. In 1961, the eye of infamous Hurricane Hattie which devastated Belize City, passed through the northern part of the Cockscomb Basin. It completely leveled the forest in a wide swath. Other hurricanes such as Fifi in 1972 and Greta in 1978 passed near the Cockscomb causing exceptionally heavy rains and some wind damage, but they were minor compared to Hattie.

The flora and fauna which thrive in the Cockscomb Basin today are intricately linked to the topography, geology and climate which in turn are linked to each other. Topography, for example, influences the soils, microclimate and available moisture, which determines the natural vegetation which, in turn, provides suitable habitat for specific wildlife species. The physical setting has also affected the human history of Cockscomb. Its rugged landscape made accessibility difficult, while the nutrient poor soils limited agricultural development compared to other areas in Belize.

References

Hartshorn, G. et al. 1984. *Belize: Country Environmental Profile.* Robert Nicolait & Associates Ltd: Belize City.

Kamstra, J. 1987. *An Ecological Survey of the Cockscomb Basin, Belize.* Master's Thesis, York University, Ontario, Canada.

Walker, S. H. 1973. *Summary of Climatic Records of Belize.* Land Resources Division: Surrey, U.K.

Wright, A.C., D. Romney, R. Arbuckle and V. Vial. 1959. *Land in British Honduras: Report of the Land Use Survey Team.* Her Majesty's Stationery Office: London.

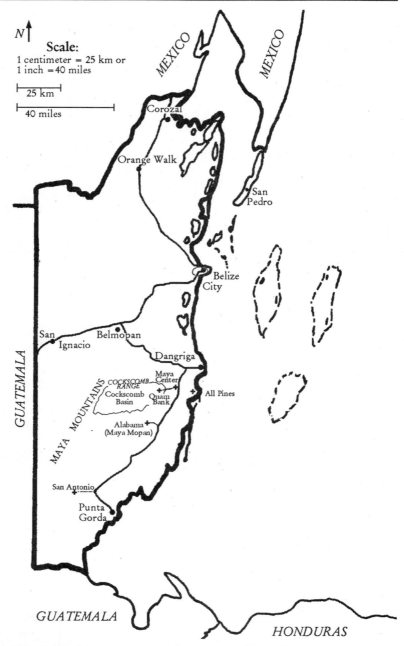

Map of Belize showing the Cockscomb Basin in relation to roads,
Belize City (◯), district towns (•) and villages
important in Cockscomb Basin history (+)

CHAPTER 2
History of the Cockscomb
Basin Wildlife Sanctuary

Ancient Maya
Judy Lumb

Like most of Belize, the Cockscomb Basin was probably utilized by preMaya people extending back at least 10,000 years. Numerous, extensive Mayan sites throughout Belize are evidence for occupation during the Preclassic period (2,000 B.C. - 250 A.D.) and the Classic period (250 - 900 A.D.). However, until very recently only two sites were known in the Cockscomb Basin.

While conducting his jaguar studies, Alan Rabinowitz stumbled onto Cuchil Balum, a minor center deep in the heart of the CBWS. The site contains four rectangular mounds, two of which are on a raised platform, a stone altar and two oblong stones. None are carved, but they may have been painted or decorated with plaster.

The Pearce Ruin was discovered by Lee Pearce, a mahogany contractor. It was officially reported by the British Museum in 1931, but was never published and subsequent attempts to locate it were unsuccessful.

Then, in the Spring of 1995, the Maya Mountain Archeological Project (MMAP), led by Peter Dunham, performed a preliminary reconnaissance of the Cockscomb Basin and rediscovered the Pearce Ruin. It is a very sizable site, among the largest in the southern half of Belize. Situated on a bluff, it consists of four major plazas surrounded by a number of massive structures and half a dozen reservoirs. The main plaza is immense, larger than 100 m square. There are also ten plain granite monuments, including a completely unique one that is shaped like a giant stone egg. A workshop where monuments were made was found nearby, along with a large carved serpent.

In addition, the MMAP team encountered two smaller, but substantial sites. Both consist of a single large plaza surrounded by sizable structures and several plain granite monuments. The MMAP crew named one of these *Hun' Tul Mo'*, meaning "one macaw" in Mopan Maya, after a single scarlet macaw that was observed there. Like other parrots, macaws mate for life and it is unusual to see one alone. The other site was named *Xa'a Yil Ha'*, "many rivers" in Mopan, because it is at the confluence of various creeks.

These sites were likely major centers in the exploitation and exchange of granite for grinding stones, essential items in every Maya kitchen. Granite was a preferred material and the Cockscomb is among few such deposits in the entire Maya area. Several grinding stones were recovered at the Cockscomb sites that appear to be made of local granite.

Maya occupation of the CBWS was evidently quite extensive, as the numerous and widely scattered obsidian blades, projectile points, pot shards, and house mounds suggest.

Expeditions to the Cockscomb Mountains
Judy Lumb

While not high as mountains go, Victoria Peak and the surrounding Cockscomb Mountains are an impressive mass of rock that rise abruptly from the lowlands, and stand above everything else. This, combined with the fact that Victoria Peak was thought to be the highest point in Belize, made them attractive to adventurers.

The first expedition to the Cockscomb Mountains in modern history was in 1888 led by then Governor Roger T. Goldsworthy. An account of the expedition by J. Bellamy, one of the scientists, was published in the Proceedings of the Royal Geographic Society of London in 1889. They began at the mouth of South Stann Creek with 15 Garifuna men (Caribs) in 5 dories. He describes how they got past the big falls as they proceeded upstream.

"At 10.30 we reached the big falls, where we were obliged to make a portage, hauling the dories over with ropes, and carrying baggage and provisions by land. The scene was a most exciting one, the mighty din of the torrents rushing between its narrow walls, the Caribs, some standing up to their armpits in the water above the falls, hauling on the ropes, others at the foot apparently regardless of the rush of water, tilting the canoes until they almost stood on end, others perched on the rocks and boulders at various points to fend off as the dories were hauled past them."

Several days later, they approached what they thought was Victoria Peak, the highest mountain in the Cockscomb Range and in the entire country of Belize.

"With great difficulty we succeeded in reaching a shoulder some 600 or 700 feet from the summit, but at this point further progress was found impossible for some of the party. Having a good rope with me, I decided to go on, and managed to scale the precipice, and having reached a projecting piece of rock, made fast my rope and assisted Mr. Allen and three Caribs to get up, Then by the aid of gnarled and stunted fig-trees, and occasionally by the rope, we succeeded in reaching the summit, and having recovered sufficient breath, celebrated the event by giving three cheers for the Queen and the Governor. . .

"The top of Mount Victoria is a thorough peak, with but little room for moving about, and an extensive view is obtained on all sides . . .

"This mountain or hill district we had explored, although so near the coast, had never been visited, and had always been enveloped in a cloud of mystery. The native imagination had peopled it with evil genii and all kinds of mysterious creatures and the main peak was said to be surrounded by a lake and unapproachable by man. It is at least something to have broken down these absurd traditions and fears, and to have shown that there is a highland district within three days' journey of Belize which might be made available as a sanatorium . . . The one thing wanting is a good road."

In 1927 and 1928, there were three expeditions into the Cockscomb Mountains. Informed by the reports from the Goldsworthy Expedition about the hazards of the river, all three started from All Pines on the coast and travelled overland using pack horses as far as they could. Herbert T. Grant, accompanied by two Kekchi Indians, Ramon and Placido Tesecun, climbed Holland Peak, but not Victoria Peak.

"About us I looked in vain for the elusive mountains. But, chancing to look up, hundreds of feet above our heads towered a tremendously steep cone-shaped peak. We were on the Cockscombs. The elevation was now 1900 feet . . . The Indians were disinclined at first to go further, being alarmed at the steepness, but I was able to persuade them . . . I shed my impedimenta, retaining only camera and instruments. To show how seriously the Indians viewed what lay ahead, they for the first time put their boots on . . .

"The summit we had reached I later identified from the 1888 map as Holland Peak . . . Ramon and Placido Tesecun were beyond praise in their loyalty, tirelessness, and bushcraft. In their company, if and when opportunity occurs again, I hope to make a fuller exploration."

He was to fulfill this wish the next April, but only after a detailed mapping expedition was conducted in February and March by J. M. Oliphant, Conservator of Forests and Duncan Stevenson, Deputy Conservator of Forests. They found that the peak climbed by the Goldsworthy Expedition was not the highest peak, and therefore, not Victoria peak.

"We were accompanied by Mr. Charles Westby, kindly lent by the Tidewater Lumber Co. for the period of the tour; the three Qeqchi (Kekchi) Indians, Ramon Tesecun, Juan Tul, and José Chuk; and Samuel Alfred and Charles Bevan in charge of the animals."

"[T]he pinnacle behind it may be the one they named Victoria; but [it] is not the highest point of the range, which lies farther to the west . . .

"Climbing up, we emerged on the main ridge (3060 feet . . .), expecting to find Victoria to the eastward. All that could be seen in that direction, however, was a continuation of the ridge on which we were standing without any marked rise in its elevation. But turning westwards we were confronted by a bold group of three peaks, separated from us by a long descending saddle, all of which were considerably higher than the point of observation, and the farthest in all reasonable probability the highest point of the range.

"This led to an immediate revision of our preconceived ideas. We assumed the third and highest mountain to be Victoria . . .

"[A]t first sight [we] were somewhat daunted by the inhospitable appearance of the eastern face of the latter. On further study the ravine or flue on its north-east side . . . looked as if it might prove negotiable . . .

"At one point in the stream-bed, foot and hand-holds were few and far between and we were glad to use the rope as an auxiliary. Thenceforward all was fairly easy going until about 100 feet from the summit, where a steep moss-covered bank afforded inadequate purchase for climbing. Ramon tackled this with help from below, and fastened the rope about 50 feet up; within a few minutes we were on the top (3680 feet) at 2.35 p.m (March 18, 1928) . . .

"We were rather aggrieved that our arrival on the summit should have coincided with the first shower of rain encountered on the trip. Visibility was not too good, and observations, photography, and sketching were all hampered to some extent . . . A paper with the signatures of the party was enclosed in a small medicine jar and, with a handkerchief, tied to a bush at the highest point. Short of building a cairn of stones there was no means of leaving a permanent mark, as any small object would soon become lost in the moss which covers the elongated summit knee-deep."

When Herbert T. Grant returned to the Cockscombs in April of 1928, he was accompanied by Placido Tesecun and Francisco Kib. They also climbed the highest peak by the same route used by the Forestry expedition.

"Reaching a point from which the summit could be seen about 100 feet above, Placido scaled a short moss-covered rock face without assistance; following, a large fragment of moss broke clear away under my feet and I was left hanging without foothold, arms buried in the moss, until Francisco threw the rope up to Placido. Except at this point, the rope was not used. From the altitude recorded here, 3620 feet (time 9.15 a.m.), I should have inferred that we were on the highest peak, although nothing was to be seen but the immediate summit, a sea of mist surrounding our feet. A handkerchief drew our attention to a little blue jar of the vaseline container type, with the signatures of the party which had been there on March 18. We added a slip of paper with our own signatures to the jar (April 19)."

Both 1928 expeditions describe the top of the highest peak as flat and elongated, not sharp as Bellamy described it. Clearly, whatever peak the Goldsworthy expedition climbed, the name "Victoria Peak" was given to the highest peak of the Cocksomb Range, the identity of which is no longer in doubt. However, it is not the highest point in Belize. That honour belongs to Doyle's Delight in the Toledo District.

In 1935 the first zoological expedition to the Cockscomb Basin was sponsored by the Carnegie Institute and led by Emmet R. Blake and Charles T. Agostini. They collected 113 birds, 15 mammals (mice, bats, squirrels, and an opossum), and 10 herpetological specimens (frogs, lizards, a toad, and a snake). Blake's report of the expedition appeared in the Carnegie Magazine —

"Modern scientific exploration in tropical lands necessitates a variety and quantity of paraphernalia unsuspected by the layman. Material required even by a modest expedition attains startling proportions in spite of one's best efforts at reduction, and the harassed expeditionist soon finds his major difficulties arising from problems of transportation in the field. . . Inland travel is practically limited to the several navigable rivers or to pack train over tortuous trails. Where these do not exist, as in the Cockscomb region, one must create and maintain one's own means of transport as best he can . . . [J]ust as it appeared that our expedition would founder beneath its own weight, arrangements were made through the ever-helpful government officials for the importation of a dozen Indians from the Maya Mountains of the southwest to serve as porters. These were hand-picked men, hardened packers and experienced woodsmen - the best that could be had . . . Our men were led by the Tescum brothers, famed Maya woodsmen . . . who had visited the Cockscombs some years previous with a government party . . .

"Agreeing upon All Pines, a well-nigh deserted outpost on the coast due east of the Cockscombs, as our rendezvous, we established a camp upon the beach . . .

"The party slowly threaded its way through the parched pinelands and finally entered the virgin wilderness of the interior. There is probably no tropical forest on earth which more richly deserves the name of 'bush' than does this primeval rain forest of the Caribbean lowlands. The vegetation is the rankest in growth and every yard of one's trail must be hewn with a machete. . .

"Only at dawn and at dusk does the forest become fully awake with unseen songsters and the sky dotted with flocks of raucous parrots. Later, as the heat of day becomes oppressive, a mighty silence descends upon the earth . . . [T]he only sounds may be the hum of insect hordes, the steady thwack, thwack, of flashing machetes and the laboured breathing of one's cargadores . . .

"No monotony attends the activities of a naturalist in the field, but there is much irksome labor undreamed of by the layman. With the collecting of specimens, one's work has just begun. Each day long hours must be spent at the skinning table preserving the rare and hard-won material. Nor does nightfall guarantee undisturbed repose. Observations of the day must be recorded in detail and a constant vigil maintained against insects and moisture lest the work of weeks be destroyed in an hour of carelessness.

"Of all the discomforts which try the patience and stamina of the museum naturalist in tropical lands none are more persistent and difficult to circumvent than are insect and allied pests. . . Among the worst offenders are sand flies, doctor flies, horseflies, bottlas flies, chiggers, seed ticks, and warree ticks; each having a special modus operandi and period of attack. Most dreaded of all, however, are beef worms, larvae of a little-known fly of the interior whose life cycle is begun with the deposition of eggs upon one's clothing or person. These soon hatch and the minute larvae, unseen and unsuspected, bore beneath the skin. There they develop into great, hairy brutes and may cause death by blood poisoning if not properly removed . . .

"A daily ritual was the removal of these parasites by an elderly Indian - an operation which held the entire camp spellbound. The appearance and subsequent eviction of each was greeted by enthusiastic exclamations of approval from the sympathetic spectators and groans from the patient. . .

"Agostini was host to thirty-nine beef worms while I escaped with one less. . . Unfortunately, several of my wounds became badly infected in spite of all precautions and I had to seek surgical attention in distant Belize. Agostini remained in the mountains with one Indian to complete the work begun and rejoined me at All Pines later. . . So ended the Carnegie Museum's expedition to the Cockscomb Mountains."

Logging
Judy Lumb

Logging has been extremely important in the history of British Honduras. Logwood and mahogany were first exploited in the lowlands of the northern half of what is now Belize. When these were depleted, loggers headed into the more rugged lands of the Maya Mountains where the job was more difficult.

Loggers may have come to the Cockscomb Basin in the eighteenth century, the era of the English buccaneers, but the first official report was from the Goldsworthy expedition in 1888 which noted that a logging presence had already been established. The 1928 exploratory expedition by the British Honduras Forestry Department was undertaken primarily to assess the area for forestry. They found that the lower part of the South Stann Creek Valley had already been depleted of mahogany near to the streams, but they suggested there may be exploitable wood farther up the valley.

From 1937 to 1962, the timber concession for the Cockscomb Basin was held by the Hulse family, first Greville Hulse and then his sons, Mervyn Hulse and Melvin Hulse. They worked both the South Stann Creek and Swasey Basin areas, cutting mahogany and cedar. Logs were floated down South Stann Creek until 1943 when a proper road was built. Then the logs were trucked out to Regalia on the Sittee River to be towed by tugboat to Belize City and loaded onto ships for export.

They had a network of roads through both the East and West Basins, including a road that went through Swasey Canyon, all of which were passable until the early 1960's. Many of the camps shown on the maps, such as Don Pedro, Go to Hell, and Middle Camp, were named by the Hulse family.

The operation employed from 140 to 300 people at any one time. Before the road was built, the headquarters of the logging operation were in Martin Bank (6 miles upstream from Locust Bank). In 1947 Cacao Branch on the Sittee River became the headquarters.

In 1961 Hurricane Hattie hit the Cockscomb Basin directly, leveling almost the entire forest and ending the Hulse logging operation in the Cockscomb Basin.

"You could walk from tree to tree without ever touching the ground," said Melvin Hulse, Sr. "Twenty-seven bridges were washed out. The Forest Department hired us to cut a fire break so if a fire would start, it would not burn the whole basin. That was the last thing we did in the Cockscomb Basin. Then we moved our operation to the Bladen Branch area which was not damaged by the hurricane."

Logging resumed in 1970 when Louis Lindo of the Cockscomb Enterprise was granted the forest concession in the Cockscomb Basin. He had worked for the Forest Department for 23 years, starting as a Forest Guard and advancing to the position of Chief Forest Officer by 1967.

"In the old days the cutting for the log trade was very selective and wasteful. They would cut down a mahogany tree, but if there was the slightest flaw, they would leave it to rot because it could not be exported as a log. But I had a small sawmill, so I used everything, cutting the logs into lumber, especially banak and mahogany. For the first two years I had my sawmill at Quam Bank, but I had a fire and lost a good inventory of lumber. I could not get insurance up there because I did not have equipment for fighting fires, so I moved the sawmill to Freshwater Creek on the Southern Highway. I still cut logs from the Cockscomb Basin and took them out to the sawmill.

"In 1970 I realigned the road [now CBWS Access Road] using a bulldozer. The next year I hired Jimmy Lindo, who had a road grader, to grade the surface of the road.

"Even with the improved road, the dry season was very short down there. We worked intensely for 6-8 weeks. I had to get other permits to work outside the Cockscomb to keep the operation going, I continued logging in the Cockscomb Basin until 1976."

The Cockscomb Minter Sawmill was established in 1978 in Quam Bank, the site of the current CBWS Headquarters by two American brothers, James and Don Smith. The sawmill was in a large building on the south side of the road. Most of the structures now used as bunkhouses were built by this logging company. In 1983, Don Smith left and took all his equipment.

Ignacio Pop, who was living in Quam Bank during the early 1980s, describes what happened next.

"A man named Warren started cutting, but he did not stay long. Next was a Mr. Kennedy who had a small, portable sawmill which he put under the building that had housed Don Smith's large one. But he had trouble getting workers because there was no housing and he did not pay enough. Then his sawmill burned and he left."

Above: *The view looking south of the CBWS Access Road in April 1986 showing the open field left by the logging camp.*

Below: *The same view looking south of the CBWS Access Road in November 1994. Vegetation has grown, limiting the long range view. The traps used by Alan Rabinowitz to study jaguars are displayed. No trapping of jaguars has been done since that study was completed. While the study provided initial information useful for the establishment of the Sanctuary, these traps did not prove totally satisfactory for live trapping. Several of the jaguars died from injuries sustained in the trap.*

The last timber concession was granted to William Depaw in November, 1984, for the area that had been declared the Cockscomb Basin Forest Reserve, an activity allowed under that status. He planned a big operation including the manufacture of plywood. Jimmy Lindo was given a contract to upgrade the roads. He had just started when Mr. Depaw came to see for himself and realized that there were not enough logs, so he decided that it was no longer financially feasible to conduct logging in the Cockscomb Basin. His conclusion was confirmed by a study of the Cockscomb Basin by the Melinda Forest Station in August of 1985 in which transects were made and no timber of commercial value was found.

Establishment of the Sanctuary
Judy Lumb

The hunting of jaguars in Belize by both Belizeans and foreigners was common until the 1980s. Bader Hassan was a big game hunter who had permission to guide such high-paying foreign clients as the Shah of Iran, even using a caged tame jaguar as bait to insure success of the hunt.

James Hyde, then Permanent Secretary for the Ministry of Natural Resources, reported that in the early 1980s a citrus farmer named Jamie Usher came to his office saying that twice he had come face to face with jaguars when harvesting his crops. He was aware of the 1945 forest ordinance limiting the hunting of wildlife, but wanted permission to shoot jaguars for his own protection. Mr. Hyde wondered why this would happen and asked the Belize Audubon Society for a study of jaguars.

About the same time, Archie Carr III, Assistant Director of the International Division of the New York Zoological Society (now Wildlife Conservation Society, WCS), found references to jaguars in Belize in hunting magazines. He concluded that there must be a sizable population of jaguars in Belize, which was welcome news because jaguars had declined significantly throughout much of their global range due to loss of habitat and hunting. He informed WCS International Division Director George Schaller and contacted Dora Weyer of the Belize Audubon Society (BAS) in 1981 to see if a jaguar study was desired.

Dr. Alan Rabinowitz, having just completed his doctoral degree at the University of Tennessee, was recruited by WCS Director Schaller to do a study of jaguars in Belize. He first surveyed the entire country to determine the status of the great cats. He found that Belize had a surprisingly healthy population of jaguars.

More than anywhere else in Belize, Rabinowitz was impressed with the Cockscomb Basin because of its remarkably high jaguar densities and its topographic configuration, rugged terrain protected by mountain ridges on all sides. So, he chose the Cockscomb Basin for his two-year (1983-4) jaguar study.

At that time the Cockscomb Basin had few human inhabitants, only one small Mayan village (see History of Maya Center) and a declining logging operation. The logging operation had constructed primitive roads which provided access into the remote areas and the people of the Mayan village became Rabinowitz's friends and supporters. These experiences provided material for his book, *Jaguar: One Man's Battle to Establish the World's First Jaguar Preserve*, which drew attention to the remarkable Cockscomb Basin.

Rabinowitz trapped seven jaguars and put radio collars on each one so he could determine what they needed to survive - how much area each one required, what they ate, and how their territories overlapped with other jaguars.

Using the results of his study Rabinowitz, with the help of Archie Carr III and members of the BAS, persuaded the Government of Belize that the Cockscomb Basin was unique and should be set aside to preserve habitat for jaguars. In 1984 the Cockscomb Basin Forest Reserve was established with a "No Hunting" declaration.

But, the forest reserve status allowed timber concessions and one had been granted, so, although the "No Hunting" declaration protected the jaguar itself, their habitat was not protected.

Hon. Dean Lindo, Minister of Natural Resources, signs the Statutory Instrument that created the Cockscomb Basin Wildlife Sanctuary in 1986 as Belize Audubon Society Executive Director Walter (Mickey) Craig looks on.

In a meeting with Chief Forestry Officer, H. C. Flowers, and Permanent Secretary of Natural Resources, James Hyde, the BAS learned that 1,456 hectares (3,640 acres) had been excluded from this timber concession. Representatives of the BAS, World Wildlife Fund of the United States (WWF-U.S.), *Centro Agronomico Tropical de Investigacion y Enseñanza* (CATIE) and WCS requested that it be designated as a wildlife sanctuary.

The Cockscomb Basin Wildlife Sanctuary (CBWS) was created by Statutory Instrument No. 32 of 1986, and was signed into law by Hon. Dean Lindo, Minister of Natural Resources, on February 26, 1986, at the Belize National Conservation Conference, in the presence of many Belizean and international dignitaries. This historic occasion was the first time a Statutory Instrument was signed outside of the Parliament.

The next August, for the sum of $5,000 BZ, the BAS purchased the buildings remaining at Quam Bank from the lumber company, two timber houses and two concrete houses. All four of these structures have been used as bunkhouses for visitors at the CBWS Headquarters.

Hon. Florencio Marin, Minister of Natural Resources, signs the Statutory Instrument that expanded the Cockscomb Basin Wildlife Sanctuary in 1990.

Rabinowitz wrote to the Belize Audubon Society in 1986—

"I met with Prime Minister Manuel Esquivel. He expressed pleasure at the publicity that Belize has received in the United States through popular magazine articles about Cockscomb Basin and the jaguar project, and pledged once again to do everything he can in helping us to set up the Cockscomb Basin for tourism."

But the 1,456 hectares of the Sanctuary was hardly sufficient. In fact, it was only enough to support one jaguar. Belizean environmentalists continued to lobby for expansion of the Cockscomb Basin Wildlife Sanctuary. Their efforts came to fruition on November 6, 1990, when Hon. Florencio Marin, Minister of Natural Resources, signed the Statutory Instrument which expanded the CBWS to include the entire Cockscomb Basin, a total of 40,800 hectares (102,000 acres).

In 1995 some 16,000 hectares were added to connect CBWS with Bladen Branch Nature Reserve to the south. This provides a contiguous, combined protected area of over 100,000 hectares.

The Cockscomb Basin Wildlife Sanctuary has received international recognition. In 1988 the IUCN declared the Sanctuary

*"The Major Achievement in
Cat Conservation for the Triennium."*

The CBWS was honoured by a visit from H. R. H. Prince Philip, President of World Wildlife Fund – International, in November of 1988, when he presented WWF's Conservation Award to Ignacio Pop for his work to establish the CBWS. At that time, H.R.H. planted a mahogany tree which has grown over 30 feet in the past 7 years and now graces the CBWS Headquarters.

Development and Management of the Sanctuary
Judy Lumb and Ignacio Pop

In 1984 the Government of Belize (GOB) asked the BAS to manage the protected area which was to become the CBWS. A memorandum of agreement written by James Hyde, then Permanent Secretary to the Ministry of Natural Resources, formed a unique partnership between the GOB and the BAS to manage protected areas declared under the National Parks System Act of 1981. This agreement was amended in 1987 and expanded in 1995. The Forest Department under the Ministry of Natural Resources handles the official administration such as approving permits to do research. All other tasks are carried out by the BAS and its staff at the site.

The initial development of the CBWS was led by Walter Craig (Mickey), the Executive Director of the BAS from 1985 to 1988. He describes the early efforts —

H.R.H. Prince Philip planting mahogany tree in 1988 | *The same tree*
with Therese Rath and Ernesto Saqui watching | *in 1995*

Ignacio Pop with his award from the World Wildlife Fund

"From the beginning, the CBWS was supported by WWF. The first grant was funded in 1985. The first Management Committee was appointed in 1985 by the BAS Board and Ignacio Pop and his son, Pedro, were hired as the first Wardens. We took in some carpenters from Scotland Half-Moon and began to fix up the buildings left from the timber operations for use as bunkhouses and Park Headquarters.

"Mike Konecny helped a lot. He was there doing research sponsored by the National Geographic Society. He and some students from Goshen College cleared the first trails. In the beginning the problem was transportation, but Mike had a 4-wheel drive Toyota. He left the Toyota at the end of his studies and the National Geographic Society donated it to the BAS, the first vehicle ever owned by BAS.

"At first it was possible to drive as much as 13 km beyond Quam Bank. You were really getting into the wilderness back there. But there was a flood in August of 1985 which washed away the timber bridge west of the CBWS Headquarters, so that was the end of vehicular access beyond the Headquarters."

The United States Peace Corps assigned Volunteer Daniel Taylor, a specialist in wildlife management, to the CBWS in September of 1986. His project was to make the CBWS functional as a wildlife sanctuary and accessible to visitors. The basic facilities were developed, including a bunkhouse with cooking facilities, bathroom, rainwater collection vat, and trails. The first operational plan was developed in 1987 and a brochure prepared to inform the public about the CBWS.

The Park Director, Ernesto Saqui, was hired in May of 1987 and continues in this position today. Other wardens have included Pedro Pop, Ignacio Pop, Elegorio Sho, Hermelindo Saqui, Alfonso Ical, Maricio Bolan, Galvino Pau, Emiliano Pop, and Pedro Pixabaj.

The Cockscomb Basin attracted other scientists, including Ben Nottingham (for whom Ben's Bluff is named) and James Kamstra, all of whom helped to develop the CBWS.

A Canadian biology student, Melanie Watt, was instrumental in attracting support from Jaguar (cars) of Canada by drawing the connection between the jaguar cats and the jaguar cars. She came to Belize in 1985, and participated in the Cross Country Classic, Belize's Easter bicycle race, to raise funds and call public attention to the new CBWS. She conducted research in the Cockscomb for 5 months and wrote about her experiences in *Jaguar Woman: One Woman's Struggle to Preserve the Jaguars of Belize.* Through her efforts, a contribution of $50,000 US was made by Jaguar (cars) to the World Wildlife Fund designated for support of CBWS.

Ignacio Pop and his family were among the Mayans that were living in Quam Bank when Alan Rabinowitz arrived to do his jaguar study. He tells of the scientific studies—

"Mike Konecny start to trap jaguarundi before Alan leave. He put little chickens in his trap. He caught armadillo, gibnut, tayra and, finally, jaguarundi.

"I help Ben Nottingham with another study. He measure land into several quadrants and put many little trails. We look at every little piece for tracks. He ask me question about what each track is. The farthest piece was 3 mile away. We even watch these pieces in the night. If you see a spider, an owl, a frog, you have to mark it down.

"While Mike is here, that's the time they hire me as a watchman in Maya Center. They have a cable gate and I have to stop every vehicle and ask what they would do. I tell them it now a Sanctuary and they cannot hunt. It was funny! They all surprised, want to know what I doing stopping traffic on the road.

"The sawmill had a watchman for the equipment they had left until the Mennonites bought it and take all they can. That was the end of logging. Then I and my son, Pedro, do all the work (in Quam Bank) - clean the cabins, clean the yard and such.

"Then Mickey Craig (Executive Director of Belize Audubon Society) bring Dan Taylor. He asked me who could do the job of Director. Who is educated good and can run the park? I know only **Ernesto Saqui is.**"

CBWS Staff in November, 1994. (from left) Galvino Pau; Emiliano Pop; Ernesto Saqui, Park Director; Ignacio Pop; Osmany Salas, Belize Audubon Society Protected Areas Manager; and Hermelindo Saqui. (Alfonso Ical not shown)

On March 29, 1993, a new Visitor Center was opened with a museum display created by Peace Corps Volunteer Bonnie Gestring. Depicted are the geology, climate, history, flora and fauna of the CBWS. The number of visitors to the CBWS has increased each year from 256 in 1986 and 1,540 in 1987 to over 5,000 in 1994.

The CBWS has been supported from many sources. In 1992 Sharon Matola led a fund-raising event for the CBWS called "Women on the Top." Women in administrative positions from the Belize Center for Environmental Studies, Programme for Belize, and the Belize Zoo climbed Victoria Peak, raised $4,000 for CBWS, and placed a new Belize flag on the top of Victoria Peak.

Support has also come from many other sources, including donations from visitors, fees charged, and the sale of items such as this book. A number of volunteer groups have made steps, bridges, benches, picnic tables and trails, including the Belize Youth Conservation Corps, Raleigh International, Rainforest New York, and the British Forces in Belize.

A recent grant (1994-96) from the National Resources Management and Protection Project, jointly funded by U.S. AID and WWF, supported a major upgrade of visitor facilities and the CBWS Access Road.

Research in the Sanctuary
Judy Lumb

Many research projects have been carried out in the CBWS on a variety of subjects. After the first expedition by Blake and Agostini in 1935, Stephen M. Russell collected birds in 1958 and 1959. The jaguar study of Alan Rabinowitz with Ben Nottingham's assistance was from 1983 to 1984. Timothy McCarthy, M.L. Reed and W. B. Burton collected small mammals in April of 1984. Michael Konecny studied the smaller cats, jaguarundi, ocelot, margay, and the tayra. Daniel Taylor did a reptile study during his tenure as a Peace Corps Volunteer, and studied bats in 1994. Jan Meerman and Tineke Boomsma have studied butterflies, dragonflies and damselflies. Philip Elliot netted and banded birds. Christina Colon surveyed attitudes of the nearby community of Maya Center in regard to the CBWS. Jonathon Lyon initiated a phenology study which has been continued by the CBWS staff. Jeremy F. Jacobs collected mammals in May of 1995.

Several research projects have been used directly in the preparation of this book. James Kamstra did a complete ecological survey of the Cockscomb Basin in 1986. His Master's Thesis has been used ever since by scientists working in the CBWS and much of this information is now included here. In 1992 Katherine M. Emmons conducted environmental education research which is the basis for her many contributions to this book. The recent translocation of black howler monkeys, which was directed by Fred Koontz and Robert Horwich, is described in detail in Chapter 8.

CBWS welcomes research projects which aim to increase scientific knowledge and are consistent with its primary purpose as a wildlife sanctuary. Projects must fit within the limits set by the laws of the Government of Belize concerning protected areas. The CBWS is not to be disturbed in any way. The following activities are prohibited: hunting; fishing; removal of plants (even dead wood), rocks, or cultural artifacts; land clearance; exploitation of any forest product; introduction of any plant, animal, chemical or mineral. No instrument for hunting or trapping may be brought into the Sanctuary. Only under special circumstances by special permit can samples of any kind be removed for analysis. Potential researchers should contact the BAS for more information.

History of Maya Center
Ernesto Saqui

The history of Maya Center is also my history. My ancestors are Mopan Maya (*Mopaneros*) who moved from Guatemala to establish the village of San Antonio in the Toledo district of Belize over 100 years ago. The Government of Belize granted them land as an Indian Reservation. For many years we practiced our sustainable rotating milpa farming system on this land. But the boundaries were never defined. By the early 1970s other individuals were encroaching on the land we thought was reservation land. The available land was no longer enough to feed all the people.

In 1973 my uncle, Elogio Sho, went north into the Stann Creek District to look for land. He settled in Alabama, a banana plantation which had collapsed just before he arrived. Gradually 10 households from four families joined him, including the Shos(3), Bolons (4), Pops(2) and the Saquis(1).

We called it Maya Mopan and established a church, a school and a clinic there. But we did not thrive in this area. First, it was too far from the main highway and we had no transportation to get our produce to market.

Also, we had a dispute with the Tush family, another group of Indians, both Kekchi and Mopan who had come from Pueblo Viejo in the Toledo District after we did and settled on the other side of Waha Leaf Creek.

So we decided to leave Maya Mopan. My uncle took some of us on January first, 1976, to find another place to establish a village. We went 16 miles north to Cabbage Haul Creek, the site of the current village of Maya Center.

We stayed and built a camp while my uncle went back to Maya Mopan for the others, all the people, dogs and chickens, everything. By January fifth we were all living on Cabbage Haul Creek.

We had come to this new place and knew it as part of the Thornton estate. One day Donald Hoo from Jamaica visited my uncle. It seemed he had recently bought that part of the Thornton estate where we were squatting. He did not drive us off, but he made it known that we were illegal.

We appealed to the Government of Belize which bought 1,000 acres on the east side of the Southern Highway from Donald Hoo for us to use as farmland and 50 acres on the west side of the highway for a village site. We named the new village Maya Center because we wanted to identify ourselves as a Mayan group.

Following the establishment of Maya Center, Elogio Sho appointed himself Chairman of the first Village Council. A dedicated member of the People's United Party (PUP), he was later elected and held the post until 1984. But his support was not universal. In 1978 four families moved up to Quam Bank, the current location of the CBWS Park Headquarters, because they did not agree with his leadership and because they wanted to make their traditional milpa plantations in rolling hills like the land they left behind in San Antonio. Other families from Maya Center moved to Quam Bank in 1982. Some of the men worked for the logging company but most had small farms and hunted for a living. They all kept their own separate life according to their traditions.

The settlers remaining in Maya Center had built a church and a school out of natural materials like their houses. I was the initial unpaid teacher. I had started high school in Punta Gorda, but had to leave without finishing when my family moved north.

In 1978 the Roman Catholic Church of Dangriga took over support of the school and a principal named Norris Williams was hired. The school achieved official government recognition with an enrollment of 22 students.

I was given the opportunity to finish high school at Ecumenical College in Dangriga and sent to a Youth Forum in Memphis for leadership training.

In 1982 Baptist missionaries came to Maya Center and changed Elogio Sho's way of thinking. He no longer supported the Catholic Church and the school. I ran against him in the 1982 Village Council election, but because of the PUP strength in the country, the people voted for my uncle.

After the United Democratic Party (UDP) won the general election in December, 1984, the people of Maya Center demanded that Chairman Sho be impeached. The Minister of Local Government, the Honorable Philip Goldson, dissolved the 7-member Village Council and appointed Ignacio Pop, a Justice of the Peace, as the temporary Chairman. In January of 1985 I was elected Village Council Chairman, a post I still hold.

Elogio Sho moved near Belmopan on the Hummingbird Highway because he could never allow anyone to rule over him.

Four families moved with him, but two returned the next year and were accepted back by the people of Maya Center village.

I have always admired my uncle for his leadership and his power. Even now I check on him through other people and I am told that he also checks on me. I hope he is proud of what I have accomplished. He used to say of me, "I pulled you out of the garbage and made something of you." I hope that one day he and I can drink from the same cup again.

At the same time Elogio Sho was packing to leave Maya Center, the group of families living in Quam Bank had been told they had to leave because the area had been declared the Cockscomb Basin Wildlife Sanctuary.

The Baptist missionaries had also converted them and their leader, Margarito Bolon, was now a Baptist minister. They wanted to return to Maya Center under my leadership, but now there was a religious dispute. When they left in 1978 they were Catholic, but now they were Baptist. In this case, however, a compromise was reached. They said they could work with us, but they would not worship with us.

After 1985 Maya Center flourished. The government built a new school, replacing the one made of natural materials, a football field, wells with pumps, a health clinic, latrines, a community center and 2 feeder roads.

As the villagers attempted to better their lives they wanted to apply for loans from a government agency called the Development Finance Corporation (DFC). Proof of land ownership was required as security, so in 1989 the land was subdivided to give each family 25 - 30 acres and a lot in the village.

Since 1993 the village has gotten a water system, electricity, streets in the village, and telephones.

Community Conservation
Ernesto Saqui

When the Cockscomb Basin Wildlife Sanctuary was first established, the removal of several families that were living in Quam Bank generated some resentment. The story of the evolution of attitudes of the people of Maya Center toward the Sanctuary shows what can be accomplished by communication, patience, understanding and cooperation. It is a model of community-based conservation. Ignacio Pop tells what happened to him—

"One day we get a paper from the Government saying we have to leave at a certain time. They don't even give help to move. We just have to go. That's all.

"I am mad for awhile. When they hire me as a warden, I start to feel good. But only I and my son, Pedro, get hired. What about all the others? They have no benefit from the place. In Maya Center, if you make a plantation, nothing grows, only citrus and that takes chemicals. But up in Quam Bank where it is a little hilly, everything grows.

"Then I read a book, *Natural History of Costa Rica* by Dan Janzen. This made me realize it (CBWS) was good. In Toledo now you cannot get fish to eat. What destroy it is they use net and trawler. It used to be in the forest you get tapir, deer, but now they scarce.

"When we first come to Quam Bank, every day we fish plenty fish. You want to hunt - see antelope, easy. Then I see they are finishing. No more fish in the river. You have to go up further and further to find deer.

"What destroy it is we. In Toledo there is only small bush, no forest. I see how my children will never see these wildlife except we save it. I always thank for what Alan has done. Without him, it would be all gone. Now for our children we have a nice place for the future.

"Some of our visitors tell me they take this place like heaven. They don't want to go back home. There is lone tall buildings - everything build up.

"If I had not read that book, I don't know what I would think now. I see that country (Costa Rica) profit out of it, the government and the people. Now the people come here and buy carving or basket. Why should we kill all the wildlife, brush down the forest? You cut a tree you never know if you are destroying a medicine. In this area we have a lot of bush medicine.

"When I start to work, still they come to hunt. Then they stop hunt in the park because they see the benefit. For the starting nothing come out good, but for the longer time it come out better."

At first I (Ernesto Saqui) saw that conservation was a foreign idea to the villagers of Maya Center. The people felt that one man came and took away everything. A strange thing had been started and nobody knew why. They said —

"The jaguar is protected but people are disregarded. Why would you protect the jaguar and give them this beautiful place? They will be there anyway. They always have been, so they always will be. How will the Sanctuary make my life better? Make me a better person?"

The transition took three years, but they eventually changed their minds. How did it happen? First, a local person has to be in charge. No matter how much a foreigner may be liked, they will always be foreign. I understand the way the villagers think. I am one of them. The fears they feel, I feel. Their concerns are my concerns, too. The same questions they ask, I ask myself, too. That is what makes us come closer together.

We can empower each other. We are designing these things ourselves and want to make them work to our advantage. We create conditions for fellow members that eventually work to our own advantage. If I were to talk with them in English, I would never hit the points. This is grassroots work in the mother tongue.

The second ingredient is the community approach. After H.R.H. Prince Philip left, I brought all the Village Council leaders, the ones who ask the questions, up to the Sanctuary, along with the officials from the Forest Department and the BAS. The meeting did not really change any minds, but it started them thinking.

For the entire community, I developed a community awareness program with slides and a video made for the TV program *Belize all* *Over*. I held a series of discussions in Maya Center and the surrounding villages, Red Bank, Maya Mopan, San Roman, Santa Cruz, and Georgetown. I went to the schools in the same villages and civic groups such as the 4H, Girl Guides, and the Scouts. I let them tell me what they think about the Sanctuary. The schools did tree-planting. It took eight months in 1988 and into 1989, until I went to the United States for a 4-month internship in Wildlife Management.

Gradually, Maya Center villagers began to see the advantages of the Sanctuary for them. Some people found employment as wardens and guides in the Sanctuary.

Tourists were coming and the villagers found that they bought Mayan crafts. At that time the gate was at Ignacio Pop's house and everyone went there to sell their crafts. It was clay bead city! The children did not want to go to school. We had to stop that, so we decided to make a building.

That's how the Maya Center Women's Craft Cooperative began in August of 1988. The first year was not so good, but after two years, it looked like they could do business. By then about twenty women and their husbands were involved. They said it was good. They saw the economic benefit to them. But there is another reason behind the arts and crafts project, the preservation of culture. It represents who we are in this modern age.

These women also monitored the gate and registered visitors to the Sanctuary. The cooperative had a crisis in 1989 when jealousies based on political, religious and economic differences led to a partial burning of the cooperative building on September 30, 1989. However, in recent times the community has been able to pull together and its economic future looks bright as new ways are being discussed to obtain benefits from tourism.

The success of Maya Center made the other communities jealous. So, I had another meeting with them. They said that it was time to divert some of these tourists to their villages.

They had several suggestions for their own tourist operations. Some people want to take tourists up the Swasey Branch to see scarlet macaws. There is a nice waterfall in the buffer zone. Maya Mopan has a small Maya ruin. Others want to rent bicycles or conduct horseback rides. As a result of that meeting, the Craft Shop in Maya Center now also sells crafts made in these other villages.

Maria Pau and Dora Pau, two members of the Maya Center Women's Craft Cooperative, with Maya crafts available for sale in the Craft Center

The Role of Conservation
Katherine M. Emmons

Wildlife sanctuaries, reserves and national parks are all protected areas that help us conserve natural resources. The Cockscomb Basin Wildlife Sanctuary exists not only to protect our favorite species of wildlife, but to also protect an entire web of life. Cockscomb is most famous for its jaguars. Yet, the protection of these large cats depends on the health of their environment. The jaguars depend on the availability of their prey for survival. In turn, the prey (deer, armadillos, peccaries, and other animals) rely on the availability of their own food, such as vegetation and invertebrates. The jaguar can be successfully protected only if every link in its food chain is preserved.

Conservation is especially important in light of the rapid rates of deforestation throughout Central America. Belize is one of the few countries where choices can still be made to conserve the forested areas and to resist converting every bit of land into pasture or crops. Cockscomb may receive a lot of attention for its role in allowing plants and animals to live naturally, but it serves even broader purposes. By protecting the forest, the diversity of life in the area is also maintained. Without it, species that have never been studied for possible use to humans could be lost forever. Plants with medicinal value, for instance, can never be tested if they are all destroyed without thought to the future. In addition, allowing the vegetation in the Cockscomb Basin to grow naturally protects the water resources of a large area of Belize. The forest cover holds the soil in place and allows it to soak up the heavy rains like a sponge. In deforested areas, runoff causes severe erosion locally, and flooding and siltation downstream can affect everything from agriculture to sea fishing.

The purpose of Cockscomb can be easily understood when it is contrasted with the purpose of a zoo. One of the main purposes of a zoo is to exhibit animals for visitors to see. Zoos also play important roles in education and in animal breeding, but they are not able to maintain the intricate relationships between plants, animals and microorganisms that are found in nature. The animals in zoos have either been removed from nature or born in captivity. They rely on humans for all their basic needs. Zookeepers provide these animals with food, water, shelter (including protection) and living space. A veterinarian attends to them regularly. In contrast, animals at Cockscomb are not exhibited so that visitors can easily see them. They are wild and they come and go as they please. They must find their own food and protect themselves and their young from predators. The multitudes of species of plants, microorganisms, insects, birds, fish, reptiles, amphibians, and mammals all interact in complex processes which keep the web of life healthy. The removal of one of these components can affect the rest forever.

References

Bellamy, J. 1889. Expedition to the Cockscomb Mountains, British Honduras. *Proc. Roy. Geogr. Soc. London* 11: 542-552.

Bill of Sale, Minter Naval Stores, Ltd. to Belize Audubon Society, August 8, 1986.

Blake, E. R. 1935. The Invincible Cockscombs. *The Carnegie Magazine* 9(4): 99-104.

Colon, C.P. 1990. An Investigation into the Status of Environmental Conservation Education in Belize, Central America. Master's Thesis. New York University: New York, N.Y.

Cockscomb Management Committee, First Report to the World Wildlife Fund (1 February 1985 - July 15, 1985).

Coe, Michael D. 1987. *The Maya.* Thames and Hudson: London.

Conway, Greg. Maya Mountain Archeological Project. Interview by Judy Lumb, May 6, 1995.

Craig, Walter. Interview by Judy Lumb, November 22, 1995.

Dunham, Peter. Memorandum to Osmany Salas, May 23, 1995.

Grant, Herbert T. 1927. The Cockscombs Revisited. *Geogr. J.* 70: 564-572.

Grant, Herbert T. 1929. A Second Cockscombs Expedition in 1928. *Geogr. J.* 73: 138-144.

Hulse, Melvin, Sr. Interview by James Kamstra, April 24, 1986.

Hyde, James. Memorandum of Understanding M16/7/6/84 (95) to the Belize Audubon Society, December 7, 1984.

Hyde, James. Interview by Judy Lumb, March 2, 1995.

Janzen, D.H., ed. 1983. *Costa Rican Natural History.* University of Chicago Press: Chicago, IL.

Lindo, Louis. Interview by Judy Lumb, November 15, 1995.

Neal, R.H. Amended Memorandum of Understanding M16/7/6/84 (95) to the Belize Audubon Society, April 16, 1987.

Oliphant, J. M., and Duncan Stevenson. 1929. An Expedition to the Cockscomb Mountains, British Honduras, in March, 1928. *Geogr. J.* 73:123-137.

Protected Areas Management Agreement between the Government of Belize, the Forest Department, and the Belize Audubon Society, November 15, 1995.

Pop, Ignacio. Interview by Judy Lumb, November 9, 1994.

Rabinowitz, A.R. 1986. *Jaguar: One Man's Battle to Establish the World's First Jaguar Preserve.* Arbor House: New York, NY.

Rabinowitz, A.R. 1986. Report to the Belize Audubon Society.

Timber Concession to William Depaw, November 8, 1984.

Waight, Lydia. 1986. Belize National Conservation Conference. *Belize Audubon Society Bulletin* 18 (1): 1-2.

Waight, Lydia. 1990. CBWS Expanded, Protected Area Now 102,000 Acres. *Belize Audubon Society Newsletter* 22 (3): 1,5.

Waight, Lydia. Interview by Judy Lumb, March 2, 1995.

Watt, Melanie. 1989. *Jaguar Woman: One Woman's Struggle to Preserve the Jaguars of Belize.* Key Porter Books, Ltd: Toronto.

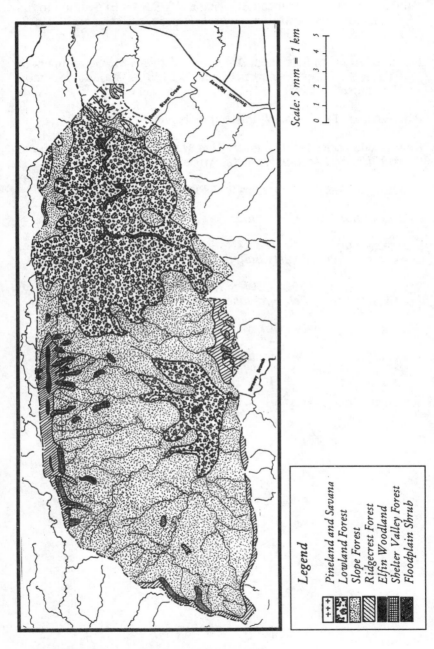

Scale: 5 mm = 1 km

Legend

Pineland and Savana
Lowland Forest
Slope Forest
Ridgecrest Forest
Elfin Woodland
Shelter Valley Forest
Floodplain Shrub

Vegetation of the Cockscomb Basin

CHAPTER 3
Vegetation of the
Cockscomb Basin
James Kamstra, Katherine M. Emmons,
Scott Silver and Judy Lumb

The vegetation pattern of any area is a reflection of climate (precipitation and temperature), soils, topography and disturbance. With a warm year-round climate and abundant precipitation, the Cockscomb Basin is covered by a broad-leaved evergreen tropical forest. Elevation differences result in temperature and moisture variations which in turn contribute to a diverse range of plant species associations. In addition, Cockscomb has a varied terrain including river floodplains, slopes and ridge crests. Each of these creates unique habitat conditions and, therefore, unique plant communities. Soils on the forest floor are granite-based; they are lower in nutrients than the limestone-based soils which are typical of many areas of Belize.

Continuous forest stretches across the Cockscomb Basin but nearly all of it has been affected by disturbance of one kind or another. Five types of disturbance have contributed to the present vegetation pattern. Wind storms, flooding, and some fires are natural events. Other fires, shifting cultivation and lumbering are human-induced.

It has been estimated that when Hurricane Hattie passed through the basin in 1961, 90% of the canopy trees were toppled in a 50 km wide swath. One of the logging operators reported that most of the basin was a chaotic tangle of logs and debris following that storm. Regrowth has been remarkably rapid in the lower basin since then. On some of the higher ridges, however, vegetation has been slower to reestablish itself. This is most apparent in the upper Cockscomb Mountains where fire followed the hurricane. Without vegetative cover, the steep slopes and abundant rainfall eroded away much of the soil. Forest has not returned there to this day.

Because Belize lies in a hurricane belt, the incidence of occasional severe wind storms has influenced the natural forest structure here. It is sometimes called "hurricane climax forest" since nearly all areas are eventually hit. Perhaps averaging no more than once every several hundred years on a given site, this is frequent enough to influence structure or species composition. In other tropical forest regions such as Costa Rica or the Amazon Basin, where hurricanes virtually never happen, the forest is taller with more prominent emergent trees and a less tangled understory.

A distinctive type of thicket vegetation is adapted to frequent flooding. During periods of high rainfall, the larger creeks of the lower floodplains overflow their banks, inundating adjacent lands. Fast flowing flood waters will even knock down or uproot trees.

Fire's influence is most apparent on Cabbage Haul Ridge at the eastern rim of the Cockscomb Basin. Here, well-drained sandy soils create a dry microclimate that is more prone to fire. Occasionally fires will move over the ridge, burning the accumulated long grasses, brackens, shrubs and even trees. Caribbean pine (*Pinus caribaea*), being more tolerant of fire than most trees, dominates the landscape. Since silty or clay rich soils, which hold moisture better, underlie most of the basin, other areas are less affected by fire.

Shifting cultivation was practiced in the vicinity of Quam Bank until 1985, just prior to establishing the Sanctuary. Natural succession is very rapid and after a few years there are no obvious signs of former milpas (temporary plantations) other than an absence of large trees. Even the thatch-roofed structures soon decay under the humid canopy of young trees.

Logging operations have disturbed most of Cockscomb at one time or another. Selective tree cutting was employed where a few high value species such as mahogany, cedar and banak were sought out and removed. Numerous roads and log skidder trails had to be pushed through to access the targeted trees which meant that many non-target trees were damaged or destroyed in the process. Since large scale clearcutting did not occur, the forest was able to regenerate rapidly in the gaps following the disturbance. In the more affected East Basin, there are few tall emergent trees, a profusion of shrub and vine tangles in the understory, patches of tall thickets and an abundance of early successional tree species.

No forestry operations have worked the West Basin since Hurricane Hattie hit in 1961. Today, visitors would find little evidence of the activities that once occurred there. The experienced eye, however can still pick out the old skidder trails by ruts on the forest floor and by the linear understory thickets. Even in the East Basin where logging continued until the mid 1980s, the signs left by the chainsaw and lumber truck are diminishing year by year. The Victoria Peak Trail that heads west from Quam Bank, formed the main logging road. A few years without maintenance allowed the wooden bridges to collapse and the jungle to reclaim the roads. Any linear tangles in the forest understory are sure to have been logging tracks.

Broad-leaved evergreen tropical humid forest typifies the Cockscomb Basin Wildlife Sanctuary. No one has yet determined all of the species of plants which grow here. There are undoubtedly hundreds of tree species alone, and countless vines, shrubs, epiphytes, herbs, mosses, ferns and fungi. The vegetation pattern is highly complex with such a varied topography, disturbance history and rich diversity of species. The pattern of vegetation communities found in the CBWS is shown on page 34.

Pines on Cabbage Haul Ridge, the eastern edge of the Cockscomb Basin

Pine Forest

Pineland is restricted to the easternmost part of the reserve, primarily Cabbage Haul Ridge and vicinity. Caribbean pine (*Pinus caribaea*) dominates the landscape, giving a temperate zone appearance to this tropical setting. The pines may grow in an open woodland or be widely spaced, forming a pine savanna. Open grassland, occasional shrub tangles and glades with bracken-like ferns three meters tall occur among the pineland.

The pineland grows on well-drained, poor sandy soil overlying granitic bedrock. Fires occur at irregular intervals, normally every 5 to 15 years. The plants that grow here, including the pines, are adapted to these periodic fires. As a result, pineland contrasts the rest of the basin not only by its openness, but also its low species diversity.

38

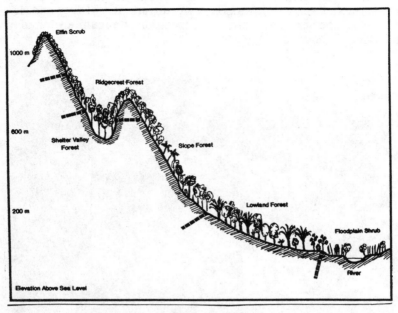

Vegetation in relation to elevation

Lowland and Slope Forests

Lowland and slope forests are both broad-leaved forests, the most widespread vegetation in the Cockscomb Basin. It consists of a diverse mix of evergreen with some semi-evergreen tropical hardwood species. While the canopy is composed of many different trees, some co-dominant species are apparent. The cohune palm (*Attalea cohune*) is one of the most numerous and conspicuous. Cohune-dominated forest occupies about 80% of the East Basin and about 20% of the West Basin. Some of the co-dominants include mountain trumpet (*Pourouma aspera),* ironwood (*Dialium guianense*), quamwood (*Schizolobium parahybum*), negrito (*Simauruba glauca*), prickly yellow (*Zanthoxylum kellermanii*), polewood (*Xylopia frutescens*) and yemeri (*Vochysia hondurensis*). This forest varies in structure and species composition across the Cockscomb Basin, influenced by slope, wetness, age, and elevation.

Much of the landscape, particularly in the West Basin, occurs on steep slopes which support a somewhat different type of forest than the level lowlands. Tree ferns, for example, grow best on undulating terrain. Many tree species grow within certain elevation ranges. The cohune palm grows primarily below 200 meters, whereas the santa maria (*Calophyllum brasiliense*) occurs mainly above this level. The entire flora, in fact, including ferns, mosses, shrubs and vines varies with elevation.

Ridgecrest Forest and Elfin Scrub

The Cockscomb Basin exhibits the greatest elevation range of anywhere in Belize. As such, its vegetation shows some of the best examples of altitudinal variation in the country (see elevation profile on p. 38). Climatic conditions become cooler and often wetter with increasing altitude, thereby influencing plant life. The Maya Mountains may not be very high as mountains go. Victoria Peak, the second highest point in Belize, is only 1,120 meters above sea level.

On the more exposed slopes of prominent hills and ridges, a ridgecrest forest has developed. Heavy mists at some times of the year and the drying influence of prevailing winds at other times create unique growing conditions. In addition, soil on ridge crests are more leached and less fertile than soils further down slope. The forest canopy is quite low, typically 8 to 15 meters tall. It is dominated by trees of the genus *Clusia* which possess thickened waxy leaves to reduce water loss. Epiphytes such as orchids and bromeliads are more abundant here than in lower elevations, likely because of higher humidity. Dense growths of moss and beard lichens sometimes adorn the tree branches. Bare exposures of rock appear on some ridge crests. Thick mats of sphagnum moss cover portions of the rock, especially on the Cockscomb Mountains.

Elfin scrub - Clusia with Beard Lichen

Generally the higher the ridge, the more stunted the tree canopy, which is more a factor of exposure and wind than true elevation. Ridgecrest forests can occur anywhere from 400 to 900 m above sea level (a.s.l.), if it is an exposed hilltop. The most stunted form of elfin vegetation grows on the crest of Victoria Peak, where *Clusia* and teabark (*Myrica cerifera*) form dense thickets only 1 to 2 m tall. On the steep slopes just below the crest (at about 850 to 1,000 m a.s.l.), long grass and occasional shrubs grow among fallen and some standing charred tree trunks, a reminder of a more magnificent forest which grew here before the devastating blow of Hurricane Hattie in 1961. A beautiful orange flowering orchid, *Epidendrum radicans*, is abundant among the grasses.

Shelter Valley Forest

The least disturbed vegetation to be found in the Cockscomb Basin today grows in some of the sheltered ravines on the south slope of the Cockscomb Mountains and on the east slope of the Maya Mountains at the western extremity of the reserve. The remoteness of these sites explains why they are still here. Somehow the topographical configuration of the deep ravines was sheltered enough to escape Hurricane Hattie's wrath, and steep enough to elude the loggers. Ranging from about 1 hectare to 1 square kilometer in area, and growing in the 400 to 800 m elevation range, these pockets approach what may be considered 'climax' or primary forest. This is likely the maximum biomass that the ecosystem can achieve. Many of the emergent trees attain heights of 40 m or more and a trunk diameter of 2 m. The understory is quite open with fewer vines and a lack of shrub tangles so prevalent in most of Cockscomb's forests. Lianas adorn the largest emergent trunks while a wide range of epiphytes festoons the upper canopy branches. Presumably, shelter valley forest is a remnant example of a forest type that was more prevalent in the Cockscomb Basin prior to 1961.

Floodplain Thicket

A distinct vegetation community that is dependent on periodic flooding can be found on a narrow riparian belt of flat land immediately adjacent to the largest creeks. Such flood plains are primarily in the East Basin along Juan Branch, Sittee Branch and South Stann Creek, and a small area of the lower Swasey Branch in the West Basin.

The creeks overflow their banks following periods of heavy rain. In some years, torrential rains accompany the start of the wet season in June. The creeks may rise several meters in a few hours, spilling over onto their banks. Trees may be knocked down and uprooted by the force of flowing water or by moving debris. The floodwaters also deposit alluvium and organic materials onto the riparian lands creating the most fertile soils in the basin. The plant life which thrives here is adapted to the natural disturbance regime as is the wildlife which abounds here.

Most characteristic of this community are the flats dominated by dumb cane (*Gynerium sagittatum*). This robust grass closely resembles sugar cane and may attain a height of six meters but is usually two or three. Heliconias (*Heliconia spp.*) may also abound in groves. Semi-herbaceous shrub thickets form almost impenetrable tangles among scattered pioneer tree species such as the trumpet tree (*Cecropia obtusifolia*) and balsa (*Ochroma lagopus*). The vegetation is mainly low but the occasional umbrella-like crown of a tall ceiba (*Ceiba pentandra*) creates a distinctive landmark on the floodplains. Bribri (*Inga edulis*) groves typically overhang creeks where gravel bars are present.

Main Plant Forms

Vines

Vines are a common rainforest feature, and a variety of families of plants has species that have adapted the ability to cling, climb, and grow quickly. Flexible, green-stemmed vines are usually distinguished from the tough, woody-stem lianas that otherwise share many characteristics with vines.

Vines of the genus *Monstera* give the rainforest understory a leafy, attractive character. *Monsteras* and similar vines are well adapted for the shade. They begin as leafless shoots that grow several feet to find a supporting tree. Once this is accomplished, small leaves are produced. As the stem continues up the trunk, it produces larger and larger leaves that stick out from the trunk like umbrellas. At this stage the shiny leaves may develop holes, slits, or large clefts that give them an ornamental appearance. *Monsteras* are often favored as houseplants as they require little care and tolerate the shade.

Other types of vines have different growing strategies. The passionflower vines (*Passiflora* sp.) would never gain a foothold on the shady forest floor. Instead they grow on riverbanks and in other disturbed areas where they can find more sunlight. There, they climb anything they can. In some cases they completely envelope trees that are then unable to compete for sun and water and eventually die. Cecropia trees often have Azteca ants that dutifully clip off the clinging intruders and save their host from being swallowed by a green tangle.

Tear-coat or haul-back vines are also sun-loving vines that have the added strategy of clinging to tree hosts with many sharp thorns. As the common names suggest, they also cling to passers-by, tripping their feet and tearing their clothing.

Some vines grow to gigantic size, competing with the canopy trees for the sun. One example is a legume, related to the bean. Indeed, these large vines look as if they came straight from the fairy tale, "Jack and the Beanstalk"! The seed pods look like gigantic bean pods, and the seeds inside are deep brown and wonderfully smooth. The seeds float, which helps in seed dispersal. During the rainy season, water vine seeds can float safely to other areas of the forest and find new places to germinate. A number of these large vines are found in the kaway swamps on the Wari Loop.

Lianas

Lianas are vines that are woody like trees, not green and flexible like many other types of vines. Lianas loop from branches and coil around tree trunks to access the sunlight above the canopy. Some lianas, like the water vine, grow quite large. They grow slowly in diameter, so the presence of thick lianas indicates an undisturbed section of forest. Lianas have an unimpressive beginning. Many are tender, leafless seedlings that sprout upright from the forest floor. Others start life as epiphytes that soon send slender shoots down to the ground. They grow rapidly only after they find an appropriate host. The many types of lianas contribute greatly to rainforest diversity. They provide additional sources of food and shelter for animals, providing habitats for more species than would a tree standing alone.

Epiphytes

Epiphytes are also called air plants. Instead of growing on the ground, epiphytes grow on other plants, especially on trees. Most epiphytic plants do not extract nutrients or water from the tree, and therefore do not harm it as would a parasite.

Epiphytes often send out roots from a position on a branch or the bark of a tree, trapping soil and nutrients from run-off and the air. A root mat will often collect soil over time, making a bed that traps more nutrients and water.

Some epiphytes are hosts to ants or other insects, which provide the plant with nutrients gathered elsewhere. A few epiphytes can actually help the trees upon which they are growing. New studies of epiphyte soil and root mats have revealed that some trees send root structures into the soil mats collected by epiphytes. This means the symbiotic relationship between trees and some epiphytes resembles mutualism rather than commensalism.

Many different kinds of plants are epiphytes, including thousands of orchids and bromeliads, as well as ferns and mosses. The presence of epiphytes in a forest greatly contributes to its diversity. Epiphytic plants are a vibrant microhabitat for all kinds of other forest life and they provide habitats and resources to other species that could otherwise not survive in the treetops. For example, some birds nest in bromeliads, and frogs and mosquitoes raise their young in ponds trapped between bromeliad leaves. Beautiful orchid and bromeliad flowers attract all kinds of pollinators, from humming-birds and insects to bats. The seeds are dispersed throughout the treetops by canopy-dwelling birds and other animals.

Trees

The most dramatic plants of the rainforest are, of course, the trees. Trees of the rainforest have several different strategies for dealing with the thin, nutrient-poor soil. Their roots must spread widely to obtain sufficient nutrients and to provide stability for the tree to grow upright.

Some trees have **radial roots**, which radiate out in all directions from the base of the tree.

Prop roots are stilt-like roots that radiate from the tree trunk at various heights above the ground down into the soil.

Many large trees found at Cockscomb display curious structures called **buttress roots**. They are a true root structure, flaring out from the trunk sometimes as high as 10 m up and spreading wide at the base. Buttress roots are common on trees growing along rivers and streams, and on trees that have no main tap-roots. Many trees with buttress roots are also canopy trees.

Large buttress roots of quamwood tree in CBWS

Herbs

Smaller herbaceous plants are rooted in the ground and most abundant in clearings or under gaps in the forest canopy since many are sun-loving early succession plants. They are often found in dense growth along the edges of trails and the CBWS Access Road. Other species are shade-tolerant and grow on the forest floor or treefall gaps.

Common Plant Species and Families

The following descriptions of particular plant species of importance in the Cockscomb Basin are divided into **ferns** and **gymnosperms**, which have a simple reproduction system involving spores rather than flowers, fruits and seeds; **monocots**, which have a single cotyledon (first leaf which grows out of the seed) and **dicots**, which have two cotyledons. Within these three categories specific plant descriptions are given in alphabetical order by Family.

FERNS
Family *Cyatheaceae*

Ferns reproduce via spores rather than from flowers and seeds, as higher plants do. Sporangia (the cases that enclose spores) can often be seen in rows on the underside of fern leaves. Each new leaf unfurls from a coiled structure in the center of the plant called a "fiddlehead" because of its appearance. After the leaf has been completely unfurled, ferns are not capable of secondary growth. The leaves of ferns vary according to how many times they are divided. Leaves once divided are called pinnate, twice divided leaves are bipinnate, etc., as shown below. Divided leaves give ferns their typical delicate, frilly appearance.

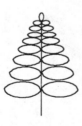

Undivided   *Divided once*   *Divided twice*
                           (Pinnate)   *(Bipinnate)*

Tree Ferns (*Alsophila mysuroides*)

Fiddlehead on a Tree Fern

Tree ferns are ferns that look like trees because they grow on a tall, thick, single stem, but they are not really trees at all. The many-divided leaves of tree ferns are large fronds that emerge umbrella-like from a scaly trunk. They are common in the understory, especially on the slopes of hills and the higher elevations of the CBWS. Tree ferns are not terribly strong or stable because the stem is not wood and the roots are not well-anchored.

The stem is actually made up of masses of roots and various other tissues. Hummingbirds and other birds use the trunk materials for their nests. The foliage is not eaten by animals or insects.

GYMNOSPERMS

Gymnosperms produce spores that are carried inside cones. The cones are actually swirls of leaves, each of which contains a sporangium full of spores.

Family *Pinaceae*

Caribbean Pine (*Pinus caribaea*)

The Caribbean pine is one of two native conifer species in Belize. It occurs both in low-lying savannas and mountain areas, but in the CBWS it is found only on the eastern ridge. Its needles are in bundles of three. Trees on some of Cockscomb's hillsides are of medium height, and reach no more than 20 m. Pine forests are very unlike rainforest habitats, making the convergence of the two ecosystems interesting to study. Pine forest trees are sparse and sunlight can easily reach the forest floor, where ferns and shrubs grow. Fire helps to preserve this ecosystem, and adult Caribbean pines are fairly resistant to it. Elsewhere in Belize, pine forests have long been managed and logged because the wood is prized for construction.

MONOCOTS
Family *Araceae*
Philodendrons and Other Arums

Philodendrons and similar plants called arums are a common feature throughout the Cockscomb Basin. The leaves of many of these plants are shiny and thick and easily shed water to help reduce rot. They also provide a strong support for the eggs of tree frogs. New leaves emerge rolled-up like a tube from the top of the plant. Flowers also emerge rolled up in a boat-shaped sheath called a spathe. The flowers are very

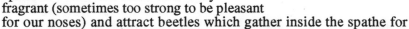

Philodendron

fragrant (sometimes too strong to be pleasant for our noses) and attract beetles which gather inside the spathe for reproduction. The beetles also help in the reproduction of the plants because they transfer pollen from one flower to another.

Some arums, including *Dieffenbachia* and *Spathiphyllum*, grow on the shady forest floor, their leaves and flowers emerging upright in a mass of thick leaves. Other arums are climbers. Many species of *Philodendron*, *Monstera*, and *Syngonium* climb and cling to rainforest trees. The word "philodendron" means tree loving. As young plants, they are very shade tolerant and actually grow toward the shadow of a tree. Once they find a suitable tree, they eventually grow up into the sunlight, where they sprout their large, shiny leaves, one after the other. The large, lovely leaves of the arums usually appear healthy and untouched, a sign that they have some sort of protection. Indeed, the sap of these plants has a high concentration of caustic poison that can burn the mouth. Some caterpillars are adapted to feed off certain arums, however. Many birds and other animals enjoy the fruits. Fruits of the climbing arums in particular provide food for collared aracaris and other canopy feeders.

Family *Bromeliaceae*
Bromeliads

The family *Bromeliaceae* contains about 2,000 species worldwide, including pineapples. Bromeliads have tough, spine-tipped leaves that deter browsers. Those growing on trees as epiphytes have no contact with the ground. This would be a rather

hostile habitat but bromeliads have adapted in two
notable ways. Some have a tank adaptation that
allows them to collect water runoff in their bases.
The shape of the leaves channels water directly
to the roots. This not only lessens the problems
of water shortage, but it allows the plant to
collect important nutrients by luring a variety of
life forms to the collected water.

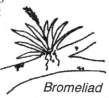

Bromeliad

   In the rainforest, bromeliads are mini-worlds of life. Resident
microorganisms, insects, tree frogs, and even crabs contribute waste
products that can be immediately utilized by the bromeliad. Thus, the
plant makes up for its lack of soil by creating its own miniature
ecosystem. Other bromeliads have adapted a hair-like covering that
helps them absorb water and nutrients directly from rain, runoff and
the atmosphere. The hairs almost serve the same role as roots in
other plants, directing the water and nutrients into the leaf interior.
Bromeliads produce colourful flowers that attract hummingbirds and
other pollinators.

Family *Gramineae*
Dumb Cane (*Gynerium sagittatum*)

   This inedible grass
looks a lot like sugar cane.
Large colonies can be
found growing in sunny
areas along riverbanks and
places once cleared by
humans. Be careful of the
sprouts. The tip is as sharp
as a spear and you would
not want to fall on one.
Once they sprout leaves,
dumb cane shoots are no
longer dangerous.

   The thick habitat of
dumb cane is home to
many small birds and other
animals. Peccaries and
other animals beat
tunneled paths through
dumb cane stands that lead
them under cover to their
favorite watering holes.

Dumb Cane on Victoria Peak Path

Family *Musaceae*
Heliconias (*Heliconia spp.*)
Other Names: waha, wild banana

Heliconias are an interesting group of plants related to the banana and the plantain. Most heliconias like the sunlight and commonly occur along streams and in forest gaps. They are often part of the successional vegetation of secondary forest. Groups of heliconias growing together may actually be a single plant with each shoot connected to the others by an underground stem. The flowers of heliconias have brilliant orange, red, and yellow colours. These are not actually single flowers, but a series of bracts that each holds several tubular flowers. As the plant grows, a new flower bract emerges from the top of the last one. The flowers within each bract ripen one at a time, each containing a rich supply of nectar.

Hummingbirds visit heliconias to drink this sweet meal, attracted by the bright colours. In return, the birds serve as pollinators for the plant. Hermits have long, curved bills that are well adapted to feed at many types of heliconia flowers. They are highly territorial, each defending its special group of flowers from intruders.

Heliconia fruits are berries with three seeds. A variety of birds enjoy them, including tanagers and flycatchers. They swallow the seed along with the fruit and disperse it elsewhere where it lies dormant until the rainy season begins. Birds also use fibers from the leaves as nest building material, and many types of animals use the young unfurled leaves as shelter, including insects and small bats such as Spix's disc-winged bat (*Throptera tricolor*). People use heliconia plants as well. The strong, broad leaves make a good wrap for tamales.

Family *Orchidaceae*
Orchids

Orchids provide a classic example of rainforest ecological inter-actions, as they depend on mycorrhizal fungi for seed germination and growth of seedlings, on insects for pollination, and on trees for living space. Yet much about orchids remains a mystery and rapid tropical deforestation threatens future research.

Orchid flowers are easy to recognize because they have three sepals and three petals, but one petal is usually a different size and shape than the other two. However, specific identification is not easy because of the multitudes of different species and because many grow high in the tree canopy as epiphytes.

Epiphytic orchids have various adaptations to collect nutrients in their arboreal environment. Some attach themselves tightly to their host to collect water and nutrients that run down the tree trunk. Other orchids form baskets with their roots and collect leaf litter and other debris which attracts other life forms. Decomposition in these baskets provides nutrients for the orchids. Some orchids also benefit from resident ants that leave their nutrient-rich waste for the plant to absorb. Insects pollinate the plants, and in turn receive nectar, fats, and sweet-smelling oils.

Orchids are very diverse, and cross-breeding (hybridization) sometimes occurs naturally. Some unusual pollination strategies decrease the chances of hybrids occurring. One such strategy is shape of the flower on bee-pollinated orchids. When the bee crawls into a flower with a certain shape, pollen will stick to a certain part of the bee's body. If the bee then crawls into a different species of orchid with a different shaped flower, the pollen is less likely to rub off. Instead, it hangs there until the bee encounters the correct flower. In this way a bee can act as a delivery van for several species at the same time, with the correct type of pollen collected and deposited at the appropriate flower. In other cases all plants of a

Black Orchid (Encyclia cochleata) *Belize's National Flower*

particular orchid species will flower at the same time. This strategy increases the chances that the insects browsing in the area will pollinate individual flowers with the correct type of pollen. Orchid seeds are like dust. The winds carry them to neighboring trees where, with the help of mycorrhizal fungi, they can grow.

Family *Palmae*
Cohune Palm (*Attalea cohune*, formerly *Oribignya*)
The beautiful cohune palm is plentiful in Cockscomb's lowland forest, and is abundant, particularly in the areas disturbed by logging. It is a hardy tree and can survive fire and defoliation. Yet when a cohune palm tree falls, it rots very quickly and leaves a neat round hole in the forest floor.

The cohune palm bears small, stiff flowers on tough branching stalks. The loud buzzing of pollinating bees will tell you if the tree is in bloom even before you see the flowers. During the winter rains, large bundles of egg-sized nuts fall. They have a very hard shell protecting a coconut-like meat. Rodents such as agouti, paca, and squirrels are able to chew through this shell to access the white interior. Large herds of white-lipped peccary, locally called wari, come near to the CBWS Headquarters to eat these nuts, leaving an obvious wide trail. A beautiful example of a cohune palm is found behind the bath house in the CBWS Headquarters.

In Belize, the cohune palm has many uses to people. The nuts are often used in cooking, and the long fronds are used to thatch roofs, like the one on the Visitor Center.

Pokenoboy Palm (*Bactris major*)
A common understory species, the pokenoboy palm is a slim, spiny plant with rather sparse fronds that are not thick or fan-like as on other palms. Pokenoboy palms can be a hazard in the forest because the extremely sharp spines can stick right into the leg or hand. People sometimes use these spines as cooking tools. The fruits of the pokenoboy are edible and they are enjoyed by forest animals.

DICOTS
Family *Anacardiaceae*
Cashew (*Anacardium occidentale*)
The cashew tree is not found naturally in the CBWS forest, but several trees have been planted in the Headquarters area. The fruit of the cashew is not a true fruit, but an enlarged stem called a hypocarp. It is extremely juicy with a bitter taste, and is avidly consumed by bats, birds, and people (raw or in wine). The cashew nut (which is technically the fruit) hangs from the bottom of the cashew hypocarp. The nut has a highly toxic oil that blisters the skin and must be roasted before it can be eaten. The leaves of the cashew tree are

fairly long and shiny. The strong wood is sometimes used to make small items, but the tree itself is not especially valuable for lumber because it rarely grows over 10 m tall.

Family *Bombacaceae*
Ceiba (*Ceiba pentandra*)
Other names: cotton tree, kapok tree

The ceiba is truly a giant tree, with broad, almost horizontal branches. Its crown often emerges above the forest canopy. The ceiba is common along riverbanks, and is also often the only species of tree left when land is cleared for pasture. Majestic solitary specimens grow along South Stann Creek where Montezuma oropendola build their nests.

The ceiba does not flower every year, but when it does, it blooms at night to attract pollinating bats. The flower closes up during the day, but birds and insects still scavenge among them. The seeds of the ceiba germinate quickly, as long as light and moisture are available. As a result, the species often plays a key role in forest succession. Cone-shaped spines cover the trunks of young ceiba trees. The palmate-shaped leaves fall off in the dry season, apparently to conserve moisture, to rid the tree of disease and parasites, and to expose the flowers to their pollinators.

A notable feature of the ceiba tree is the thick, buoyant, cottony material inside the seed pods. This is kapok, which helps in seed dispersal by wind. Humans have found other uses for kapok, for stuffing couches, pillows, and life preservers. The small black seeds contain an edible oil that can also be used for making soap and lamp-oil. The tree has a soft wood that is not valuable for lumber. However, it is appropriate wood for making dugout canoes. In fact, ceiba comes from an Arawak word for boat. Marker 7 on the Self-Guided Nature Trail is a large ceiba tree.

The ceiba tree plays an important role in Mayan cosmology. It is believed that the ceiba tree connects the gods of the underworld below with the gods above. The branches are as clouds looking over the gods of the underworld providing shade so the living soul can ascend into the sky above. The tree is also a fertility symbol. Rituals are conducted beneath its branches for souls in thanksgiving that the god above is there to balance the gods of the underworld. That is why ceiba trees are seldom cut down and one often sees an open pasture with only one ceiba tree still standing.

Balsa (*Ochroma lagopus*)

Balsa is a fast-growing tree with a very lightweight, buoyant wood (the word "balsa" is Spanish meaning "raft"). It has large round-shaped leaves and can be spotted along the CBWS Access Road, on the River Path, and in other cleared areas.

Balsa trees bear dark brown seed capsules about 20 to 25 cm long covered by a fuzzy brown wool, which helps the many seeds to be dispersed by wind. While still on the tree, they look like wooly corn dogs, but on the ground they resemble a furry animal skin.

This wool has also been used by people for stuffing pillows and mattresses. The lightweight wood of the balsa rots easily, but it can grow quickly to dominate light-gaps as a pioneer. Like the cecropia, balsa occurs in disturbed areas, and can be harvested after only 5 to 7 years. The seeds are able to survive for many years, and can germinate after burning or clearing. The flowers are whitish and are pollinated by bats. The lightweight wood was very important during World War II for making life rafts and airplanes. Today it is used in ocean tankers as an insulation against wave action.

Family *Burseraceae*
Carbonwood (*Tetragastris panamensis*)
Other name: red copal

The carbonwood tree belongs to the copal family, which for centuries has provided the indigenous Maya with a resin that is burned as incense during rituals. Carbonwood is a common tree along CBWS trails. The bark has a smell like a temperate cedar.

Most noticeable are the beautiful fruits that drop from the branches onto the trails. These fruits have three sections that open up before falling to reveal a bright red inner flesh and a faint sweet smell.

Gumbolimbo (*Bursera simaruba*)

Gumbolimbo trees have a reddish bark that peels off in paper-thin flakes, revealing a greenish layer beneath it. The peeling of the bark may be a mechanism to rid the tree of unwanted vines. Gumbolimbo trees are deciduous and thus, lose their leaves in the dry season to help prevent loss of water.

They grow to a moderate height, and have been planted in many areas as an ornamental. The wood is fairly lightweight and perishable and is more useful for living fence posts than for construction. Gumbolimbo trees can be seen in the Campground and along the Access Road.

Gumbolimbo bark

The leaves, branches and small fruits have a rather pungent odor when crushed, due to the tannins they contain. Crushed leaves are soaked and used to relieve the effects of poisonwood. Gumbolimbo resin (sap) is used as glue, varnish, and medicine.

The tiny greenish-white flowers attract small bees, flies, and ants. Monkeys, birds, squirrels, and other treetop feeders eat the seeds and disperse them to new areas. Peccaries eat the fruits whole when they fall to the ground.

Family *Guttiferae*

Santa Maria (*Calophyllum brasiliense*)

The Latin name for this tree means beautiful leaf and it certainly does have attractive foliage. The leaves are dark green with lines running cross-ways all the way up the leaf, perpendicular to a single vein down the middle. On older trees, the bark is yellowish with a diamond pattern. When damaged, the bark bleeds a yellow sap.

Santa maria is a rainforest tree with an incredibly tough wood. This characteristic helps it survive against rot and insect invaders, but also makes it very valuable as timber.

Family *Leguminosae*
Legumes

Legumes are plants that have a symbiotic relationship with bacteria of the genus *Rhizobium* that live in their roots. These bacteria are able to fix atmospheric nitrogen and make it available in the soil for the legumes and other plants to use. Some legumes are trees like bucut, ironwood, kaway, quamwood, guanacaste and bribri; others are shrubs or vines, including edible peas and beans.

The seeds of legumes grow in long pods. They usually have a high protein content, which makes them valuable in the diets of a variety of rainforest fauna and some of the most important foods in the human diet.

Subfamily *Caesalpinioideae*
Bucut (*Cassia grandis*)
Other names: stinking toe, beef feed, mucut (Maya)

The bucut tree is a legume. It has noticeably large seed pods that grow up to three feet long, an important food source in the forest. Although the pods have a rather disagreeable smell, this does not deter many animals (including people) from breaking them open and eating the seeds inside. The bucut tree has 10 to 30 oblong leaflets, each about 3-5 cm long. The leaves fall in the dry season to make room for many beautiful pink flowers. The tree can grow large and reach canopy height. Extracts of the bucut have properties that can be used to treat fungal skin infections. It is not found in the forest in the CBWS, but has been planted in the Headquarters area.

Ironwood *(Dialium guianense)*

Ironwood is a large leguminous tree with a very hard, heavy wood that does not float. The ironwood resists decay, and has thus been favored for building houses in Belize. A fallen ironwood is marker 2 on the Self-Guided Nature Trail, still visible after many years as a standing dead tree and four years after it has fallen. Although it is a much sought-after timber tree, ironwood trees are quite common in the CBWS forest.

The leaves have alternate leaflets that are about 3-7 cm long. It has low buttresses from which it grows very straight. Bunches of green to brown marble-sized fruits can be seen on most of the trail from May through July.

Kaway (*Pterocarpus officinalis*)
Other names: swamp kaway, dragon's blood

The kaway is a large tree of swamp forests and stream borders. The kaway has enormous, plank-like buttresses measuring as wide as five feet across and reaching even higher up the trunk. These buttresses may help prevent the tree from toppling in deep mud, especially because the kaway tree thrives best in a habitat that is periodically flooded. However, a dry season is necessary for new seedlings to establish themselves.

Kaway swamp on the Wari Trail

The dark red sap of the kaway has given it the name dragon's blood. This sap can reportedly be used as an astringent and to stop bleeding. At times, you may see this sap oozing out of wounds on the trunks. It solidifies very quickly, so sticky sap indicates a very recent injury. For the tree, the sap serves the function of protecting wounds from invasion by fungi or insects.

The fruit of the kaway is a winged pod that is dispersed by both wind and water. Being very buoyant, the seeds travel easily. The seed itself contains an alkaloid (a toxin) which is avoided by rodent browsers, aiding in seed survival. The leaves of the tree have about 7 to 9 alternate leaflets, about 10-18 cm long. The wood decays quickly, and is thus not useful for construction.

There are two large stands of kaway trees on the Wari Loop and single trees can be found along waterways.

Quamwood (*Schizolobium parahybum*)

The quamwood is a common tree in the Cockscomb Basin. The bark sometimes has a red tint and the leaves are large and fern-like. During the beginning of the dry season the quamwood loses its leaves and then bears bright yellow flowers. Green tear-shaped seed pods soon follow, each measuring about 10 cm long. The trees have short buttresses and grow very straight. They are common along waterways. A big quamwood can be found next to the bench on the Curassow Trail and another is at marker 8 on the Rubbertree Trail.

The seeds and flowers are probably fed on by the crested guan, otherwise known as the quam (hence the name quamwood). Black howler monkeys eat the flowers and other animals also enjoy the seeds.

Subfamily *Mimosoideae*
Guanacaste (*Enterolobium cyclocarpum*)
Other names: tubroos, ear tree

The guanacaste is a leguminous tree that can grow to be quite massive with a broad, spreading crown. The guanacaste has ear-shaped fruits about 6 cm wide. These fruits fall to the ground near the end of the dry season and contain about 10-16 seeds. The reproduction of the tree is closely tied with other forest functions. Seeds will not germinate unless their coats are broken by wear, animals, microorganisms, or by passing through the gut of an animal such as a peccary or tapir. The leaves of the tubroos are made up of tiny, feathery leaflets. The tree grows quickly, yet the inner heartwood is fungus-resistant. In Belize, large tubroos trees are traditionally used for dugout canoes (dories). Two beautiful guanacaste trees are found in the CBWS Headquarters (*see photograph on the next page*).

Guanacaste tree in CBWS Headquarters

Bribri (*Inga edulis*)

Bribri is commonly found along the South Stann Creek and other waterways. Like many other trees of the genus *Inga*, the leaves have a curious shape. They have 6-12 opposite leaflets connected by a rachis or leafy bridge. A variety of insects feed on the leaves, which are not well-protected by chemicals. The bark is smooth. The brush-like flowers produce a nectar enjoyed by bats, insects and hummingbirds all of which in turn help with pollination. Fruits of the bribri are leguminous pods and are eaten by all kinds of animals, including birds, porcupines and humans. A beautiful bribri shades the picnic table at the end of the River Path.

Family *Melastomataceae*
Miconia spp.

Plants of the family *Melastomataceae* are the most numerous in the tropical rainforest. There are over 1,000 species in the *Miconia* genus alone. All members of this family are characterized by a distinctive pattern of veins in their leaves. They have a main longitudinal vein down the middle with 1-4 pairs of others near each edge of the leaf. The longitudinal veins are connected by many finer perpendicular veins. They are large, smooth, oval leaves. Most members of the family are shrubs or small trees, but a few are large. The common names of the large trees use "maya" as a last name, such as black maya, purple maya, green maya, red maya, hairy maya, and white maya. However, the tree that is locally called "white maya" in the Cockscomb Basin is a different tree than the one called "white maya" in northern Belize.

Family *Meliaceae*
Cedar (*Cedrela mexicana*)

Cedar trees can grow up to 30 m high, often with small buttresses at the base. The crown is large and rounded, often emerging above the forest canopy. The cedar is a fine tree and is very valuable for timber, like its cousin, the mahogany. Large cedar trees are rare in the Cockscomb Basin because of past logging. The wood of the cedar is golden-brown, fairly lightweight and has a very fragrant odor. Like many fine rainforest woods, it is durable and resistant to termites. It has been an important timber for local use. Cedar wood has been used in making everything from cigar boxes and furniture to dugout canoes. The bark of the cedar is an astringent and is used by some people for home remedies.

Mahogany (*Swietenia macrophylla*)

Mahogany trees grow to as high as 50 m tall, and have buttress roots. However, it is rare to find such a giant these days due to past logging. Even with the protected status of the Cockscomb Basin Wildlife Sanctuary, it will take time before mahogany trees are again obvious in the area. However, there are two growing in the CBWS Headquarters planted in 1988 by H.R.H. Prince Philip and another in front of the cabin called Balum Naj (*see photograph on the next page*). In addition, large mahogany trees are seen on the trail to Victoria Peak and other less accessible areas of the CBWS.

Mahogany leaves are variable in size and have a deep green colour. The leaves are shed for a few weeks during the dry season after which buff-coloured flowers appear. During this phase, mahogany trees are visible from a long ways away, a fact that was used by timber companies to locate mahogany trees scattered in the forests. The trees then bear brown fruits that release about 40 seeds

Mahogany tree in front of Balum Naj

to the wind. These seeds have a very unpleasant taste and animals usually leave them alone.

Mahogany has a sparse distribution in tropical forests, particularly where the forest is undisturbed. Interestingly, slash and burn agriculture as practiced traditionally by the Maya appears to produce favorable conditions for mahogany, but only when the forest is allowed to reestablish itself with a long fallow period.

This tree has played an important role in the history of Belize. Over 100 years ago mahogany was already being extracted from the Cockscomb Basin. With the invention of airplanes, trees that remained hidden from loggers could be easily discovered from the air by their buff-coloured flowers. Some people have attempted to cultivate mahogany, but typical plantation-like farms usually fail due to insect pests. Cabinetmakers all over the world have prized the rich golden wood. It is very hard and durable and has served as a standard to which all other types of cabinet woods are compared.

Family *Moraceae*

Cecropia (*Cecropia obtusifolia*)
Other name: trumpet tree

Cecropias are pioneer trees found in disturbed areas, along roads and rivers, and in gaps. Look for them along the River Path and Curassow Trail where there was a former milpa. When abundant sunlight is available they grow quickly but do not usually grow taller than 20 m and live only about 30 years. The seeds are able to germinate after two years of dormancy, lying in wait for sufficient sunlight and water.

Cecropia branches are sparse with large, fan-like leaves. When they dry out and drop to the ground, the leaves roll up into brown softball-sized balls. Cecropia trees have stilt-like roots.

Cecropias have individual male and female trees. Female trees can produce as many as a million seeds each time they fruit.

Cecropia tree

Cecropia flowers are fuzzy and long, with several in one cluster. The fruits are also a cluster of long, finger-like strings of many tiny seeds. While the fruits are not particularly high in nutritional quality, birds, bats, monkeys, insects, and baby iguanas eat them readily. Monkeys also feed on the leaves. Crested guans can often be seen roosting on the branches.

The hollow cecropia trunks are home to ants that guard the tree fiercely. Although these trees inhabit sunny clearings, you will often see them free of climbing vines. The ants attack these transgressors, as well as anybody trying to cut down the tree.

Mountain Trumpet (*Pourouma aspera*)

In contrast to the cecropia which is found on the edges of the forest or in disturbed areas, the mountain trumpet is found as a co-dominant tree deep within the lowland forests of the Cockscomb Basin. While it looks very much like the cecropia, the mountain trumpet is distinguishable by its fruit which is large bunches of green, cherry-sized fruits, each containing a single seed. The fruit has a very sweet juice and is eaten by monkeys, kinkajous and toucans when it is ripe between May and September.

Fig (*Ficus* spp.)

Figs are a remarkable genus of trees that are quite common in the forests of Belize, especially along rivers. They have shiny, thick leaves and smooth bark. When a leaf or stem breaks, an obvious milky latex (sap) will ooze out. Figs have internal inflorescence, that is, the flowers are not seen, but cover the inside surface of a hollow structure. There are many species of figs and each has its own specific wasp which burrows in and pollinates the flowers so that the fruit can be produced. The resulting fruit ranges from 0.5 - 10 cm in diameter and red, orange, yellow, green or brown when ripe, depending upon the species.

Fig trees are an important food source for many types of rainforest animals. Some species will fruit several times a year, and are frequented by monkeys, birds, bats, coatis, and others. Fruits that drop into water become food for fish. Figs of the same species sometimes will produce flower clusters in sequence, to best allow their wasp pollinators to visit each tree.

Strangler Fig (*Ficus* spp.)

The strangler fig is one of the most fascinating types of plants in the sanctuary, and there are specimens within easy reach on the Curassow Trail and along the river. The strangler fig begins its life as an epiphyte in the forest canopy, sprouting from a seed deposited by birds or other animals. As the seedling takes full advantage of the sunlight available in the treetop, it soon sends down adventitious roots to tap nutrients from the ground. As it continues to grow, it sends down more of these strong and flexible aerial roots.

Once the roots become anchored in the ground, the fig has successfully occupied its host. The roots grow and thicken, and they begin to bind together around the trunk of the host tree. The host tree can no longer grow in girth. At the same time, the fig leaves effectively block the sun from reaching the host tree, and its roots compete for nutrients. With this formidable competitor, the host tree is doomed. It eventually dies and rots, leaving a tangled mass of strangler fig roots, which have become a tree trunk supporting canopy branches and leaves. By this time the fig is a fantastic specimen, very tall with a large crown.

Strangler Fig on Cohune tree

The victorious fig serves several functions in the forest. The grooves on its knobby trunk provide a refuge for reptiles, birds, insects, and even mammals. Its sweet and tasty fruits are very attractive to all kinds of animals, including bats, birds, monkeys, rodents, and even fish (when growing near water). Canopy feeders are most useful for fig tree regeneration, since they are more likely to deposit the seeds back in the canopy to start new epiphytic seedlings.

Family *Myristicaceae*
Banak (*Virola koschnyi*)

The Banak is a tall canopy tree, a cousin of the nutmeg tree that provides us with a cooking spice. Banak branches spiral out almost horizontally from a strong, upright trunk. The inner bark of the tree secretes a watery red sap after injury. The seeds are enjoyed by birds which in turn disperse them to other areas of the forest. The banak thrives well in old-growth forest because the seedlings are shade tolerant. They grow slowly and patiently until a gap occurs in the canopy above, then they take advantage of the sunlight and grow quickly upward. Banak was exploited and removed from the Cockscomb Basin during the logging years, but several can be seen on the Waterfall Trail.

Family *Piperaceae*
Cowfoot (*Piper auritum*)

Cowfoot is a relative of the black pepper that we use to spice our food. It is a shrubby pioneer species that commonly occurs in forest gaps and cleared areas. Cowfoot has a single, main stem, sometimes with prop roots at the base. It grows to about 7 m high, and only where light is available.

The leaves of cowfoot are quite large and almost heart-shaped. When crushed, they have a pleasant licorice or anise smell and are used to flavor food or to make tea. The flowers of cowfoot are very small and grow on a stalk that generally droops. After bees or small beetles pollinate them, small fruits appear on the stalk. They are a favorite of fruit-eating bats, which help disperse the seeds to other forest areas.

Cowfoot Leaf

Cowfoot has been reportedly used to treat fertility problems. An oil from the cowfoot attracts fish, and can be used as a fish bait.

Family *Rubiaceae*
Lady's Lips (*Cephaelis tomentosa*)
Other names: hot lips
Lady's lips are shrubs that have lip-shaped orange and red flowers. As shade-tolerant shrubs they are able to survive as undergrowth. Lady's lips are common along the trails, the plants reaching about hip-high. The actual flowers are small, yellow blossoms in the middle of the lips. The flowers are visited by heliconid butterflies in the morning for pollen that provides them with amino acids important for reproductive purposes. The flowers become bright blue fruits toward the end of the dry season and a variety of birds eat them. It has been used for human birth control.

Family *Rutaceae*
Prickly Yellow (*Zanthoxylum kellermani*)
This tree has a straight trunk armed with pyramid-like spines, and has alternate leaves with 6-8 shiny leaflets, each about 15 cm long. The tree often sheds its leaves during the dry season. When crushed, the leaves of the prickly yellow have a citrus smell. The wood and roots have a yellowish colour. Prickly yellow was cut as a secondary lumber species, so it is not so common, but there are several large ones along the Antelope Loop.

Family *Simarubaceae*
Negrito (*Simaruba glauca*)
The negrito is a common but important tree. The leathery leaflets of the negrito are dark green on the top, and pale on the bottom. The black fruits are found littering the trails in April and May. They are eaten by a variety of wildlife, including monkeys, as well as humans. Vegetable oil and other products can be obtained from the seeds, and the tree is very valuable for firewood, because it burns green. Various parts of the negrito are used as medicine. Extracts have antibacterial properties and can help treat stomach disorders such as food poisoning.

Family *Sterculiaceae*
Bay Cedar (*Guazuma ulmifolia*)
Other name: cork bottom wood
The bay cedar is a medium-sized tree that exists, but is not common in CBWS. Examples can be seen on the Wari Loop just after the River Overlook. The tree produces dry, black fruits that are covered with soft spikes from March through May. The fruit are eaten by monkeys, birds, bats, and other animals, including children for whom it is constipating, accounting for the local name, cork bottom wood. The sap of the bay cedar is quite sticky and has medicinal properties. It has been used to treat elephantiasis.

Family *Vitaceae*
Water Vine (*Vitis titiifolia*)
Other names: water tie-tie
The water vine is a liana that is rooted into the forest floor, but grows thick and woody up to the canopy, draping from tree to tree. The water vine has an amazing feature that has provided it with its name. It contains a clear, tasteless sap that drips out from cut sections. Forest workers sometimes rely on this sap as a source of water.

Family *Vochysiaceae*
Yemeri (*Vochysia hondurensis*)
Other names: white mahogany, saguc, San Juan
Yemeri trees are most noticeable from April through June when their many bright yellow flowers form yellow canopies on all the hillsides, seen easily from the roads. They are very tall, very straight, and sometimes as large as a meter in diameter. An example is seen behind the bath house in the CBWS Headquarters, towering over the cohune palm.

The seeds of the yemeri are small and winged, adapted for dispersal by wind. The seeds also contain high concentrations of fats and proteins, making them an important food source for animals.

Natural Cycles and Microorganisms
All processes in the rainforest operate in a cyclical fashion. No material is actually lost or gained. Microorganisms play a subtle, but important role in the completion of these cycles. The fundamental interacting cycles are the water, carbon, and oxygen cycles. Other cycles involve all the essential nutrients such as oxygen, nitrogen, phosphorous, sulphur, etc.

Water Cycle
The water cycle involves evaporation, transpiration, respiration, condensation, precipitation and runoff. Driven by the sun's energy, water transpires from the earth's vegetation and evaporates from bodies of water, especially lakes, seas and oceans. Respiration (breathing of animals) gives off water vapor.

In the atmosphere, the water vapor condenses to form clouds. Growing heavy with tiny water droplets, the clouds eventually precipitate, returning the moisture to the earth as rain.

Some of the rain enters the soil to be used by plants; some is used by animals drinking from the streams; much is used by all the other components of the ecosystem such as insects, fungi and bacteria; and the rest soaks into ground water or runs off into creeks and rivers and into the ocean. Plants combine atmospheric carbon dioxide with water through the process of photosynthesis to make carbohydrates which are used as energy by animals and other life forms.

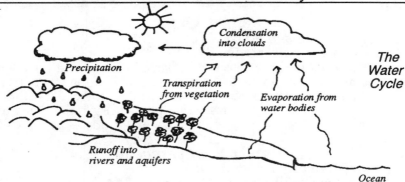

The
Water
Cycle

The water used by plants, animals and microorganisms is eventually returned to the atmosphere through transpiration, respiration and decomposition, beginning the cycle all over again.

Carbon Cycle

Carbon is an element found in all organic matter. It circulates through nature in many chemical reactions, moving from the atmosphere to plants and other life forms, and then back into the atmosphere again.

In photosynthesis, plants trap energy from the sun and use it to combine atmospheric carbon dioxide with water to produce carbohydrates (sugars and starches). Animal consumers, including humans eat the plants and use these carbohydrates as an energy source and as raw materials for growth of living tissue. Through their (our) respiration, they (we) breath out waste carbon dioxide and water vapor. In addition, carbon dioxide is released as organic matter decays or burns, or as fossil fuels are burned.

Oxygen Cycle

A side product in photosynthesis is oxygen, which is produced by plants and needed by animals to metabolize plant carbohydrates. Thus, the oxygen cycle is linked with the water and carbon cycles in that plants give off oxygen which is then used by animals. There is some concern that these natural cycles are being thrown out of balance by extensive cutting of rainforests, the main producer of oxygen, and by burning of fossil fuels which produces excess carbon dioxide and could cause what is know as the "greenhouse effect," or "global warming."

Nitrogen Cycle

Other nutrients cycle through the ecosystem, too. One of the greatest limits to the growth of plants is the amount of nitrogen available, the main component of most fertilizers. Ironically, nitrogen occurs in the most abundant gas in the atmosphere, nitrogen dioxide, but in that form it can be used by only a few bacterial species, most notably those of the genus *Rhizobium*.

Rhizobium bacteria live among the roots of plants called legumes, forming a symbiotic relationship. The bacteria are able to fix atmospheric nitrogen, that is, change the chemical form of the nitrogen into one which can be used by the legumes and other plants. This nitrogen can then be incorporated into the living material of all other organisms.

The nitrogen cycle is a complex one involving several chemical changes in the form of nitrogen from nitrates and nitrites to ammonia, each of which is catalyzed by different species of bacteria. To complete the cycle, decomposition returns nitrogen dioxide to the atmosphere to be fixed by other *Rhizobium* bacteria in the roots of another legume.

Decomposition

In the sections describing particular plants, we have emphasized the growth and reproduction of plants and the roles played by other species in those processes. However, just as important as growth is decomposition. Decomposition is the breakdown of dead plants and animals into their chemical components. The nutrients from this organic matter pass from the living to the non-living parts of the ecosystem, the soil, water, and air, and then back into living organisms again.

As bacteria and fungi feed on dead organic matter, they pass carbon, oxygen, nitrogen, phosphorous, and other chemical components through their systems, breaking them down into forms which can be used by plants, the primary producers. The high rate of decomposition allows a luxuriant green forest to grow rapidly, without leaving the nutrients in the soil for very long. While there is always a carpet of leaf litter on the forest floor, rapid decomposition does not allow it to accumulate. As a consequence, the soils of the rainforest tend to be thin and poor in nutrients.

The mold and dampness, which are household annoyances, are exactly what makes the rainforest ecosystem function so well. The warm, wet environment of Cockscomb is quite hospitable for bacteria and fungi, allowing decomposition to take place at a phenomenal rate. As soon as a tree falls, various types of fungi begin to take over, breaking down the tough fibers of the wood. Even the benches and bridges on the trails fall victim to rot.

Insects such as termites and leafcutter ants help decomposition in the forest because they cut up plants into small pieces, making the job easier for the microorganisms. Leafcutter ants transfer organic matter from one part of the forest to another and have their own fungal gardens, the waste of which is extremely high in nutrients.

Fungi

Fungi are organisms that have no roots, seeds, leaves, or chlorophyll. Each new fungus develops from a tiny spore that was released with millions of others from the parent fungus. Some fungi have a visible phase, commonly called mushrooms. Fungi were once classified in the plant kingdom, but they are now classified in a kingdom all their own.

Fungi are not able to make their own food through photosynthesis, and must rely on food produced by other plants and animals. Thus, many types of fungi are decomposers. These are the most obvious to the casual observer because they create a rich humus from the leaf litter and debris. Mildews and molds cover just about everything in the moist forest environment. Fungi even help break down wood that we would like to preserve, such as bridges and benches.

Some fungi are parasitic. They live off plants and animals, weakening and sometimes killing their hosts. Athlete's foot is a non-fatal, but irritating fungal infection of humans.

Mycorrhizal fungi live in a symbiotic relationship with the roots of many trees and other plants, such as orchids. Since the fungus is not able to photosynthesize food, it absorbs energy from the plant. In return the fungus helps the plant absorb nutrients. This relationship is the key to the survival of many different plant species, especially where the soil itself is thin and does not easily retain

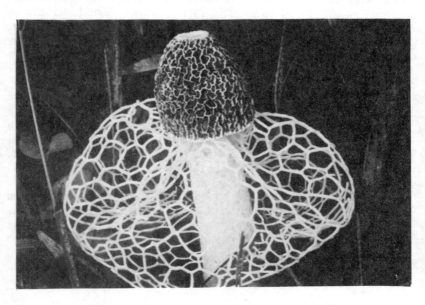

Mushroom called netted stinkhorn or virgin's veil
(Dictyophora duplicata) *in CBWS Headquarters*

On the trails, especially after a rain, many different kinds of mushrooms may be seen. They may be bright red, orange, yellow or white, moist and slimy or dry and hard. These mushrooms are the fruiting bodies of fungi that otherwise live in the ground or in rotting tissue in a microscopic form too small to be seen by the human eye.

An interesting mushroom often sprouts up overnight after a rain in the CBWS Headquarters between the road and the wooden bunkhouse building. It is called "virgin's veil" because of the lacey structure that surrounds it.

Bacteria

Bacteria are the unseen heroes of the forest. They are completely microscopic, never visible to the naked eye. However, they are the most numerous organisms in the rainforest. They are responsible for many links in the cycles. They are extremely specialized and often live on a single chemical as a source of energy and, in the process, convert it to another chemical which is used by another bacterial species, which converts it to yet another form used by other bacteria, and so on through the cycles of nature.

The most well-known of these bacteria are those of the genus, *Rhizobium,* which fix atmospheric nitrogen among the roots of legumes. They are responsible for the bulk of the natural fertilization of soils by the rotation of crops. Alternating corn with beans replenishes the nitrogen which is depleted from the soil by the corn, or any other crop that is not a legume.

In decomposition, one bacterial species may break the large molecules into smaller ones that another species can use. It takes billions of bacteria of many different species to decompose a single plant.

Bacteria are especially important in the flow of essential nutrients through the ecosystem. There are bacteria which specialize in the processing of sulfur compounds, others which use only specific forms of nitrogen for their energy sources, and still others that use phosphorous compounds. There are many, many species of bacteria but only a few have been well-studied. A whole new world awaits the rainforest microbiologist.

References

Forsythe, A. & Miata, K. 1984. *Tropical Nature: Life and Death in the Rainforests of Central and South America.* Charles Scribners Sons: New York, NY.

Gentry, A. H. 1993. *A Field Guide to the Families and Genera of Woody Plants of Northwest South America (Colombia, Ecuador, Peru).* Conservation International: Washington, D.C.

Hartshorn, G. et al. 1984. *Belize: Country Environmental Profile.* Robert Nicolait & Associates Ltd: Belize City.

Henderson, Galeano, and Bernal. 1995. *Field Guide to the Palms of the Americas.* Princeton University Press: Princeton, NJ.

Horwich, R. H, & Lyon. J. 1990. *A Belizean Rain Forest: The Community Baboon Sanctuary.* Orang-utan Press: Gays Mills, WI.

Janzen, D.H., ed. 1983. Costa Rican Natural History. University of Chicago Press: Chicago, IL.

Kamstra, J. 1987. *An Ecological Survey of the Cockscomb Basin, Belize,* Master's Thesis. York University: Ontario, Canada.

Kricher, J. C. 1989. *A Neotropical Companion: An Introduction to the Animals, Plants and Ecosystems of the New World Tropics,* Princeton University Press: Princeton, NJ.

Little E. L., Wadsworth, F. H. 1964. *Common Trees of Puerto Rico and the Virgin Islands.* Agriculture Handbook No. 249. U.S. Department of Agriculture, Forest Service: Washington, D. C.

Newman, A. 1990. *Tropical Rainforest: A World Survey of our Most Valuable And Endangered Habitat with a Blueprint for its Survival.* Facts on File: New York, NY.

Saqui, E., et al. 1990. The Cockscomb West Basin Expedition Report, June 11-18, 1990.

CHAPTER 4
Jaguars
Robert Horwich and Judy Lumb

Jaguar (*Panthera onca*)

The five cat species that occur in Belize all share the Cockscomb Basin by occupying different niches. The Basin is an especially good habitat for the largest cat, the jaguar. In other areas of its range jaguar habitat is being greatly reduced. For this reason the Cockscomb Basin Wildlife Sanctuary (CBWS) was created for the protection of the jaguar.

Jaguars are threatened with extinction by increasing human habitation with consequent deforestation. They are classified as "vulnerable" by IUCN, "endangered" by US Department of the Interior and are included in the Convention on International Trade in Endangered Species (CITES) list in Appendix I. In Belize and elsewhere, jaguars have been hunted for their beautiful skin and because they are predators that compete with humans both for wild game as well as domestic livestock. An elimination of the skin market by legal restrictions in the US and other countries has drastically reduced the hunting of jaguars.

The jaguar's reputation as a powerful, elusive animal has generated a mystique about the Cockscomb Basin. Its secretive life insures that visitors to Cockscomb are unlikely to encounter a jaguar directly. Yet the presence of jaguars is evident through tracks, scratch markings and feces (scats) on the trails or roads where they frequently walk (see Chapter 14 for details on tracks). But this elusive presence is enough to excite the imagination of those who walk the trails that are the home of one of the most powerful of cats.

Jaguars are classified along with other cats as members of the Family, *Felidae*. The jaguar is the only member of the large cat genus (*Panthera)* that lives in the Americas. Along with others of this genus, they are distinguished from smaller cats by cartilage in the hyoid throat structures that gives them the ability to roar. The jaguar is the third largest cat in the world after the tiger and lion.

Compared to the Old World leopards, jaguars are more robust, with broader heads and thicker necks and forelimbs. Male jaguars weigh between 50-100 kg with females weighing a third less. Jaguars are cryptically marked with the background color varying from pale to reddish or brownish yellow and white under the belly. They have large dark rosettes with spots inside on the back and flanks. The midline of the back is a row of elongated spots which may be fused, forming a line. They have a relatively short black-tipped tail. Jaguars also occur in a melanistic form in which the spotted pattern is barely visible on dark background.

Like other cats, jaguars are adapted for a predatory life. Their muscular body allows the quick rushes to take their vertebrate prey. Their flexible forepaws with curved, retractable claws can rotate. making them formidable in capturing and holding prey. The shortened skull with powerful jaw muscles and long canine teeth are used for killing prey and the rear carnassial teeth are adapted for cutting and chewing meat. Jaguar kills are usually made by breaking the neck or piercing the skull with the canine teeth.

Jaguar Habitat

Jaguars may inhabit a wide variety of habitats though they are most often found in dense forests and swamps with good cover and easy access to water. When they inhabited southwestern United States, they hunted in open areas as they do now in the northern part of their range in Mexico. In Central America, they inhabit coastal lowland forests including mangroves, savannas and shrubby forests. Jaguars are generally found under 1,000 meters in elevation and are most often associated with riverine forests and wetter habitats. They are excellent swimmers and have been known to traverse rivers, small lakes, and coastal lagoons.

The study of jaguar habits in the Brazilian Pantanal, which is a mosaic of wet forest and grasslands, indicated that the jaguars spent 70% of their time in the forests and were always fairly close to water. This association with water minimizes competition with the puma which likes a drier habitat.

With the rapid deforestation, especially in Central America, populations of jaguars are becoming scattered and disconnected since they require such large territories. In a 1991 follow-up to his original study, Rabinowitz estimated between 600 and 1,000 in Belize. A number of conservation organizations have been attempting to connect large reserves to decrease the disjunction of jaguar (and puma) habitats. The addition to the CBWS which connects it to Bladen Nature Reserve is an example of this effort.

Territoriality and Land Use

Although the jaguar is the largest land predator in Central and South America, it is quite elusive. Until the 1980's, very little was known of the species except from zoo animals and hunted specimens. The major research on jaguars in Central America was done by Alan Rabinowitz in the Cockscomb Basin in 1983 and 1984. The results of this research became the impetus for the creation of the CBWS as a reserve for jaguars.

The jaguars in Rabinowitz's study were captured either by treeing them with dogs or by capturing them in large steel traps which he baited with pigs. These traps are displayed in the CBWS Headquarters. The animals were then immobilized in order to attach radio collars to their necks for tracking. Five trapped adult males and a female which was translocated into the Cockscomb were studied. Three times a week, Rabinowitz ascertained each animal's location using directional antennae either from the ground, a tree or a small aircraft. Once a number of points were determined for each animal over a period of time, home ranges could be drawn from the known locations.

Rabinowitz could also determine the behavior of the jaguars based on the activity sensors in the radio collar and changes in the strength of the signal from the radio transmitter. When the animal is traveling, the signal strength varies due to changes in the level of interference from the jaguar's body, vegetation, and rock formations. The pulse rate of the signal increases as the jaguar's head moves. An active pulse rate with no signal strength change meant the jaguar was locally active, while an inactive pulse rate meant the animal was resting. Rabinowitz studied the activity by monitoring the animals at 15 minute intervals for 24 hours.

The results indicated that the jaguars were mainly nocturnal, traveling just after sunset and throughout the night. They rested during the day. The data showed more activity during the dry season than wet season. In contrast, the jaguars in Brazil were more active during the day, but their prey were also active during the day.

Rabinowitz also walked the roads and trails in Cockscomb observing tracks and scats (feces). Jaguar tracks are easily distinguishable from those of puma by their shape, but it is difficult to distinguish a young male from a female jaguar by their tracks. Sometimes individuals had unique characteristics that allowed them to be identified specifically from their tracks. For example, one male had one toe which was crooked and smaller than the other toes. In this way, Rabinowitz was able to identify another adult male and two adult females from their tracks and to plot their home ranges.

When he became aware of killed jaguars, Rabinowitz measured and took what data he could from them. He used these animals in a study of problem jaguars in Belize.

The Belize study confirmed earlier studies in Brazil that the jaguar is solitary except during breeding season. The larger male territories overlap a number of female territories. The young use their mother's home range for up to two years after which they become independent in their own territory.

The studies indicated male ranges of 25-38 square km whereas females had a territory about half that size. Four adult males that were continuously tracked for 3 to 14 months showed an average home range of 33 square km. Some males' ranges showed consider-able overlap. For example, one male's range was overlapped by at least 4 males, a female and a puma. Rabinowitz estimated an average density of one jaguar per 15 square km. Thus, the CBWS, which is almost 600 square km, might support as many as 40 jaguars.

When two of the males died during the study's first year, other males shifted into their ranges within a month, while still maintaining portions of their former ranges. One of these shifts allowed another male to move into the Basin.

Jaguar males are thought to signal ownership of their territories through urine spray marking, piled feces (scats), scratching tree trunks or leaving scratch marks in the earth. Sometimes they leave both urine and feces in scrapes of piled litter. However, the Cockscomb studies showed that the jaguars used feces only in these scrapings, with no detection of urine.

Despite the overlap in their territories, males showed few scars which indicated that there had been few fights between males. Tagged males were rarely noted in close proximity of each other and there were no fresh signs of more than one male in an area. However, all scats and scrapes in the ground were found in overlap zones between the territories of two males.

Roaring is also thought to inform other males of the presence of the calling male. Females may also roar. Old time hunters of jaguars in Belize could call in male jaguars with a jaguar caller. A caller consists of half of a calabash gourd covered by animal skin. A horsehair or other long reed is attached to the center of the drum head skin. The index finger and thumb are slid over the reed in the natural cadence used by a calling male emitting a low-pitched cough or grunt-like sound. The roar pattern consists of three or more slow coughs followed by a rapidly accelerating series of coughs.

Jaguar Prey

Despite their size and power, jaguars in the Cockscomb Basin often select small prey. This might reflect size to some extent because jaguars that inhabit the rainforest may be smaller than those in more open areas. Although jaguars can climb, most hunting occurs on the ground. Prey is often cached, or hidden for future consumption.

By analyzing hair and bone fragments in 228 scats, Rabinowitz determined that the jaguar's favorite food is the armadillo. Armadillo remains accounted for 53%, paca and anteater each accounted for 9%, followed by lesser amounts of red brocket deer, peccary, agouti and opossum.

In a related study, Rabinowitz and Nottingham determined the relative abundance of the various prey species by making transects and noting signs, such as tracks, armadillo diggings, and agouti and paca gnawings on cohune nuts. They found that armadillo and paca were the most numerous prey in the Basin, followed by red brocket deer and agouti.

In other areas jaguars are known to take fish. They attract fish with their moving tail after which they swipe the fish out of the water with a powerful paw. Other prey may include monkeys, tapir, birds, turtles and their eggs, frogs, and small rodents.

Alan Rabinowitz measuring jaguar tracks on the CBWS Access Road.

The Role of Jaguars in Mayan Culture
Judy Lumb

Jaguars have been present in the environment of the Mayan people for many centuries and are represented in traditions that have been handed down from generation to generation. Jaguars often appear as tricksters or clever clowns in their myths and legends. In one story told by Julio Saqui of Maya Center Village, the jaguar tricked the man so that he could steal the man's woman.

In 1989 I was privileged to witness the traditional Mayan Deer Dance in the village of San Antonio in the Toledo District of Belize, the village from which the people of Maya Center migrated. The Deer Dance was performed for 9 days, each day at a different home in the village. Each morning the sound of the drum announced the procession to the dance location. Leading the procession was the Holy Deer and the Tiger (jaguar), followed by the other characters of the dance and the marimba being played by one man while being carried by two others.

The marimba player directed the dance. The twelve dancers faced the marimba in two lines. Those in the left line were said to be the older brothers or sisters of those in the right line. Heading the lines were two men in red, called "Bacabs," the guardians of the directions, then the Holy Deer on the left and the Tiger on the right, followed by another pair of bacabs, the women (played by men), the dogs and, finally, the hunters, who were dressed in black. The bacabs and the hunters played rattles and chanted.

The entire dance was repeated each day, beginning with the story of the Tiger. The Tiger danced around each of the other dancers and then chased and was chased by each of the bacabs. The Tiger played the clown, improvising and teasing the hunters throughout the dance, stealing their hats or their rattles. Finally, the Tiger was captured by the hunters and the dancer stepped out of the skin of his costume and out of the dance. The hunters pantomimed the killing and skinning of the Tiger.

In contrast, the story of the Holy Deer was danced with reverence instead of comedy. The Holy Deer danced grandly around, acknowledging the other dancers and then ran away to hide in the woods. The hunters sent their dogs after him. Eventually, the Holy Deer was chased back by the dogs and the hunters captured the skin as the dancer slipped out of it. The hunters killed the deer, skinned it, and gave it to the women to end the dance.

The dance seemed to be a hunting ritual and, like most other Mayan traditions, was combined with a Christian ritual, namely the celebration of the Saint Day for San Luis, August 25.

*The jaguar in the traditional Mayan Deer Dance
in San Antonio, Toledo District, Belize, August, 1989*

Conflict With Humans

As the human population increases with accompanying deforestation, the conflict between humans and jaguars in Belize will continue to intensify. But this is not a new issue. E. R. Blake remembered his 1935 experience in a 1987 memorandum—

> "This (or several) jaguar had been harassing scattered marginal plantations, etc., along the Sittee River several miles from the coast for months and seemed to concentrate on dogs, allegedly killing quite a few. There was mounting fear that sooner or later it (they) would take small children. . .
>
> "As the attacks were widely scattered and unpredictable, Agostini and I staked out a small hound dog covered by our two shotguns and waited for them to be triggered. On the third night my gun went off in the wee small hours and the jaguar was killed instantly by a blast of #4 shot. It was skinned out as a rug which I won from Agostini by the flip of a coin, long since worn out and discarded. In hindsight, I should have turned it in to Carnegie as a specimen record."

While attacks on humans are extremely rare, predation by jaguars on livestock is a problem, especially where there is cattle ranching. From the available literature on jaguar livestock depredation, it seems probable that only certain "problem jaguars" are guilty of killing livestock since, when they are killed, the livestock deaths cease. However, it is sometimes difficult to determine which is the problem jaguar and non-problem jaguars are killed along with those that hunt the livestock.

In addition, the number of problem jaguars may increase if some are wounded. In Rabinowitz's 1986 study of jaguar predation on livestock, most of the 13 problem jaguars were previously injured jaguars. Ten had prior injury to the head or body, including at least one broken or missing upper canine, old shotgun wounds, pellets in the skull and old pellets in the body. Two of the three animals without old injuries were subadults.

Rabinowitz also found that healthy jaguars ranged near livestock without killing them. —

> "Healthy adult jaguars seemed reluctant to cross man-made boundaries into pastures or villages, despite the presence of potential domestic prey. However, there was no reluctance to prey upon domestic animals when they were left untended within the jaguar's range. Pigs placed in the forest were quickly killed, yet these same jaguars never came into nearby villages for pigs or dogs."

Thus, if livestock are allowed to range into the forests they are at risk. Proper livestock management can do a great deal to reduce depredation of stock. Rabinowitz reported in 1991 that "where livestock are managed and kept in pens or open pastures, problem jaguars are few."

Blake and Agostini kill a problem jaguar in 1935

Translocation does not seem to be a viable way of containing problem animals, since they show a propensity to return to their original range and to continue to kill livestock. Additionally, translocating them into another's range will only cause stress and disorientation within the normal population.

In 1995 Rabinowitz described a general strategy for conservation of jaguars and for dealing with problem jaguars —

"creation of more extensive protected areas within the jaguar's range . . .
"education in livestock management for ranchers . . .
"government assistance to individuals with jaguar problems . . .
"stricter penalties and enforcement for the illegal killing of jaguars . . .
"jaguar conservation education."

A recent study done for the Government of Belize by Round River Conservation on the conservation and management of Belize's jaguar population recommends that:

- provisions of the existing Wildlife Protection Act of 1981 be enforced, especially the requirement for hunting licences,
- education on jaguar conservation and the laws of Belize be provided to hunters, tour guides, and the general public,
- government agencies responsible for wildlife protection should participate in discussions about development projects that would affect wildlife habitat,
- conservation officer capabilities be strengthened by additional training,
- livestock management techniques be improved by adequate training of ranchers,
- wildlife research needed for policy and management be identified and prioritized, and
- increased funding for all of the above activities be obtained from licencing fees, taxes on guns and ammunition, and shared fees charged for use of Protected Areas.

The following procedure is to be followed in the event of a problem jaguar anywhere in Belize.

Procedure for Problem Jaguars in Belize

1. Contact the Belize Forest Department.
2. They will investigate and determine the best solution, whether to translocate the animal or destroy it.
3. The carcass and skin of any destroyed jaguar remain the property of the Belize government and will not be sold for profit.

References
Blake, E. R. 1935. The Invincible Cockscombs. *The Carnegie Magazine* 9(4): 99-104.

Blake, E. R. Memorandum to Timothy McCarthy, May 18, 1987.

Janzen, D.H., ed. 1983. *Costa Rican Natural History*. University of Chicago Press: Chicago, IL.

Macdonald, D., ed. 1984. *The Encyclopedia of Mammals*. Facts On File: New York, NY.

Macdonald, D., ed. 1984. *Carnivores*. Torstar Books: New York, NY.

Nowak, R.M. and J.L. Paradaiso. 1983. *Walker's Mammals of the World*. The Johns Hopkins Press: Baltimore, MD.

Rabinowitz, A.R. 1986. Jaguar predation on domestic livestock in Belize. *Wildlife Society Bulletin*, 14: 170-174.

Rabinowitz, A.R. 1986. *Jaguar. One Man's Battle to Establish the World's First Jaguar Preserve*. Arbor House: New York, NY.

Rabinowitz, A. R. 1995. Jaguar Conflict and Conservation, A Strategy for the Future. p. 394-397 in *Proc. Frst Int. Wildlife Management Congress*. The Wildlife Society: Bethesda, MD.

Rabinowitz. A.R. and B.G. Nottingham. 1986. Ecology and behaviour of the jaguar (*Panthera onca*) in Belize, Central America. *Journal of Zoology*, 210: 149-159.

Rabinowitz, A.R. 1991. New Jaguar Study. *Belize Audubon Society Newsletter* 23 (3): 4-6.

Round River Conservation Studies. 1995. Results of Investigations to Undertake Jaguar and Wildlife Research in Belize. Submitted to the Forest Department, Government of Belize.

Schaller, G.W. and P.G. Crawshaw. 1980. Movement patterns of Jaguar. *Biotropica*, 12: 161-168.

Seidensticker, J. and S. Lumpkin, eds. 1991. *Great Cats*. Rodale Press: Emmaus, PA.

CHAPTER 5

Other Cats of the
Cockscomb Basin
Robert Horwich

Puma (*Puma concolor*)

The pumas found in the Cockscomb Basin, locally called red tiger, are a smaller subspecies of puma that is limited to the Yucatan peninsula. Despite their small size, they are sometimes referred to as "upstart cats" in Belize because they hold their ground when encountering humans. While jaguars have only been known to show curiosity toward humans, never attacking them, puma have, on rare occasions, attacked children.

Despite their large size pumas do not have the ability to roar like jaguars. But they do purr like a domestic cat in friendly social situations. Puma colouration differs markedly from that of the jaguar. Adult pumas have no spots. Their coats are tan with lighter underbellies. The young are spotted cryptically for protection, but they lose their spotted coat at 6-8 months. Pumas have long tails and small heads.

Although jaguars and pumas are found in the same general areas in Belize, they have different habitats. Jaguars prefer wet riverine forests, but pumas frequent drier areas. Thus, pumas are found in the open pine ridge areas at the eastern end of the Cockscomb Basin.

Pumas are generalists and have a very extensive range, inhabiting a variety of habitats and altitudinal levels. They are agile climbers and, although they do not prefer water, are good swimmers. Despite this adaptive nature pumas are not common within their range.

Pumas may prey on the some of the same animals as jaguars, but they also divide up the food sources by size and type. Rabinowitz collared one male puma and analyzed a few scat samples. The puma feces contained small rodents and four-eyed opossums which were rarely found in jaguar feces. Elsewhere pumas are known to feed on pacas, armadillos, coatis, monkeys, tapirs, agoutis, porcupines, and peccaries.

Habitat also determines the prey species. In many areas puma prey on deer, but not the red brocket deer of the forest, Instead, they hunt in more open habitats frequented by white-tailed deer.

Puma

   Pumas are powerful predators, stalking and capturing prey in a short chase with their large clawed forepaws. With larger prey they may move the unfinished carcass to a secluded place and cover it with leaves, sticks or other debris. They may return a number of times or they may abandon the cache.

   Pumas establish territories of about 25-50 square km for males or 10-40 square km areas for females. Males have fairly rigid boundaries that are maintained by scent marking but their range may overlap with more than one female. Pumas move a great deal covering sometimes 50-70 km in a night.

   Scent marking can function both to bring animals together or space them. They leave urine or feces on trees or in scrapes of piled litter. In Cockscomb studies by Rabinowitz and Nottingham, pumas left urine in the scrapes half of the time. Anal scent glands leave other smells in the pile. These scrapes are round piles about 30 cm wide and 12 cm high and are occasionally seen along the road. Pumas also leave scratch marks on tree trunks or fallen logs. These consist of 2 parallel scrapes 20 cm long.

   Female pumas attain sexual maturity at 2.5-3 years. There does not seem to be a main breeding season. The puma's high-pitched legendary scream, which has a human quality, is thought to be emitted by the female during the breeding season. Gestation takes three months and litters of one to four spotted kittens are concealed in crevices or hollow trees. The mother suckles the young for three or four months. Then she brings them food she has caught and later takes them directly to the kill. They remain with their mother for over a year or longer.

Small Cat Study

Three small, endangered cats are found in the Cockscomb Basin, jaguarundis, ocelot and margays. They overlap throughout their ranges in Mexico, Central America and most of South America. In addition, ocelots and jaguarundis are found, along with jaguars, as far north as the southwestern United States. Margays are more tied to their arboreal niche in the rain forests that begin around Veracruz, Mexico.

In order for these three similar cat species to coexist together in the same habitat, there must be some distinguishing habits to allow for different niches. This was the subject of a study by Mike Konecny in the Cockscomb Basin from 1985 to 1986. Very little was known about the habits of these species and this study was one of the first attempts to use radio telemetry with these animals.

Cats were captured in large wire traps baited with live chickens. The trapped animals were anesthetized and fitted with radio transmitter collars so they could be followed. Prey species were determined by examination of scats (feces), since the size, shape, odor and surrounding tracks allowed identification of the species which defecated it.

All three species of cats traveled about 6.5 km in an average 24 hour period. Home ranges varied considerably, ranging from 10 to 99 square km, and the size of the home range was not related to the size of the animal or the species.

All three species preyed on other vertebrates, especially other mammals, with such prey comprising 95-98% of their diet. However, there was some difference in temporal habitat use. Jaguarundi hunted in the daytime and the other two cats hunted at night. The larger ocelot took larger prey than the margay, and the ocelot's niche was primarily on the ground while the margay was arboreal, reducing the competition between the species.

Jaguarundi (*Herpailurus yagouaroundi*)

Jaguarundis or halaris, as they are called locally, are different in appearance from the other Cockscomb cats. Their slender, elongated bodies (over 1 m) are supported by such short legs that they are only 25-30 cm high at the shoulder. This elongated appearance accentuated by a long tail (0.5 m) and small, flattened ears makes jaguarundis look more like a weasel than a cat. Weighing 4-8 kg, jaguarundis occur in two color phases, a dark gray phase that can even be black and, more rarely, a deep reddish brown.

The jaguarundi's unusual body type is reflected in a different capture strategy. Instead of stalking like most cats, they run down their prey. They are primarily ground dwellers, although they have been known to climb trees after fruits. The animals are secretive and, if you see one, it will usually be for only an instant before it disappears.

Jaguarundi

Three jaguarundis were captured, collared and followed by Konecny. They were mostly active in the daytime, but some activity was noted at night, especially on moonlit nights. There was no difference between the sexes in how they travel. They follow a single directional path each day rarely doubling back and consequently end up far from where they started each day.

The female occupied an area of about 13 square kilometers; and the two males lived in areas of 30 and 100 square km. Compared to other cats, the home range of the male jaguarundi seemed too large. This cannot be due to competition with other species, because Konecny's results indicated that there were sufficient differences in temporal activity, size of prey species and species taken by each carnivore species to avoid competition. Thus, it is more probable that the large territory size of the males allowed them to monitor a number of females for breeding.

Differing from the small spotted cats, jaguarundis seemed to prefer riparian (river) habitats and located their dens along stream banks. They were most commonly found in disturbed second growth, such as former milpas, but they used mature forests also. In other areas of Belize they may be found in open savanna, lowland forest edges or dense brush, especially near water.

Their habitat determined the type of prey jaguarundis hunted which included rodents (48% of scats) small birds (21%), and opossums (13%). Vertebrate species comprised 95% of the bulk of their diet, but some arthropod remains were found in most scat samples. Seeds were also found in their scats indicating vegetable matter was used as a diet supplement. In other parts of their range jaguarundis feed mainly on small mammals and birds, although they have been known to prey on reptiles, especially iguanas, and stranded fish along a stream bank. In Belize they are often thought of as pests since they prey on domestic chickens as well.

Ocelot (*Leopardus pardalis*)

The two smaller spotted cats, margay and ocelot, both called tiger cats in Belize, are closely related and look alike except for size. A medium-sized cat, the ocelot may reach 1 m in length and weigh as much as 16 kilograms. Two black stripes on the cheek and spots on the side forming longer bands characterize ocelots. Both ocelots and margays may occur rarely in melanistic forms.

Ocelot

Ocelots inhabit a variety of habitats from dry scrub to tropical rainforest but hunt mainly on the ground although they can climb as well. Their size and ground dwelling habits allow them to exploit a different niche from the closely related margay. Ocelots are thought to be especially suited to preying on ground-dwelling birds. They hunt using quick rushes and acrobatic leaps to capture these larger ground birds as they attempt to escape in flight. Ocelots are prone to pluck birds before eating them, which characterizes an adaptation for preying on birds.

However, Konecny's Cockscomb study showed that bird remains were less frequently found in the scats of ocelots than in any of the other cats studied. Instead, these ocelots fed primarily on small and medium-sized mammals. Their prey was larger than that of margays. They most frequently consumed opossums and armadillos but also ate brocket deer, tamandua, peccaries, birds and reptiles.

Konecny captured, radio-tagged, and followed one male and two female ocelots. They were mostly active at night, but some activity was seen during the day, especially on overcast or rainy days. Even their nighttime activity was composed of a couple of active hours followed by an hour of inactivity. Ocelots often hunt in pairs, mewing to keep in contact with each other.

The ocelots maintained territories that they used intensively, continually backtracking as they moved. They used second growth areas extensively with some movements into older secondary forest. Ocelots are thought to maintain territories by marking them with fecal scrapes, scratching trees and urine spray, but none of these were observed by Konecny.

Margay (*Leopardus wiedii*)

Margays, the smallest and most arboreal of the small cats, are a little bigger than a domestic cat and have the ability to rotate their hind limbs and feet so that they can grasp the tree trunk with their long claws to descend trees head first like a squirrel. Their long tail aids in balance as they climb and leap in the canopy branches. But their arboreal life must restrict reproduction because margays have only one pair of teats for nursing and give birth to only 1 or 2 kittens.

This adaptation to an arboreal life allows the margay to prey on smaller arboreal prey. Although the margay may be active during the day it is much more active at night, resting during day in the trees. This arboreal, rainforest niche separates the margay from the other small cats which may move through open country. Thus, margays are very susceptible to the rainforest destruction which is occurring throughout their range.

Konecny captured two margays and followed only one young adult male for six months. The facts that few margays were captured and few signs of margays were seen during the study indicate a low population level of margays in the Cockscomb. The study confirms

Margays

the general knowledge that they are nocturnal and rest during the day in trees 7-10 meters from the ground usually in a tangle of vines and lianas or in the bole of a cohune palm. They vary their resting spots but will return to them on occasion.

Observed movements in the Cockscomb were always on the ground but margays have been reported to move through the tops of canopies in other parts of Belize. The collared animal confirmed a general preference for older secondary forests.

The scats were covered with leaves and dirt rather than being deposited in conspicuous places. In line with their arboreal habits, margays took more birds and fewer terrestrial mammals than the other cats studied. They showed over 96% of prey bulk to be arboreal mammals. Arboreal rodents found include rats (48%), squirrels (22%), mice (19%) and opossums (19%). Some scats also showed arthropods, birds and fruit.

References

Emmons, L.H. 1987. Comparative feeding ecology of felids in a neotropical rainforest. *Behavioral Ecology and Sociobiology*, 20: 271-283.

Emmons, L.H. 1989. Ocelot behavior in moonlight. In *Advances in Neotropical Mammalogy*, pp. 233-242. K.H. Redford and J.F. Eisenberg, eds. The Sandhill Crane Press: Gainesville, FL.

Guggisberg, C.A. 1975. *Wild Cats of the World*. C.A. Taplinger Publishing: New York, NY.

Janzen, D.H. (ed.) 1983. *Costa Rican Natural History*. University of Chicago Press: Chicago, IL.

Konecny, M.J. 1989. Movement patterns and food habits of four sympatric carnivore species in Belize, Central America. In *Advances in Neotropical Mammalogy*, pp. 243-264, K.H. Redford and J.F. Eisenberg, eds. The Sandhill Crane Press: Gainesville, FL.

Macdonald, D., ed. 1984. *The Encyclopedia of Mammals*. Facts On File: New York, NY.

Macdonald, D., ed. 1984. *Carnivores*. Torstar Books: New York, NY.

McCarthy,T.J. 1992. Notes concerning the jaguarundi cat (*Herpailurus yagouroundi*) in the Caribbean lowlands of Belize and Guatemala. *Mammalia*, 56: 302-306.

Nowak, R.M. and J.L. Paradaiso. 1983. *Walker's Mammals of the World*. The Johns Hopkins Press: Baltimore, MD.

Seidensticker, J. and S. Lumpkin, eds. 1991. *Great Cats*. Rodale Press: Emmaus, PA.

Sunquist, M.E. and D.E. Daneke. 1989. Ecological separation in a Venezuelan llanos carnivore community. In *Advances in Neotropical Mammalogy,* pp 197-232. K.H. Redford and J.F. Eisenberg, eds. The Sandhill Crane Press: Gainesville, FL.

Tinesley, J.B. 1987. *The Puma, Legendary Lion of the Americas*. Texas Western Press: The University of Texas, El Paso, TX.

CHAPTER 6

Other Mammals of the Cockscomb Basin

Katherine M. Emmons, Robert H. Horwich, Timothy J. McCarthy, and Judy Lumb

Mammals (Class *Mammalia*)

Mammals are warm-blooded vertebrates, which means the body regulates its own temperatures and uses energy from food to keep warm. Mammals have hair and claws or nails, and are able to nurse their young from mammary glands. Humans are mammals, along with dogs, peccaries, monkeys, and jaguars, to name just a few.

Opossums (Order *Marsupialia*)

Opossums are marsupials, mammals in which the young are born as a tiny embryo after a very short gestation. Each is immediately attached by its mouth to one of the mother's nipples where they stay until they are well-developed. Most, but not all, species have pouches to protect the young while attached to the nipples.

Opossums have very short legs, long noses and long tails. There are four species of opossum recorded in the Cockscomb Basin. They are exclusively nocturnal and can sometimes be seen on the trails at night with a flashlight. Their eyes look small and far apart in a bright reflection of the light.

The common opossum (*Didelphis marsupialis*) is the largest of Cockscomb's opossums. The body is 32-42 cm long and the tail is about the same length. It is mostly black with lighter yellowish underparts and face. The tail is naked and black with a white tip.

The grey four-eyed opossum (*Philander opossum*) gets its name from the distinct black mask around its eyes and over the top of its head. Pale spots over the eyes look like eyebrows. The upper part of its body is grey with cream-coloured underparts. The tail is dark grey with a white tip and has fur on only the quarter nearest the base.

The Mexican mouse opossum (*Marmosa mexicana*) is the smallest of Cockscomb's opossums, the body being only 8-15 cm long, and the only one that does not have a pouch. It is reddish brown with prominent black eye rings.

The water opossum (*Chironectes minimus*) is fairly common in the Cockscomb Basin and may be seen swimming at night in South Stann Creek or its tributaries. It is silver grey with wide black bands across the back, connected with a narrow stripe along the spine. The face is dark with a pale stripe running from ear to ear across the brow.

Bats (Order *Chiroptera*)
Other name: ratbat

Bats are an extremely beneficial component of tropical eco-systems. Twenty-five species have been documented in the CBWS, but there may be more because there are 65 in the entire country of Belize. In fact, bat species constitute 53% of mammal species in Belize.

Bats are the only mammals capable of true flight. Their wings are made of strong, flexible skin supported by a greatly modified hand. Elongated finger bones provide considerable wing flexibility. To reduce weight, bats have very weak legs with few muscles. As a result, most bats cannot walk or stand and hang upside down to rest. This position allows them to use gravity to provide the energy for takeoff on their next flight and to rest out of the reach of predators.

Bats use a form of sonar, or echolocation, to determine the position of nearby objects. They emit high frequency sounds which echo back to be received by their ears. This allows the bat to navigate at night through the dark forest understory, as well as to determine the whereabouts of prey. Most bats have an excellent sense of smell and can see very well, but are color blind.

Bats do not deserve their negative reputation. They only bite to defend themselves and do not fly into people's faces or hair. Bats have few natural predators, but humans can do great damage to bat populations by destroying their roost sites and through excessive use of chemicals in agriculture.

Neotropical bats evolved from insect-eating ancestors but diverged into various other feeding habits. Today there are bats that eat insects, fruit, nectar, vertebrates, and blood.

Insect-eaters are the largest group of bats. Some scoop up mosquitoes and other winged insects that are active at dusk. As many as 1,800 flying insects can be consumed by one individual bat in one night. Other bats are specialized to detect large insects like katydids perched on vegetation. Their catch is eaten at a secure roosting site.

The tiny, insect-eating Spix's disc-winged bat *(Throptera tricolor)* roosts in unfurled heliconia leaves. The Cockscomb Basin is the only place in Belize where this bat has been seen.

Frugivorous bats (fruit eaters) play a crucial role in dispersing seeds. They often pick fruit from a tree and fly to a roost to eat, spitting out large seeds and indigestible matter. Smaller seeds pass through the digestive system of the bat and are defecated, dispersing them. Many frugivorous bats also eat some insects.

True nectar-eaters are small bats with long tongues, but, when nectar is abundant, other bats will frequent accessible blossoms. Some are found in gardens as well as in forests. Bats are very important for pollinating trees like the ceiba, balsa, and calabash. As they lap the nectar from the blossoms, they also collect pollen and pass it from flower to flower. Many bat-pollinated plants have large, whitish flowers that are easy for the bats to see at night, and have a fragrant scent that attracts the bats. Most nectar-eating bats also eat some fruit, and catch insects to satisfy their protein needs.

Vertebrate-eaters are quite specialized. The greater fishing bat (*Noctilio leporinus*) uses its sonar to locate fish that break the surface of streams. It grabs the fish with its claws, then returns to a roost to eat the fish. The bulldog bat also feeds on insects.

Greater Fishing Bat

Carnivorous bats like the wooly false vampire bat (*Chrotopterus auritus)* species eat small animals such as lizards. Others species eat rodents, birds and reptiles as well as large insects. They locate some of their prey by scent.

Blood-feeders are known as vampire bats. Of all the bat species known in Belize, only two are vampire bats. The common vampire bat (*Desmodus rotundus)* feeds on mammals. In deforested areas it feeds on domesticated livestock like cattle, angering farmers. It will feed on human blood as well, but this is rare if easier prey is nearby.

Vampire bats crawl on their hind legs and wrists, and do not need a sophisticated echolocation system. They do not suck blood, but instead painlessly cut the skin with razor sharp teeth (upper incisors) and lap up the blood as it flows. Their saliva contains an anticoagulant coenzyme which allows the blood to flow freely. Scientists are studying this compound as a possible heart medication, because it opens the arteries faster and better than medications in use today.

Vampire bats must be controlled where they pose problems to livestock. Unfortunately, many people believe all bats are vampire bats and kill them indiscriminately.

Edentates (Order *Edentata* or *Xenarthra*)

Edentates are a group of mammals which have either weak, peg-like teeth or no teeth at all.   The meaning of edentate is "without teeth." They are the last of a large, ancient group of species that evolved in South America when it was an isolated continent.

Two edentates, armadillo and tamandua, are very common in the Cockscomb Basin. Both species live on a specialized low energy diet and, therefore, show a low metabolic rate and sluggish movement.

Nine-Banded Armadillo

Nine-Banded Armadillo (*Dasypus novemcinctus*)
Other name: dilly, hamadilly

Armadillos have weak peg-like teeth for chewing insects. They thrive in warm areas where there are no extended cold periods to limit their insect prey. Because of their wide range of habitat use and a high breeding rate, they are a successful species with a very wide, expanding range from southern United States through central South America, as well as in some Caribbean islands. Their abundance at Cockscomb and throughout Belize may account for their use by the jaguar for food.

The word "armadillo," means "little armored one" in Spanish. The armor is an almost hairless external shell, which is arranged in bands connected by flexible skin. It develops from the skin modified to provide a double-layered covering of strong bony plates or scutes, overlaid by a layer of horny epidermis. These bands cover most of the upper body and tail, with some protection afforded to the head and limbs against thorny shrubs and from predators.

The armadillos' digging abilities and keen sense of smell allow them to locate and capture small vertebrates and invertebrates. They probe the earth and leaves with their long noses, searching mainly for insects, but they also eat reptiles, amphibians and a limited amount of plant material and carrion. Since their jaws are weak with reduced teeth, their diet must be small and soft.

Armadillos dig long underground burrows with powerful forelegs and then kick the loosened dirt toward the entrance with their hind legs. Burrows are often located in streambanks. Armadillos emerge at dusk after resting in burrows during the day.

When chased by a jaguar or other predator, armadillos first attempt to escape with a quick burst of speed toward their many burrow holes where they dig and anchor themselves underground. If caught above ground, they draw up within the armor, a futile gesture when confronted by the powerful jaws and teeth of a jaguar.

Although armadillos are known to live as long as 15 years, the average lifespan is four years. They mature at one to two years and breed during July and August. Though conception occurs at that time, the embryo does not implant in the uterus until November. From then gestation is 4-5 months. The normal litter is identical quadruplets of the same sex. The young are born able to see and move around the burrow on their own. However, the shell does not develop until much later, so the infants are very soft and vulnerable to predators.

Except females with litters, armadillos are mainly solitary. Females maintain fairly exclusive home ranges, perhaps to safeguard their litters, whereas males show considerable overlap in an area as large as 25 acres. A good sense of smell helps armadillos to communicate with each other. They mark territories using numerous scent glands located on the ears, eyelids, soles of feet, as well as around the anus.

Northern Tamandua (*Tamandua mexicana*)
Other names: collared anteater, antsbear

Tamanduas are medium-sized animals weighing between 3-7 kg. They have pale, yellowish heads and legs with a black "vest" covering the belly, lower back and shoulders. Their prehensile tails, naked at the tip, are adapted for climbing in the trees. Tamanduas forage on the ground or in trees either during the day or night.

Like other anteaters, tamanduas eat insects that congregate socially in nests, such as ants, termites and, rarely, bees. Their long tongues are perfectly suited for reaching into holes and crevices and trapping the prey with sticky saliva. Tamanduas have no teeth and instead grind insects in their muscular gizzard. They may eat termites away from the nest as well, since the insects have fewer defenses from the soldier termites on the trails.

Tamandua

The three large, powerful middle claws of their forefeet allow them to tear open wood or ant and termite nests. These claws are also used for defense. When not in use, the large claws curl under and in toward the center and the animal walks on the outside of its hand and knuckles.

Tamanduas mate around September or October and have only a single young six months later which rides on its mother's back as she moves through the forest. As the mother forages the baby climbs down to inspect potential food alongside of her. It is probable that a tiny relative, the silky anteater (*Cyclopes didactylus*) shares the Cockscomb forest with the tamandua, but its nocturnal, arboreal lifestyle does not make it easy to observe.

Primates
Central American Spider Monkey (*Ateles geoffroyi*)
Other name: monkey

Spider monkeys are not usually encountered in accessible parts of the CBWS, but live in the remote areas of the Basin. For example, two were seen on May 4, 1995, by hikers climbing Victoria Peak. This monkey weighs up to 8 kg. It is more slender than the black howler monkey and has long, thin legs, arms, and tail that help it move about in its arboreal home. Using hand over hand locomotion the monkey can swing quickly around in the branches. The prehensile tail can support the weight of the animal which frees the monkey's hands to eat or care for its young. The fur may be black, brown, or red-brown, with lighter fur on the underside. The face is pale and hairless.

These monkeys are very social and tend to travel through the tree tops in small groups that merge and split again as the animals forage for fruits. They disperse the seeds of many different fruits, especially figs.

Spider monkeys make several sounds, including a loud scream and a dog-like bark. If the monkeys perceive a threat on the forest floor, they will shake branches and bomb the intruder with plant matter, urine, and feces.

They are diurnal and rest quietly in the treetops at night. Baby monkeys cling to their mothers' bellies when they are very small. After one or two months the baby moves to the mother's back until it is large enough to move on its own. It begins to sample solid food at this time but continues to nurse for about a year. A new baby is born to female monkeys every two or three years, timing which allows a long and close association between the young animal and its mother.

However, due to this low birth rate, spider monkey populations have a slow, difficult recovery after depletion due to hunting or illness. Thus, they are very sensitive to human disturbance and decline rapidly when people enter a remote area. It is illegal to kill or capture monkeys for either food or pets. Some people like the idea of having a monkey for a pet, but they are wild animals that do not belong in captivity. Moreover, they become messy and mischievous as they get older.

Yucatan Black Howler Monkey (*Alouatta pigra*)
Other names: baboon

The black howler monkey is a large neotropical monkey found only in Belize and in southeastern Mexico and Guatemala. Howler monkeys get their name from their loud vocalizations. They howl in the morning and evening, when it rains, and when their territory is threatened. The sound is a hoarse roar, not what you would expect from a monkey.

Baboons have hands and feet that they use for getting around their treetop homes. The prehensile tail is like a fifth limb, grabbing hold of branches for extra support.

Baboons eat leaves, flowers, and fruits, and have an important ecological role as seed dispersers. They generally eat new leaves, which have lower concentrations of toxic tannins

Black Howler Monkey

and alkaloids. This forces them to browse on a wide variety of species, so they require a habitat with many different kinds of trees.

Baboons live in troops of 4-8 individuals, with one primary male, a few females, several young and, possibly, additional secondary males. The size of the territory depends on the available food supply and the size of the troop.

The females reach sexual maturity at about 4 or 5 years of age, and give birth to single infants after a gestation of 6 months. Infants cling to their mothers for about three months, then begin to play and socialize with other troop members.

The baboon is an endangered animal, threatened by habitat destruction and hunting. It is illegal to hunt baboons in Belize for either meat or pets. Black howler monkeys were common in the Cockscomb Basin until the 1950's. Melvin Hulse, Sr. reports that both spider monkeys and baboons were seen in the Cockscomb Basin until 1956-7 when he saw monkeys dying and falling out of the trees, apparently due to yellow fever. Loss of habitat from the effects of Hurricane Hattie in 1961 probably also contributed to their demise.

An ambitious reintroduction program began in 1992 to restore this species to the CBWS. Over a three-year period, 62 baboons were transferred from the Community Baboon Sanctuary in central Belize to the CBWS, equipped with radios to track their movements. Over 90% of the original animals survived and many babies have been born in the Cockscomb Basin (Chapter 7).

Rodents (Order *Rodentia*)

Fifteen percent of the species of land mammals of Belize are rodents, including squirrels, rats, mice, agouti, and paca (gibnut). *Rodentia* is the largest order of mammals in the world. The teeth of rodents are adapted to gnaw and grind hard food items. Canines and premolars are lacking, but the incisors continue to grow throughout life and are chisel-like in structure. Gnawing and cutting activity wears the hard surfaces of the incisors. The molar teeth provide a grinding surface with hard enamel folds and ridges. These teeth wear without replacement during the life of the rodent.

Deppe's Squirrel (*Sciurus deppei*)

Squirrels are rodents that are well-adapted for climbing trees. Their sharp claws cling to the tree bark and their flexible joints allow them to climb down head first. These climbing rodents especially like vine-covered trees. Squirrels are diurnal animals that move about quietly to satisfy their omnivorous diets. They feed on nuts and seeds, soft fruits, fungi, insects, and an occasional flower or leaf. Their chisel-like teeth are excellent tools for gnawing through the tough exterior of cohune nuts.

Tropical squirrels have not been studied extensively, but they probably have about two young. The young keep to a nest in a tangle of vines or tree hole until they are large enough to explore their surroundings. Deppe's squirrel (*Sciurus deppei*) is brown with a grey belly, and grey front legs and shoulders.

The Yucatan squirrel (*Sciurus yucatanensis*) is polymorphic, that is, its fur colour varies. It may be black, brown or grey. The tail is bushier than Deppe's squirrel and black, with frosty grey highlights. The belly is usually pale. Though the Yucatan squirrel has not been reported in the CBWS, it has been documented nearby and is presumed to be there.

Forest Spiny Pocket Mouse (*Heteromys desmarestianus*)

The forest spiny pocket mouse is a common species in the lowland and upland forest of Belize. It is quite distinctive in appearance among the rodents in Belize. The coarse fur contains modified stiff hairs with more flattened hairs dorsally (on top of the back). The fur on the back and forelimbs is dark brown to blackish contrasted by a white belly. The tail is longer than the head and body and has large scales. This tail is easily broken, which may be a defensive mechanism to avoid predation. The largest males reach 335 mm in total length and weigh about 105 grams; males are larger than females. Spiny pocket mice produce as many as five litters annually with an average of three young each.

While a reasonable climber, the forest spiny pocket mouse dwells primarily at ground level where it is a granivore feeding on seeds. Seeds are temporarily held in the cheek pouches while foraging and then hoarded in their nests or in caches elsewhere within its territory. Nests have been reported associated with ground holes and decomposing tree falls. *Heteromys* is the only genus that possesses fur-lined cheek pouches.

Big-eared Climbing Rat (*Ototylomys phyllotis*)

There are two species of big-eared climbing rats, *Ototylomys phyllotis* and *Tylomys nudicaudus,* but only *O. phyllotis* has been documented in the Cockscomb *Basin.* However, it is anticipated that further studies will reveal the presence of *T. nudicaudus.*

The fur of both species is long and soft, contrasting a completely white belly with a brown to greyish-brown back that is darker in the middle. The tails are long (approximately equal to body-head length) and naked (without hair cover) with large scales. The total length of an adult *O. phyllotis* can exceed 50 cm in Belize,

Big-eared climbing rats range from southeastern Mexico to central Costa Rica, where they frequent both dry and moist tropical forests. They forage both on the ground and in trees. What is known about food habits suggests a diet of fruit and leaves. Females have several litters of about three young each year with the number of pregnancies increasing during the dry season. These rats nest in ground level burrows with entrances beneath rocks and ascend the trees at night.

This rat is the principal reservoir in Belize for a parasite, *Leishmania mexicana*, which causes cutaneous leishmaniasis or bay sore, a human disease carried by sandflies.

Hispid Cotton Rat (*Sigmodon hispidus*)
Other name: Pine Ridge Rat

The pine ridge rat, as its name suggests, inhabits the more open grass/sedge and brushy habitats of Belize, such as that on Cabbage Haul Ridge. It invades the eastern basin of Cockscomb along the grassy corridors created by roads, trails, skidder tracks, secondary vegetation, and areas of human habitation. Consequently, its occurrence in forest habitat reflects disturbance. Pine ridge rats are active during the day, constructing trails through the cover of the grasses. Nests are made from grass.

Older pine ridge rats from Cockscomb measured 25-30 cm in length and weigh 100-130 grams. The sparsely haired tail is shorter than the body. The body is robust with a dense fur of short and rather coarse hair. The coloration is not uniform but has a "salt and pepper" grizzled appearance. The ears are short and rounded.

The teeth and digestive tract of this rodent are adapted to chewing and digesting grasses, sedges, and young plants, besides eating seeds, fruits, insects, etc. Pine ridge rats were found to be reproductively prolific with litter sizes ranging from 2 to 10 young.

Mexican Porcupine (*Coendou mexicanus*)
Other names: hairy porcupine, prehensile-tailed porcupine

This mammal has an undeserved reputation for being dangerous. True, its modified hairs, called quills, are sharp and will detach into the face or mouth of a biting aggressor. But the porcupine does not shoot or throw its quills, nor does it purposefully attempt to stick a passerby. Quills are most visible on the head and neck where the hair is thinner and shorter. They are yellow in colour, and stick out a little from under the black or dark brown fur. Arboreal predators like the margay learn from an early age to leave porcupines alone.

Unlike North American porcupines, the hairy porcupine has a prehensile tail that provides the animal with an extra grip as it forages in its tree-top habitat for fruits and foliage. The hairy porcupine is a nocturnal animal. It sleeps throughout the day in a hollow tree and people rarely en-counter it.

Mexican Porcupine

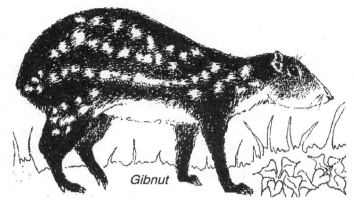

Gibnut

Paca (*Agouti paca*)
Other name: gibnut

Gibnuts are large rodents weighing 4 to 8 kg. They have a heavy stocky body with extremely short, stubby tails. They differ from the smaller agoutis by the reddish color, four noticeable rows of white spots, and white underparts. Gibnuts are nocturnal and their widely spaced eyes give a bright yellow or orange eyeshine. Gibnuts can sometimes be heard walking noisily through the leaves.

Gibnuts prefer habitats near streams and swamps, sleeping in large burrows in the river banks, on slopes or among tree roots which usually have more than one exit for escape. They swim readily and may try an escape through the water. They feed on fallen fruits, nuts and other plant materials such as leaves, stems and roots. Their large bodies allow them to store food as fat.

Gibnuts have enlarged skulls that act as a resonating chamber to amplify loud grinding sounds, which may be used to communicate with one another or to scare potential predators. They share a territory with their mates but forage and sleep alone. Gibnuts mate and produce one or two young born in the dry season. They may also have two additional pregnancies in the same year. Young gibnuts are lively soon after birth and follow their mother through the forest.

Gibnuts are an important food source for rainforest carnivores. With their heavy bodies, they are not adapted to run from predators. Instead, they run a short distance to a dark place, freeze and remain motionless until it is safe. Their cryptic spots make them difficult to see in the nocturnal forest. They may also take refuge in water remaining immersed for a considerable time. They are frequently hunted for meat, making them scarce in populated areas. Although their potential domestication is controversial, there is some indication that they could be raised commercially.

Central American Agouti (*Dasyprocta punctata*)
Other name: bush rabbit, Indian rabbit

Agoutis are smaller than gibnuts, about the size of a small house cat. Their coarse, glossy fur is greyish black with buffy underparts. They have small round ears and no tail. Agoutis live in forests, secondary growth and savannas, and are usually associated with water like the gibnut.

Agoutis fill an important niche in the forest as seed dispersers because they often bury or cache nuts and seeds and then forget to dig them up. Although both gibnuts and agoutis are fruit and seed eaters, agoutis can cut through harder seed covers. They rest on their haunches, freeing the forepaws for seed manipulation, and gnaw on one spot. They also eat fungi, leaves and insects. Agoutis are most active in early morning or late afternoon and otherwise rest in hollow logs or burrows.

Socially they differ from the gibnut, forming long-lasting mated pairs with 1-2 hectare territories that include their breeding nests, sleeping spots, feeding areas and a stretch of the river. Males defend the territory aggressively by erecting their long rump hairs in display and thumping the ground with their hind feet. They may chase the intruder as it flees and bite it on the rump. Smell is important in communication and their trails and sleeping areas are marked with their anal glands.

Breeding occurs throughout the year with a greater number of young being born from March through July when more fruit is available. Those young born during this fruiting period are most likely to survive. Mating courtship involves the male spraying the female with urine after which she eventually allows him to mate with her.

Usually one or two young are born and occasionally three. Like the gibnut, they are born with their eyes open and have the ability to run within the first hour after birth. The young are born in the mother's sleeping area but later she leads them to potential nest sites which have small entrances to protect them from predators. The young agoutis select a small burrow and line it with leaves. Since the mother is too large for their small burrow, she calls them out only to be nursed or cleaned. Aggression by the parents causes the young to leave after the next litter is born because food supply becomes limited.

Agoutis provide an important food source for predators like jaguars, ocelots and coatimundis. While heavy-bodied gibnuts freeze in response to predators, agoutis are slim, fast and agile. When startled, agoutis bark alarmingly and may stamp their feet or run off at a fast pace. Although rodents, both agoutis and gibnuts have hoof-like nails on their toes allowing them to escape rapidly. Agoutis are also hunted by humans and are often eliminated in areas of high human habitation.

Carnivores

Grey Fox (*Urocyon cinereoargenteus*)

The grey fox is a wild relative of the domestic dog. Foxes mark their territories like dogs, by spraying urine on rocks or plants or by leaving feces in obvious places. Foxes are small, weighing no more than 6 kg. They prefer to hunt along forest edges and in cultivated areas and are found in the pine ridge area of the eastern CBWS. Foxes do like to be near trees, however, and are adept at climbing them, unlike others of the dog family. They have long, sharp claws that help them grip the trunk, and strong hind legs that propel them up into the tree branches.

As carnivores, foxes catch and eat rodents and other small animals, or they eat carrion. Like many other tropical carnivores, foxes vary their diet with fruits and seeds. Fox parents occupy dens in protected hollows, under tree roots or rocks. They have litters of 2 to 6 young and care for them for five or six months.

White-nosed Coati (*Nasua narica*)
Other names: quash, coatimundi

Quash are cat-sized animals related to kinkajous and raccoons. They forage on the forest floor and in tree branches during the day. They are omnivorous, that is, they eat most anything, including small animals, invertebrates, fruits, and flowers. They use their long noses to poke into holes and cracks, and tear the soil and logs with their claws. Their rear claws allow them to climb with agility.

Females bear their young in an arboreal nest. Mothers and their young from the previous two years live in family groups of 4 to 30 animals. Members of these family units groom each other, but do not share food with one another. Mature males usually live alone.

Quash have few predators, but boa constrictors, hawks, and cats will eat them on occasion. Where humans have encroached on their native habitat, quash are pests because they enjoy corn and other crops.

A rare relative of the coatimundi, the cacomistle (*Bassariscus sumichrasti*), has been seen in the higher elevations of the Cockscomb Mountains.

White-nosed Coati

Kinkajou (*Potos flavus*)
Other name: nightwalker

Kinkajous are exclusively nocturnal members of the raccoon family. They frequent the treetops in search of fruits, insects, honey, and even flower nectar. They use their relatively short forelegs to bring food to the mouth. The colour of the kinkajou is brownish or red-grey with a red-brown or black head and face. Kinkajous are common in the CBWS and can be encountered when walking the trails at night. They are more often heard than seen, however, for they clamor noisily in the treetops, frequently dropping fruit.

Kinkajou

The kinkajou's prehensile tail acts as an extra limb, wrapping around branches for support and balance. It holds on tightly with its tail to reach out for food, even hanging upside down. The kinkajou does not often come out of the trees. When startled, they have an unusual vocalization that sounds like a cross between a loud sneeze and a bark. Their eyes are large and have an orange eyeshine. During the day kinkajous rest in tree hollows.

Tayra (*Eira barbara*)
Other name: bush dog

The tayra is not related to the dog but to the weasel, otter, and skunk. The fur of this animal is a lovely, glossy brown, grey or black, generally with a tan or yellowish face, head, and neck. The tayra is about the size of a large house cat, with relatively short front legs and a muscular body. The tail is thick and bushy, and is used for balance as the animal climbs trees or runs along logs and branches.

Tayras are crepuscular animals, that is, they hunt at dusk and dawn or on overcast days, searching in holes, logs, and under leaves for rats, agoutis, insects, lizards, eggs, and fruit. The tayra hunts anywhere that prey is found, both on the ground and in trees. Tayras adapt well to human encroachment and sometimes live near fields and pastures. In these cases they may hunt at night to avoid people and are blamed for killing chickens. Tayras raise their young in a den under tree roots or in a hollow trunk.

Neotropical River Otter

Neotropical River Otter (*Lutra longicaudis*)
Other names: water dog, Central American river otter,
Southern otter

Neotropical river otters, or water dogs, are usually found in or near water. They are strong and graceful swimmers. On land, otters waddle awkwardly but use mud slides on the river bank to propel themselves quickly into the water. They are very elusive and are not easy to spot. They go about their daily business alone or with one partner. Otters may pop their heads out of the water to take a look, but are gone again in a split second. They like clear, fast moving streams and rivers and find a very favorable habitat in South Stann Creek and some of the larger streams.

Otters weigh from 4-10 kg, the males being much larger than the females. They have beautiful shiny, dark coats, with light tan or yellow on the belly.

The diet of otters consists of fish and crustaceans such as crabs. They consume the entire prey and later deposit feces full of fish scales or crab shells on the tops of large river rocks. Otters probably find shelter in dens in the banks of the streams and rivers. They have been widely hunted for their beautiful coats, but that has been illegal in Belize for some time.

Perissodactyls

Baird's Tapir (*Tapirus bairdii*)
Other name: mountain cow

Belize's largest terrestrial mammal, Baird's tapir, is the National Animal of Belize. Although tapirs are called mountain cows locally, they are more closely related to horses. The Central American tapir is dark black or brown in colour, with short hair, very thick skin, a low mane, lighter colored ears, lips and sometimes a white throat patch. Although they weigh as much as 200-300 kg, their body shape, short tail and short powerful legs allow them to move rapidly through the thick underbrush of the forest in which they live.

The most noticeable features of the tapir are the snout and upper lip which form its short trunk with nostrils at the tip. The trunk can be stretched and contracted in all directions for use in feeding. Leaves or branches are grasped between the inner upper lip and the trunk tip. Although tapirs may eat some fruits and nuts or graze on grass with their trunk contracted, their main food is leaves. They eat a wide variety of different plants, including aquatic plants. While leaves are chewed by the adaptive molars, most seeds pass whole through their gut and are defecated in the forest or in the river where they may float away. Thus, tapirs have a role in seed dispersal.

Tapirs are able to digest plant cellulose with the help of stomach microorganisms that break down the plant matter. They spend most of their waking hours foraging to get enough to eat.

Tapirs

Tapirs inhabit the humid tropical rain forests and emerge mostly at night to feed in open areas with grass and shrubs. They prefer early successional vegetation and riverine forest found on floodplains. Areas that have been selectively logged like the East Basin and other disturbed habitats with a large proportion of herbaceous plants are better for tapir than forests with closed canopies.

Tapirs are very shy and are not often seen or heard. They stay clear of the CBWS Headquarters, but tracks can be seen along the banks of more remote streams and, occasionally, along the trails. Tapirs are excellent swimmers and like to live near water. They submerge themselves in water and in mud wallows to cool down. They also take refuge in the water when they feel threatened. They can dive and walk on the bottom of streams.

Tapirs may live as long as 30 years. Females reach sexual maturity and breed at 3-4 years. Courtship involves sniffing each other's rear and the male uses urination in the ritual as well. The male also sniffs the female's urine giving a lip curl like other hoofed animals to assess whether the female is in heat.

Gestation in the tapir lasts 13 months. Females give birth in a squatting posture and then lick their calves as they nurse from the two teats between her hind legs. The young tapir, which is more vulnerable to occasional attacks by jaguars, has a different appearance from its mother until 6-8 months of age. It is colored like a gibnut, a chestnut background with white stripes and spots that help to camouflage it. Tapir mothers have one baby that is able to walk and follow them soon after birth. Though normally shy, mothers defend their calves and can attack with their teeth or rush violently and knock a threatening predator down to trample it. Calves may stay with the mother for as long as a year, until they attain adult coloration.

Tapirs are asocial, occurring only in mother-calf groupings or in pairs during the breeding season. They produce a number of sounds which they use in communication, including a contact squeal, a pain squeal, a greeting click and an alarm snort. Males mark territories by spraying urine backwards and depositing feces on land and in the water.

In Belize the tapir has a history of fascination for humans. Since there are several temples in which Chac, the Rain God (also called by the Teotihuacan name, Quetzalcoatl) is prominently displayed with a trunk like that of the tapir, one might conclude that the ancient Maya revered the Central American tapir. Despite the tapir's status as Belize's National Animal and its legal protection, tapirs are occasionally hunted in Belize, both for food and to protect farms from its depredations. Even though the meat is extremely fatty and not very tasty, tapirs are still hunted in most of Central America and, as a result, are very rare in populated areas. The tapir is a highly endangered species.

Artiodactyls

Peccaries (*Tayassu* spp.)

Peccaries are common residents of Cockscomb that are closely related to domestic pigs. They have long flexible snouts for rooting up tubers and other foods for their generalized diet. Peccaries have teeth, jaws, and digestive tracts adapted to their omnivorous habits. They root aggressively under leaves and in soil looking for food, which includes fruits, tubers, rhizomes, bulbs, acorns, grasses, green shoots, and a variety of small animals. They crunch most seeds completely with strong molars so they have little role as seed dispersers. They assume the same niche in the American tropics as the pigs in the Old World tropics. They have an unusual pouched glandular stomach to transform cellulose to fatty acids which allows them to utilize plant roughage.

There are two species of peccaries living in Cockscomb. Both species may be hunted by jaguars and are important game for human hunters outside of the Sanctuary. The white-lipped peccary (*Tayassu pecari*), locally called wari, is the larger of the two, weighing up to 30 kg. It is dark brown or black and has an obvious white area on its jaw. Waris travel in large herds of 50-100 animals over long distances without returning to the same area very often. In November and December, when the cohune nuts are falling, large herds of wari, or the evidence of their having passed, are seen near the CBWS Headquarters. Waris are known to be aggressive and should be treated with respect.

White-lipped Peccary

More commonly encountered is the collared peccary (*Tayassu tajacu*), locally called peccary. Its hair is long, coarse and greyish black in color. A noticeable "collar" of lighter hair rings its neck and shoulders. The collared peccary has a very short tail that is not visible. Adults weigh about 15-18 kg. They usually travel in groups of 5-10 animals but sometimes as many as 20 will walk single file on trails or scatter in the immediate area to browse.

Collared peccaries have wide ranging behavioral adaptations which enable them to survive in a variety of habitats, including desert, semi-desert, oak woods, and lowland tropical rain forests, from very wet to very dry areas.

Herds of collared peccaries have territories or defended home ranges of between 60-200 hectares with overlapping zones which are only used by one herd at a time. Peccaries often rest in contact with each other. They use vocalizations for communication within the herd.

Scent glands that protrude from the hair on their backs emit smelly secretions which are used in herd bonding and to mark territories. Peccaries deposit the scent by rubbing the gland against objects within their territory or by mutually rubbing head to rump, thus anointing each other's heads. Herd members may also anoint their heads from another herd member by rubbing their cheeks against previously marked posts. They also mark trails by scratching the ground and defecating.

Collared peccaries have no breeding season but can breed throughout the year. Females first come into estrus at 11 months of age and cycle every 23 or 24 days. After a five-month gestation period she gives birth to one or two piglets which can follow the herd soon after birth. Newborns are tan to yellowish-grey with a dark back. The mother nurses the piglets for about six weeks and aggressively defends them with growling and tooth chattering. Mothers and their young keep in contact with a purring sound and adults use a grunting sound for similar reasons. The young form close surrogate relationships with others in the herd.

Peccaries are formidable fighters. They growl and make a sound by rubbing their canine teeth together in aggressive encounters in which the large sharp canines are displayed.

Collared Peccary

White-tailed Deer (*Odocoileus virginianu*)

Deer are slender, graceful animals that move quickly and quietly through the forest. They browse on leaves, grasses and other tender foliage and include some fruits and flowers in their diet. The digestive system of deer is equipped to deal with this plant matter and uses a process of cud-chewing, regurgitation and fermentation.

White-tailed deer (*Odocoileus virginianus*) are found mostly in the open pine ridge at the eastern end of the Basin. Deer that live in open habitats form herds for protection against predators and develop social rituals. For example, the male of this species has large, branched antlers for interlocking wrestling battles. These elaborate antlers would easily be caught in the lianas and brush if they lived in the dense forest, but are appropriate for open country.

Should they be broken in the battles, the antlers are usually replaced every year. However, antler cycle is controlled by levels of male hormones in the blood which respond to daylength. In higher latitudes, where there is more variation in daylength, antler cycle is well-defined. But in the tropics, where there is less variation in photoperiod, antlers may be shed at any time of the year and even carried longer than a year.

Deer have many scent glands that they use for communicating within the herd and for marking territory. There are glands between the eyes and the antlers, at the base of the ears, on all four legs and between the hooves. When deer paw the ground to threaten an opponent, they are also marking with the scent glands between the hooves. Glands are often opened in dominance and courtship displays or when alarmed.

Red Brocket Deer (*Mazama americana*)
Other name: antelope

Much more common in the rainforest of the Cockscomb Basin, is the red brocket deer (*Mazama americana*). It is a small deer weighing 20-35 kg with a reddish brown body and a grey head. The males have two short, straight antlers which cause no trouble in the underbrush. They frequent river banks and swamps and have been spotted along the road and trails at Cockscomb where their two-toed tracks can often be seen. Although they are commonly hunted for meat in Belize, only the large cats hunt them in the Sanctuary.

Little is known about red brocket deer because their nocturnal behavior and dense forest habitat make them difficult to study. Studies on a related species in Surinam indicate that they may be quite numerous in a forest environment with a density of one per square kilometer.

Forest types like the red brocket deer are smaller, show more uniform coloration and have smaller antlers than animals that live in open areas. Smaller animals with smaller antlers can more easily move about in the dense forest. Such animals are generally solitary nocturnal browsers and, therefore, show less conspicuous social behavior. Tropical deer have longer tails, bigger ears and lack a mane, compared to deer that live in cooler climates. The longer tails and bigger ears provide more surface area to dissipate heat.

Although they may breed throughout the year, births are most frequent in November through February, coinciding with the winter rainy season. Females usually carry one fawn for a gestation period of 218-228 days, though twins may occur. There may be a post-partum estrus, 1-5 days after giving birth.

Males first show small antler nubs at 8-12 months of age and breed when antlers are fully grown. As with other deer, the antlers are developed anew each year and are initially covered with velvet. The blood vessels in the velvet provide the nourishment for antler growth. The velvet is rubbed off when no longer needed.

Stiletto-like antlers like those of the red brocket deer are weapons used to defend their food resources. A male deer points his antlers at an opponent in a threatening manner. If the opponent stands his ground, the two may try to poke each other, often causing injury.

Solitary species like brocket deer mark their territory with urine and dung or using scent glands. They are frequently seen sniffing their environment. They probably use smell for food and predator detection and in social contexts. Males are attracted to females urinating and give a response called Flehman's response, in which they hold their heads up high and draw air through their open mouths, allowing them to "taste" the air.

Red Brocket Deer

References

Barrette, C. 1987. The comparative behavior and ecology of chevrotains, musk deer and morphologically conservative deer. In *Biology and Management of the Cervidae,* pp. 200-213, C.M. Wemmer, ed. Smithsonian Institution Press: Washington, D.C.

Branan, W.V. and R.L. Marchinton. 1987. Reproductive ecology of white-tailed and red brocket deer in Suriname. In *Biology and Management of the Cervidae,* pp. 344-370, C.M. Wemmer, ed. Smithsonian Institution Press: Washington, D.C.

Burton, D.W., J.W. Brickham, H.H. Genoways, and T.J. McCarthy. 1987. Karyotypic analysis of five rodents and a marsupial from Belize, Central America. *Annals of Carnegie Museum* 56(4):103-112.

Disney, R.H.L. 1968. Observations on a zoonosis: Leishmaniasis in British Honduras. *Journal of Applied Ecology* 5:1-59.

Emmons, L. 1990. *Neotropical Rainforest Mammals: A Field Guide.* University of Chicago Press: Chicago, IL.

Forsythe, A. and K. Miata. 1984. *Tropical Nature: Life and Death in the Rainforests of Central and South America.* Charles Scribners Sons: New York, NY.

Fragoso, J.M. 1991. The effect of selective logging on Baird's tapir. In *Latin American Mammalogy,* pp. 295-304, M.A. Mares and D.J. Schmidly, eds. University of Oklahoma Press: Norman, OK.

Fragoso, J.M. 1991. The effect of hunting on tapirs in Belize. In *Neotropical Wildlife Use and Conservation,* pp 154-162, J.G. Robinson and K.H. Redford, eds. The Sandhill Crane Press: Gainesville, FL.

Geist, V. 1987. On the evolution of optical signals in deer: A preliminary analysis. In *Biology and Management of the Cervidae*, pp. 235-255, C.M. Wemmer, ed. Smithsonian Institution Press: Washington, D.C.

Hartshorn, G. et al. 1984. *Belize: Country Environmental Profile.* Robert Nicolait & Associates Ltd: Belize City, Belize.

Horwich, R. H, & Lyon. J. 1990. *A Belizean Rain Forest: The Community Baboon Sanctuary.* Orang-utan Press: Gays Mills, WI.

Janzen, D.H., ed. 1983. *Costa Rican Natural History.* University of Chicago Press: Chicago, IL.

Kamstra, J. 1987. *An Ecological Survey of the Cockscomb Basin, Belize.* Master's Thesis. York University: Ontario, Canada.

Kricher, J. C. 1989. *A Neotropical Companion: An Introduction to the Animals, Plants and Ecosystems of the New World Tropics.* Princeton University Press: Princeton, NJ.

McCarthy, T.J. 1987. Distributional records of bats from the Caribbean lowlands of Belize and adjacent Guatemala and Mexico. B.D. Patterson and R.M. Timm, eds. *Fieldiana: Zoology, new ser.* 39: 137-162.

McCarthy, T.J. 1993. *Checklist: Mammals of Belize.* Belize Audubon Society: Belize.

MacDonald, D., ed. 1984. *The Encyclopedia of Mammals.* Facts On File: New York, NY.

MacNamara, M. and W. Eldridge. 1987. Behavior and reproduction in captive pudu (*Pudu pudu*) and red brocket (*Mazama americana*), a descriptive and comparative analysis. In *Biology and Management of the Cervidae,* pp. 371-387, C.M. Wemmer, ed. Smithsonian Institution Press: Washington, D.C.

Muller-Schwarze, D. 1987. Evolution of the cervid olfactory communication. In *Biology and Management of the Cervidae,* pp. 223-234, C.M. Wemmer, ed. Smithsonian Institution Press: Washington, D.C.

Nowak, R.M. and J.L. Paradiso. 1983. *Walker's Mammals of the World.* The John Hopkins University Press: Baltimore, MD.

Putnam, R. 1988. *The Natural History of Deer.* Cornell University Press: Ithaca, NY.

Reid, F. *Field Guide to Mammals of Central America and Southeastern Mexico.* Oxford University Press: Oxford (in press).

Scheler, D.G. 1988. Armadillos make me smile a lot. *Audubon Magazine.* July, 1988, pp 72-77.

Smith, L.L. and R.W. Doughty. 1984. *The Amazing Armadillo.* University of Texas Press: Austin, TX.

Sowls, L.K. 1984. *The Peccaries.* University of Arizona Press: Tucson, AR.

Storrs, E.E. 1982. The Astonishing Armadillo. *National Geographic,* 161(6): 820-830.

Whitehead, G.K. 1972. *Deer of the World.* Constable: London.

CHAPTER 7

Reintroduction of Black Howler Monkeys into the Cockscomb Basin

Robert Horwich, Fred Koontz, Ernesto Saqui, Hermelindo Saqui, Emiliano Pop, Scott Silver, Linde Ostro, Pedro Pixabaj, Charles Koontz, and Judy Lumb

The reintroduction of black howler monkeys (*Alouatta pigra*) into the Cockscomb Basin Wildlife Sanctuary (CBWS) was conducted between May, 1992, and May, 1994, as part of a broader effort to conserve the species. Black howlers, locally called "baboons," occur naturally in southern Mexico, northern Guatemala, and Belize. Unfortunately, their range is shrinking due to habitat destruction. As a result, the species is listed as "threatened" under the USA Endangered Species Act. Black howlers were living in the Cockscomb Basin as recently as the 1960's, but a combination of yellow fever in 1956-7 and habitat destruction by Hurricane Hattie in 1961 probably accounted for the local demise of the black howler.

Restoring animal populations by reintroduction requires a great deal of planning, hard work and a skilled team of dedicated conservationists working together. The Black Howler Reintroduction Project was first suggested by Mike Konecny and Robert Horwich in 1984 and slowly developed over the next seven years with input from Peace Corps Volunteer Dan Taylor, CBWS Director Ernesto Saqui, other CBWS staff, and BAS members. In 1990, the Cockscomb Basin Wildlife Sanctuary was enlarged from approximately 4,000 acres to over 100, 000 acres by the Government of Belize, making it a more realistic size for the conservation of jaguars and a large enough area for a new population of the howlers as well.

In February of 1991, motivated by the recent expansion of the Sanctuary and the fact that there were no fully protected areas for black howler monkeys in Belize, Ernesto Saqui and Robert Horwich invited Fred Koontz of the Wildlife Conservation Society (formerly the New York Zoological Society) to join them in conducting a feasibility study for the reintroduction of black howlers in the CBWS. From the outset, the idea was to translocate wild howlers captured at the Community Baboon Sanctuary (CBS) which is located about 135 kilometers north of the CBWS. These monkey colonists would then

Above: *Adult male black howler monkey (baboon) howling*
Below: *Ken Glander aims the tranquilizer gun as the capture team waits to catch the black howler monkey in the net.*

be released into the Cockscomb Basin with the hope that they would multiply and establish a new population. The immediate challenge recognized by the team was that no similar primate translocation project had ever been attempted.

First, it was necessary to look at the surrounding area and determine if nearby howlers might colonize the Cockscomb Basin without any human intervention. If natural recolonization were not probable, were there any nearby howlers that could be moved more easily than those from the CBWS? A survey of adjacent areas showed that much of the howler habitat was being deforested for citrus plantations and that the very few howlers remaining in the area could not easily be moved. The team found that the Cockscomb Basin would be a good home for the CBS animals because the Basin has enough of the same food trees as those in the CBS.

The feasibility team concluded that the project was important for the conservation of the species and provided a unique opportunity to study primate translocation; the CBS would be the best source of animals for the reintroduction; and translocations should be carried out gradually, over a three-year period, with a total of about 60 animals moved.

Thus, in late 1991 the Black Howler Reintroduction Project was proposed as a joint project of the Belize Audubon Society, Community Conservation Consultants and the Wildlife Conservation Society. This effort was only possible because of the many villagers of the CBS who helped capture the monkeys and graciously donated them to the CBWS. Also, Belizean government officials were very cooperative and helpful, and the British Armed Forces provided a helicopter to transport some of the animals.

Much planning had to occur before the actual translocation of the monkeys. In order to give the monkeys the best chance for survival, the researchers wanted to move them when the most fruits would be available for food. Howlers eat flowers, leaves, and fruit, specifically selecting the new leaves and ripe fruit when available. Researchers and staff at the CBS had found that May was the main fruiting season and a similar study at Cockscomb indicated May was a good time for forest fruits there as well. Since May is also the driest time of the year, moving the monkeys then would insure good road travel.

The team then determined the best places from which to release the animals in the CBWS. To allow ready access into the forest, provide security for the monkeys, and enhance visitor experience, it was decided to release the monkeys from the visitor trails near the Sanctuary Headquarters. To minimize aggressive interactions between troops of released animals, release sites were located at least a kilometer apart.

It was important that intact troops be captured, moved and released together to maintain their social support system. This required that the troops be followed for a period of time prior to the translocation so all members could be identified.

Acclimation cages were designed so that each troop could be kept for a few days to make sure the animals were healthy, to observe the monitoring equipment, and to give them a chance to recover from the capture. These cages, measuring 16 feet long by 8 feet wide by 10 feet high, were built at each of the selected release sites. The team hoped that this temporary confinement would prevent panic when the animals were set free.

The first capture, translocation and release of black howler monkeys occurred in May of 1992 and was repeated in May of 1993 and May of 1994. In January and February of each year preceding the moves, the team mapped the trails and built the acclimation cages. The capture teams were headed by Drs. Rob Horwich of Community Conservation Consultants, Fred Koontz of the Wildlife Conservation Society, and Ken Glander of the Duke University Primate Center. Each year the team also consisted of persons from the BAS, the CBWS, the Wildlife Conservation Society's Bronx Zoo and the CBS villages.

The team discusses radio tracking of the reintroduced monkeys.
(from left) Robert Horwich, Fred Koontz, Hermelindo Saqui,
Scott Silver, and Ernesto Saqui

During the capture procedure, each howler in a chosen troop was darted with a chemical immobilization drug and caught in a net as it dropped to the ground. Each animal was weighed, measured and given health checks by Dr. Wendy Westrom, the team veterinarian. She also took blood samples so that genetic records and blood chemistries of the founding population would be available if needed for future research. Each adult animal was fitted with an anklet with colored beads for individual identification.

In all, 62 animals were reintroduced into the Cockscomb Basin between 1992 and 1994. They comprised 14 animals from three troops in 1992, 23 animals from five troops in 1993 and 25 animals from six troops in 1994 (Table 1). Each year two or three trips were made from the Community Baboon Sanctuary to the Cockscomb Basin by van or by British Armed Forces helicopter. Most animals were carried immediately to their acclimation cages within the Cockscomb, observed for 1-3 days and released. Four small troops, however, were not held in acclimation cages, but instead were released directly from their small carrying cages into the forest as an experimental comparison.

Adult howlers were fitted with radio transmitters so they could be monitored by tracking them with a directional radio receiver. Each female's transmitter was on a ball and chain collar. Males, because the large hyoid bones in their necks prevented them from comfortably wearing collars, were fitted with either an internal transmitter or one attached to an anklet. The battery life of the transmitters allowed the monkeys to be tracked for 6-12 months. The transmitters will eventually break off when the fasteners rust sufficiently. Hermelindo Saqui, Emiliano Pop, and Pedro Pixabaj have tracked the reintroduced monkeys, providing much valuable information on their behavior and ecology.

The reintroduced howlers adapted well to the Cockscomb Basin. An assessment of the situation as of May, 1995, is reported here. Survivability was high: 93% of the 62 howlers survived the first 30 days; and 80% could still be located one year after their release. Only two of the the translocated animals were known to have died: male # 2 (M2) was shot 9 kilometers away, near the village of San Ramon; and female # 37 (F37) apparently died of natural causes.

Monkeys mostly stayed close to their release sites, with the average dispersal being less than 2 kilometers. Eighteen babies had been born in the CBWS and at least 14 of them were still alive (Table 2). The total population was estimated between 55 and 75 animals. This high survivability, low dispersal and positive birth rate suggest that the black howler population in the Cockscomb has a good chance of recovery.

Table 1. Identification of Black Howler Monkeys Released into the Cockscomb Basin*

Troop Name	Monkey (Sex/ID#)	Age Class at capture	ID Tag Color	ID Tag Foot
1992				
Chuck's	M2	Adult	Yellow	Rt
	F1	Adult	Yellow	Rt
	F3	Adult	Yellow	Lft
	M4	Infant		
Harold's	M15	Adult	Blue	Lft
	F13	Adult	Blue	Rt
	F22	Adult	Blue	Lft
Ferry	M8	Adult	Orange	Rt
	F6	Adult	Orange	Lft
	F14	Adult	Orange	Rt
	F9	Adult	Orange/Orange	Lft
	M7	Juvenile		
	F10	Infant		
	F11	Infant		
1993				
Flowers Bank	M32	Adult	Lime	Lft
	M26	Adult	Lime	Rt
	F28	Adult	Lime/Red	Rt
	F29	Adult	Lime	Lft
	F30	Adult	Lime	Rt
	M27	Juvenile		
	M31	Juvenile		
	F25	Juvenile		
Plantation	M34	Adult	Red/White/Red	Lft
	F36	Adult	Red	Lft/Rt
	F37	Adult	Red	Rt
	F38	Adult	Red/Red	Lft
	M39	Juvenile		
Reuben's	M41	Adult	White	Lft
	F40	Adult	White	Lft
	F42	Adult	White	Rt

*Adult animals were marked with different coloured anklets on the right (Rt), left (Lft) or both (Rt/Lft) ankles and assigned a number upon capture or birth. Animals captured as juveniles or infants or born after translocation are not marked.

Table 1. Black Howler Monkeys Released into the Cockscomb Basin (cont.)*

Troop Name	Monkey (Sex/ID#)	Age Class at capture	ID Tag Color	ID Tag Foot
1993 (cont.)				
Four Group	M44	Adult	Yellow/Green/Yellow	Rt
	M47	Adult	Yellow/Green/Yellow	Lft
	F45	Adult	Yellow/Green/Yellow	Rt
	F46	Adult	Yellow/Green/Yellow	Lft
Roy's	M49	Adult	Red/Blue	Lft
	F48	Adult	Red/Blue	Lft
	F50	Adult	Red/Blue	Rt
1994				
Gang of Four	M67	Adult	Bright Red	Lft
	F66	Adult	BrightRed/Yellow	Rt
	F68	Adult	Bright Red/Yellow	Lft
	F69	Juvenile		
Pasture	M76	Adult	Lime/Blue	Rt
	F74	Adult	Lime/Blue	Rt
	F75	Adult	Lime/Blue	Lft
New	M59	Adult	White/Blue	Rt
	F60	Adult	White/Blue	Lft
	F61	Adult	White/Blue	Rt
G-7	M56	Adult	Tangarine	Lft
	M55	Adult	Tangarine	Rt
	M51	Adult	Tangarine	Rt
	M54	Adult	Tangarine	Lft
	M57	Juvenile		
	M58	Juvenile		
	M52	Infant		
Lefty's	M63	Adult	Yellow	Rt
	M65	Adult	Yellow	Lft
	F62	Adult	Yellow/Blue	Rt
	M64	Juvenile		
Creek	M72	Adult	Tangarine/Lime	Rt
	F70	Adult	Tangarine/Lime	Lft
	F73	Adult	Tangarine/Tangarine	Rt
	M71	Infant		

*Adult animals were marked with different coloured anklets on the right (Rt), left (Lft) or both (Rt/Lft) ankles and assigned a number upon capture or birth. Animals captured as juveniles or infants or born after translocation are not marked.

120

Table 2. Babies Born to Reintroduced Black Howler Monkeys as of May 1995*

Date of Birth	Death	Troop Name	Sex/#	Mother/Father	
1- 9-92	20-7-93	Ferry	F5	F9	M8
2- 9-92	5-1-93	Ferry	M12	F14	M8
25-12-92		Harold's	F16	F22	M15
30-12-92		Harold's	F17	F13	M15
16- 2-93		Ferry	F18	F6	M8
3- 8-93		Flowers Bank	M19	F30	M32
7- 8-93	missing	Flowers Bank	M20	F28	M32
17- 3-94		Flowers Bank	F21	F29	M32
4- 4-94		Roy's	F23	F48	M49
14- 4-94	missing	Ferry	M24	F14	M8/M7
1- 8-94		Ferry	F33	F6	M8
5- 8-94		Pasture	M77	F75	M76
24- 8-94		Harold's	M78	F22	M15
26- 9-94		United	M79	F3	M26
25-10-94		Flowers Bank	F80	F30	M32
27-10-94		Harold's	F81	F13	M15
6-12-94		Lefty's Troop	M82	F62	M63
20-6-94		Roy's	?83	F25	M49

*Of the 18 babies born in the CBWS, two have died and two are missing. When there are two possible fathers, both are listed (M8/M7); ? means the sex is unknown.

The 14 howler troops released into Cockscomb displayed five behavioral scenarios in regard to troop organization (Table 3). In the first scenario, four troops remained stable with no members leaving or joining, except for new babies born to the group. For example, Harold's troop, released in 1992, still included the original male and two females plus four babies born in the Cockscomb.

Four troops illustrate the second scenario in which most of the troop stayed together but one or two members left or one or two monkeys from other troops joined them. For example, Lefty's Troop was comprised of 3 males and 1 female when translocated. One male (M65) has left and formed the South Stann Creek troop across the river. One female, F38 from the Plantation Troop, has joined Lefty's Troop.

In the third scenario, two troops remained together following release, but moved to more remote areas of the CBWS. Occasional reports of howling heard by persons hiking to Victoria Peak were the only evidence of their whereabouts.

The fourth scenario was observed in four troops that split up within the first few days or weeks after release. Most of these animals, although they dispersed and left their troop, did not die and eventually joined another troop.

Finally, the fifth scenario was observed when two new troops formed from animals leaving their original troops. The United Troop is one of these new troops, and is sometimes seen from the Visitor Center.

Nine of the 12 troops were living in areas near visitor trails, and were sometimes seen or heard howling (see map below). In 1994, Scott Silver and Linde Ostro conducted a year-long study of four Cockscomb troops, so that their behavior and ecology could be compared to monkeys remaining in the CBS. The troops observed by following the monkeys quietly for many days were: Harold's Troop, Pasture Troop, Gang of Four, and the United Troop. Scott and Linde found that the size of the troops' home range increased dramatically when the monkeys were translocated. The average home range in the CBS was less than 3 hectares, but in the CBWS it was typically 16 hectares!

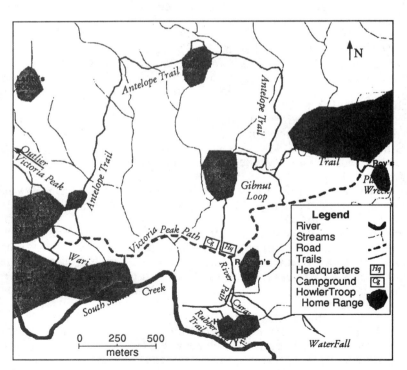

The locations of the nine black howler troops most likely to be observed by visitors to the CBWS.

The troops studied moved slowly with frequent stops to feed or rest. They spend up to 70% of the day and nearly all of the night resting. Visitors might observe that howlers are not the most graceful of animals when moving in the trees and can be heard coming from far away as they crash through the branches. The troops traveled an average of 500 meters per day, but that distance varied from 200-1400 meters and seemed to be related to their diet which varied according to the season. For example, in the heaviest fruiting season, May - October, the monkeys moved further than they did the remainder of the year when they consumed more leaves.

The group most often seen by visitors was Harold's troop, which lived near the Rubber Tree, Curassow and Waterfall Trails. From November through February they were often seen feeding in the large suclui'in tree (*Celtis schippii*) located near the bench where the Rubber Tree and Curassow Trails intersect.

The United Troop ranged from near the Visitor Center along the Gibnut Trail and inside the southern part of the loop formed by the Antelope Trail. This troop has been observed making rather spectacular leaps while crossing the Victoria Peak Path just beyond the first bridge and were often seen feeding in the large ceiba tree southwest of the Headquarters.

The Pasture Troop shared the Kaway Swamp on the Wari Loop with the Ferry Troop. The Pasture Troop also occasionally went as far as the Victoria Peak Path and the Antelope Trail. The Gang of Four also occupied areas near the Antelope Trail, so visitors must look carefully for identification tags on any monkeys and compare them to the list in Table 1.

The Flowers Bank Troop was seen on the Tinamou Trail and from the CBWS Access Road. Roy's Troop ranged between Ben's Bluff Trail and the Access Road. And Reuben's Troop wandered widely between the Access Road, the Waterfall Trail and the Antelope Trail.

Even if you do not see howler monkeys in the CBWS, you might hear them roaring. However, these howlers are much quieter than those in the CBS. They are thought to vocalize for two reasons: they howl at dawn and dusk in order to keep track of their neighbors; and they roar if they encounter another group intruding into their area. Perhaps because there is such a low density of monkeys in the Cockscomb there is little reason for them to howl. On average, howling was heard only three or four times a week in 1994. As the population grows, the howling will probably increase.

So far, the reintroduction of black howler monkeys into the CBWS has shown very promising results. We hope that researchers will continue to study the released monkeys far into the future! If you see troops, please report it to the CBWS staff. Information needed is the color of the anklet bead, the leg it is on, the sex, the time, date, and precise location, along with your name and address.

Table 3. Status of Reintroduced
Black Howler Monkeys as of May 1, 1995

Troop Name	Members	Status/Location
Scenario 1: Troop includes all the original members plus babies		
Harold's	M15, F13, F22	Rubber Tree/Curassow
born CBWS	F16, F17, M78, F81	and Waterfall Trails
Roy's	M49, F48, F50	Ben's Bluff/Access Road
born CBWS	F23, ?83	
Gang of Four	M67, F66, F68, F69	Wari Loop/Gibnut Loop
Pasture	M76, F74, F75	
born CBWS	M77	Antelope/Wari
Scenario 2: Most stayed together but a few left or joined.		
Ferry	M8, F6	River Overlook/Kaway
born CBWS	F18, F33	Swamp on Wari Trail
left	F9	joined United Troop
left	F14	joined S. Stann Creek
missing	F11, M10, M7	
Flowers Bank	M27, F25, F29,	Tinamou/Access Road
	F30, M32	
born CBWS	M19, M21, M80	
left	M26	joined United Troop
left	F28, M31, M20	seen together south of river
Lefty's	M63, M64, F62	Victoria Peak Path west
born CBWS	M82	
joined	F38	(from Plantation Troop)
left	M65	formed S. Stann Creek
G-7	M55, F51, M57,	Victoria Peak Path west
	M58, M52	
joined	F60	(from New Troop)
left	M56	seen with F61
left	F54	seen headed northeast
Reuben's	M41, F42	
left	F40	stayed 3 months, then left

124

Table 3. Status of Reintroduced
Black Howler Monkeys as of May 1, 1995(cont.)

Troop Name	Members	Status/Location
Scenario 3: Most stayed together when last seen but left study area.		
Four Group	M44, M47, F45, F46	reported howling NW
Scenario 4: Split up almost immediately		
Chuck's	M2	shot San Ramon Village
	F3 + M4	joined United
	F1	joined Ferry and later joined S. Stann Creek
Plantation	F38	joined Lefty's
	F37	dead of natural causes
missing	M34, M39, F36	
New	F60	joined G-7
	F61	seen with M56 or alone
missing	M59	
Creek	M72, F70, F73, M71	headed toward the Outlier
Scenario 5:	*Newly formed troops*	
United		Antelope and Gibnut
	M26	(from Flowers Bank)
	F3, M4	(from Chuck's Troop)
	F9	(from Ferry Troop)
born CBWS	M79	
S. Stann Creek		south of S. Stann Creek
	M65	(from Lefty's Troop)
	F1	(from Chuck's Troop)
	F14	(from Ferry Troop)

References

Horwich, R.H., F. Koontz, E. Saqui, H. Saqui, and K. Glander. 1993. A reintroduction program for the conservation of the black howler monkey in Belize. *Endangered Species Update* 10 (6): 1-6.

CHAPTER 8

Birds of the Cockscomb Basin
Katherine M. Emmons and James Kamstra

While it was the jaguar that made the Cockscomb famous, the modern visitor will certainly see much more evidence of birdlife than mammals. The Cockscomb Basin is an excellent place to see birds because of their diversity and abundance. Most of the Belizean forest species occur here, and for some the Basin is one of the best places to see them. Many of the common species can be seen by walking the trails near the CBWS Headquarters. With a little patience (and some luck) many of the less common ones can be found as well.

Early morning is the best time to see birds, particularly in open areas and along forest edges. They begin vocalizing with the first hint of daylight, and soon begin actively foraging. By midmorning, when the sun gets hot, most birds retire to the shade. In late afternoon, the frenzy of feeding activity resumes until nightfall. Deep within the forest interior, flocks of mixed species continue to forage through the day in the relatively cool shade of the understory. Forest streams act as corridors through which birds move and, therefore, offer good vantage points to look up into the canopy.

Watching flocks of mixed species interacting while feeding and slowly moving through the forest is exciting. Ten or more unrelated species such as tanagers, woodcreepers, antwrens, warblers and flycatchers may form a loose aggregation that stay together. Each species forages in a slightly different manner. Some glean leaves for insects, others search tree trunks, while yet others devour small berries. Some flocks follow ant swarms in the understory while a different group of species forms a canopy flock. Often one species, such as red-throated ant-tanager or black-faced grosbeak, acts as the core species around which others gather. Watch for large fruiting trees. Sometimes twenty bird species may be in one tree at the same time, all gorging themselves on the juicy pulp.

Watching birds in a tropical forest area like the Cockscomb can be frustrating as well as rewarding. One must frequently strain one's neck while looking up into the canopy. Birds move about in dense leafy tangles, then reveal themselves for a split second before disappearing again. Others call loudly from somewhere off the trail but lianas prevent a closer approach. But with perseverance, birds will finally appear, making the effort worthwhile.

Bird Habitats

Many bird species are specialized to a particular habitat and are not found elsewhere. Broad-leaved tropical forest dominates Cockscomb and here is where the greatest number of species is found. Many different niches are available within the forest. Great tinamou and black-faced antthrush, for example, slink elusively on the forest floor, while green shrike-vireo and keel-billed toucan forage high in the canopy; sulfur-rumped flycatchers perch patiently in the midstory; and red-throated ant-tanagers glean through the understory shrub layer. Many species rarely venture beyond the closed forest interior while others hunt along forest edges and are easiest to see along the CBWS Access Road. Squirrel cuckoo, black-faced grosbeak and many of the tanagers are typically seen along edges.

The higher elevation forests are some of the most inaccessible habitats and the birds that live here are only rarely seen by Cockscomb's human visitors. Hearing the melodious flute-like call of the slate-colored solitaire is truly one of the delights of visiting the upper portions of the Basin. The common bush-tanager is perhaps the most numerous bird, frequently forming the nucleus of mixed species flocks. Shining honeycreeper and eye-ringed flatbill are higher elevation canopy species. The tody motmot, considered a rare species in Belize, is fairly common in the 400 to 800 meter elevation range in the Cockscomb Basin. Stripe-tailed hummingbirds are found all along the higher sections of the Maya Mountains.

The open pineland on the eastern fringe of the reserve harbours fewer species than other habitats. Several distinctive species can be found here, however, including azure-crowned hummingbird, Grace's warbler and hepatic tanager. The open grassland is also favoured by open country species like blue ground-dove and grey-crowned yellowthroat.

Floodplain thickets dominated by dumb cane and shrub tangles, form a narrow belt bounded by forest on one side, and a wide creek on the other. Conditions are ideal for seeing a wide variety of species in close proximity including shrub, forest edge, aquatic and marsh dwellers. Furthermore, floodplain thickets appear to support higher bird densities than other types of vegetation. Several species are essentially restricted to the open floodplains including the grey-necked wood-rail, cinnamon becard and band-backed wren.

Some species thrive in disturbed second growth vegetation and actually benefit by human forest-clearing activities. These are the most commonly seen birds in agricultural areas and near villages. In the mid 1980s, open fields surrounded Quam Bank but this is no longer the case. Past logging and 'slash and burn' agriculture created clearings but these open areas are rapidly reverting to forest. Some of the open country species are now becoming less common. The great-tailed grackle, for example, which thrives near towns and farms throughout Belize, is now rarely seen within the Sanctuary. Many other open-country species still find suitable habitat within floodplains or pineland, however.

Waterbirds are not well-represented in the Cockscomb Basin. There are no sizable wetlands and only a few oxbow ponds and swamps created by the creeks' meandering. The larger creeks, however, harbour healthy fish populations including some large species like mountain mullet and bay snook. The wider, sunnier sections of creek are the haunts of fish-eating birds including sungrebe, limpkin, four kingfishers, and ten heron species. Smaller shaded streams by contrast, see few aquatic birds except the occasional pygmy kingfisher.

Almost 30 diurnal birds of prey (vultures, hawks, falcons, etc) have been recorded in the CBWS. One needs to find an area that provides a good vista of sky to be able to scan for soaring raptors. Ben's Bluff is a good spot. Vultures are the most common soaring birds but examine them closely. Several of the hawks are dark and will resemble them from a distance.

Migrants And Residents

During the northern winter, many species which breed in temperate North America can be seen in the Cockscomb Basin. These are mainly forest and edge species with wood-warblers being particularly well represented. They spend their winters here and often join up with the resident tropical species to form mixed foraging flocks in a habitat very different from where they spend their summers. Yellow-bellied flycatcher, grey catbird, magnolia warbler, American redstart and northern oriole are among the most abundant winter visitors. Other species such as eastern kingbird, barn swallow and prothonotary warbler winter further south but can be seen in Cockscomb during their brief migration period.

The majority of the species are year-round residents. Most of these undoubtedly breed within the Sanctuary, although actual nesting evidence has been documented for comparatively few. A small number of species, which includes plumbeous kite, piratic flycatcher and yellow-green vireo, breed here but migrate further south during the winter.

Although the climate is warm year round, most birds breed here at about the same time as the temperate North American species, between April and July. This makes good sense because nesting coincides with the start of the wet season when insects and fruit are most abundant. There is abundant food for the developing nestlings and they do not have to compete for it with the large numbers of winter migrants.

Common Bird Species

The Cockscomb Basin is a large remote area with varied topography, range of vegetation and a high diversity of birds. It is not surprising that some are rare and impressive, the kinds of birds that capture the essence of the exotic and unusual. Below we introduce the birds often encountered in the CBWS.

Tinamou (Family *Tinamidae*)

Great Tinamou

The three species of tinamous found at Cockscomb are all stout birds that live and forage mostly on the ground. Their colours are plain, blending in well with the shadows of the undergrowth as they hunt for seeds, fruits, and some insects. The elusive tinamous walk quietly and inconspicuously away from possible danger, but flutter away if startled. They do not build elaborate nests, but lay their eggs on the ground in protected, leafy hollows. The eggs have beautiful colors. After the female lays the eggs, the male takes over the entire job of incubating the eggs and raising the young. When the chicks are dry, he leads them from the nest and protects them for several weeks.

The great tinamou (*Tinamus major*) has beautiful glossy blue-green eggs. It is the largest of the family, weighing sometimes more than a kilogram. It will eat small animals as well as fruits and seeds. Every evening as dusk falls, the great tinamou's powerful, eerie whistle pierces the air.

The slaty-breasted tinamou (*Crypturellus boucardi*) is dark grey on the head, neck and breast, with a dark brown back and orange legs. It lays purplish eggs. The slaty-breasted tinamou walks slowly through dense undergrowth, sometimes using the maintained paths in the CBWS. It will walk quietly ahead of you, always just beyond a good glimpse. Its song is a pleasant two-note whistle.

The little tinamou (*Crypturellus soui*) is small with a rusty belly and grey legs. It is also very secretive, walking quietly on the forest floor. The song of the little tinamou is a series of four to eight beautiful whistles that are more highly pitched than those of the great tinamou. The female lays two glossy lavender eggs.

Herons and Egrets (Family *Ardeidae*)
Other names: gaulin

Ten species of herons and egrets live in the Cockscomb Basin. They frequent the river, steams, and oxbow ponds, especially on the Curassow and Wari Loops. These graceful birds eat frogs, fish, crayfish, or any other small animals that they can grab with their long, pointed bills. In flight, herons and egrets tuck their necks into an S shape and stick their legs straight out behind.

The boat-billed heron (*Cochlearius cochlearius*) is a stocky bird with a very wide bill, grey wings, and black areas on its head and shoulders. It hunts alone at night for fish, crabs, and frogs from the stream bank or a low branch. During the day, boat-billed herons call to each other with grunts and croaks. They nest in trees overhanging oxbow ponds and rivers and lay pale blue eggs. One pair often nests off the Wari Loop, just beyond the River Overlook.

Boat-billed Heron

The most unusual feature of the boat-billed heron is the bill for which it is named. Ornithologists have not figured out the purpose of their unusually large bill. The bird may feed by scooping or the bill may be some adaptation to its nocturnal niche. Another theory is that the bill is for making noise in a mating display. Because these birds feed and carry out most of their routines in darkness, it is difficult to observe how the birds use the bill.

The agami or chestnut-bellied heron (*Agamia agami*) stalks fish in pools of narrow, shaded or partially shaded streams. The agami heron has a chestnut belly, a green-black back, a black head, and a long bill. Rare throughout most of its range, the Cockscomb Basin appears to be one of the best places in Belize to find it, especially on the Curassow Trail.

The mature bare-throated tiger-heron (*Tigrisoma mexicanum*) has a black crown and a yellowish throat. The neck has black bars, and the belly is a brownish colour. This spectacular bird is often seen along the oxbows of the Wari Loop.

There are three white herons or egrets, in Cockscomb. The cattle egret (*Bubulcus ibis*) is the smallest, and can sometimes be seen in flocks that cover trees in white. During the breeding season, the feathers take on a buff tinge, and the bill and legs become pinkish. Otherwise, legs are yellow or brownish. Unlike the others of this family, the cattle egret feeds on land. It catches grasshoppers and other insects while following cattle or other animals which help flush out the prey.

Less common in the CBWS are the snowy egret (*Egretta thula*) with long white head plumes, black bill and legs, and bright yellow feet, and the great egret (*Casmerodius albus*), a large bird with a yellow bill.

The great blue heron (*Ardea herodias*) is a very large bird with blue-grey plumage, black shoulders, a yellow bill, and a white head with a long black eyelash plume. The adult little blue heron (*Egretta caerulea*) is dark blue-grey with dark legs and a deep maroon neck, while the juvenile is white. Though the great blue heron and the little blue heron are common in other wetlands and coastal areas, they are less common in the CBWS.

Vultures (Family *Cathartidae*)
Other names: John Crow

Vultures play an important role in the ecosystem by cleaning up dead animals (carrion) and thus accelerating decomposition. Like hawks and eagles, vultures have strong, hooked bills capable of ripping flesh. Unlike other birds of prey, their feet are relatively weak and are not usually used for catching live prey. Three species of vultures can be seen at Cockscomb. All soar overhead, trying to locate carrion by scent. The sight of vultures circling in the air does not signal the presence of carrion. If the soaring vultures detect any food, they immediately land to eat it! Vultures are often spotted perched on exposed limbs, particularly in the morning.

The king vulture (*Sarcoramphus papa*) is the largest vulture in

King Vulture

Belize. Because of the heavy forest cover, they outnumber black vultures here, but elsewhere they are declining due to deforestation. They are easily recognizable by their white feathers, black wing tips, and black tail. The featherless head of this bird is brightly coloured with orange, yellow, blue, and black. When the king vulture arrives, all other species give way and allow it to eat first. Sometimes king vultures kill small animals. Both parents tend the young, which hatch in low tree stumps or ground nests. Young birds are mostly black and acquire their full adult plumage after three years.

The black vulture (*Coragyps atratus*) is a stocky, bare-headed, all black bird. It often supplements its carrion diet with fruit, and sometimes kills small animals as well. Black vultures lay two eggs on the ground behind rocks or scrubby vegetation. Both parents tend the young.

The turkey vulture (*Cathartes aura*), the most common CBWS vulture, is longer from head to tail, but is much lighter and more slender than the other species. It has a bare red head and black feathers with grey on the bottom of the flight feathers. Young birds have black heads. Turkey vulture parents raise their two young on the bare ground in a cave, crevice, or old tree stump.

Eagles, Hawks, and Kites (Family *Accipitridae*)

All birds in this family are predators that hunt with the help of their excellent eyesight and strong talons. Raptors prey on birds, mammals, reptiles and amphibians. Female raptors are usually larger than males, but both sexes usually have similar colours. Their nests are bulky platforms of sticks located high in trees. Young birds need much care and teaching before they can fly and hunt proficiently alone. In most species, both parents help in this task.

Several types of eagles live in the Cockscomb Basin. The solitary eagle (*Harpyhaliaetus solitarius*) is a massive raptor with a large territory that is encountered only occasionally. It is rare throughout its range. It soars at great heights, and has been spotted from the CBWS Headquarters on several occasions.

The black-and-white hawk-eagle (*Spizaetus melanoleucus*) is the most frequently seen hawk-eagle in the CBWS. They sometimes fly along at treetop level while the others soar very high. The ornate hawk-eagle (*Spizaetus ornatus*) has also been spotted in the area but is not commonly seen.

The roadside hawk (*Buteo magnirotris*) is relatively small, about 40 cm long. It has a brownish-grey back, white belly, and legs barred with brown. The tail has brown and white bands. The roadside hawk often sits on roadside fence posts and trees. In the Cockscomb it calls from trees in open areas and secondary growth. It has a shrill, angry-sounding call when it is disturbed, sounding something like "kee-yaar." It normally feeds by dropping from its perch onto large insects, lizards, and other small prey. During the dry season, the roadside hawk builds its nest of twigs in a tree along a forest edge or in a pasture. The female lays two speckled eggs. Because they live and hunt in more open areas, the roadside hawks have increased with deforestation. They are commonly seen at the edge of the forest near the CBWS Headquarters.

The grey hawk (*Buteo nitidus*) is similar to the roadside hawk, but it is slightly larger and has a grey back and a barred belly and tail. The grey hawk likes to hunt along rivers and forest edges. It is more active than the roadside hawk and eats rodents and birds, but especially relishes lizards. The grey hawk soars at times but does not usually fly very high. It builds its nest of twigs high in a tree and lays two whitish eggs.

The white hawk (*Leucopternis albicollis*) is one of the most beautiful birds of prey seen at Cockscomb, with a white body, black barring on wings and tail, and bright yellow legs. White hawks are rather large, measuring 50 cm from head to tail. They build nests of twigs high up in a tree, often in a mass of epiphytes. They have a harsh, typically hawk-sounding cry. White hawks hunt below the canopy or along forest edges in hilly areas for rodents, frogs and reptiles.

The plumbeous kite (*Ictinia plumbea*) is fairly small for a raptor, with grey underparts and dark back. The long and pointed wings allow the bird to soar gracefully above the canopy and forest edges. It swoops down on reptiles, especially snakes, clinging to branches and can catch insects in flight. The plumbeous kite migrates to South America when it is not breeding, and can mainly be found in the Cockscomb during the dry season. It builds nests high in trees, sometimes exposed and easy to see, laying one egg.

Swallow-tailed kites (*Elanoides fortificatus*) are also snake hunters that sail just above canopy level in search of their reptilian quarry. They are also a migratory species and seen in the CBWS in the dry season.

Falcons (Family *Falconidae*)

Falcons are raptors, or birds of prey. They are closely related to hawks, kites, and eagles, and have strong claws and bills that are adapted for hunting and tearing meat.

Laughing Falcon

The small bat falcon (*Falco rufig- ularis*) is a treat to see as it perches on high, exposed branches and snags. From this position it scouts for bats, swifts, swallows, parakeets, and other birds that it can overtake with its powerful wings. In flight the pointed wings and square tail of the bat falcon are visible. It has a light-coloured chest and neck, and a tail barred with black and grey. The head and back are black. The bat falcon nests high in trees, in holes occurring naturally or made by woodpeckers.

The laughing falcon (*Herpetotheres cachinnans*) is a striking bird with dark brown wings, a buff-coloured chest and head with a black mask across the eyes and a barred tail. The laughing falcon, as its name suggests, makes loud, laughing calls, that get louder and louder, lasting over a minute. It prefers broken forests and forest edges, and is often seen at the CBWS Headquarters, perching on exposed cecropia tree branches or dead trees. It scans for prey while soaring and then swoops suddenly on a snake or an occasional rodent. The laughing falcon nests in tree hollows and females lay one egg during the dry season.

Forest-falcons (*Micrastur* spp.), meanwhile, rarely venture above treetop level. Their raucous evening calls give testimony to their presence.

Chachalaca, Guan and Curassow (Family *Cracidae*)

Because of their large sizes, guan and curassow are highly prized gamebirds and are hunted extensively in Belize. They are among the first species to disappear when an area is settled, but the Cockscomb Basin harbours healthy populations. The smaller chachalacas are much more adaptable and more common in Belize in general.

The crested guan (*Penelope purpurascens*), locally called quam, is a large, turkey-sized bird that is dark brown with a short feathered crest and a long slender tail. It has a red throat and matching red legs. The quam is more arboreal than the great curassow. Quams are often observed in groups of four as they jump from branch to branch in the treetops, calling loudly to each other. They pluck fruits and young foliage from the trees and sometimes collect fallen fruits from the ground. The nest of the crested guan is bowl-shaped and bulky, made of twigs and lined with leaves. The loud honking or clanking calls of the quam are often heard in the morning around the CBWS Headquarters.

The plain chachalaca (*Ortalis vetula*), locally called cocrico, is a drab, medium-sized arboreal bird with a long tail that is more often heard than seen. Entire flocks will chorus "cha-cha-LA-ca" repeatedly in the morning. The chachalaca lives in secondary growth and thick bush and is sometimes seen jumping and flapping from branch to branch in a flock of up to 10 or 15 birds. Females lay from 3 to 6 eggs during the dry season. Parents lead their chicks around low branches and the forest floor soon after they hatch. Chachalacas eat fruits (such as trumpet tree or fig fruits), seeds, leaves, and insects.

The great curassow (*Crax rubra*) measures 1 m from head to tail. The male is glossy black with a white patch beneath his tail. He has a large, curved crest and bright yellow knob on his forehead. During breeding, the male emits a loud, low-pitched call from the treetops. The female has camouflage colouring with browns, black, and white. Each handsome couple is monogamous and families remain together for protection. Females lay two white eggs in tree nests. Like the chachalacas and quams, the young of the curassow can hop around right after hatching and can fly short distances within 4 or 5 days. Curassows are most often spotted foraging on the ground, eating fallen fruit, seeds, and insects. The curassow is more difficult to find than the quam or chachalaca, which more loudly announce their presence.

Great Curassow

Doves and Pigeons (Family *Columbidae*)

Nine species of doves and pigeons live in the Cockscomb and are easy to recognize by their shape. Members of this family are wary, fast-flying and often difficult to see well enough to identify the individual species. These names are somewhat arbitrary, as doves and pigeons have similar anatomy and habits. Doves and pigeons eat seeds, nuts, and fruits, as well as some insects and other small animals. Young birds are almost naked and helpless, and must be fed regurgitated food by the parents.

The ruddy ground dove (*Columbina talpacoti*) prefers open areas and bare ground for foraging, usually in flocks of 10 or 20. It calls softly and repeatedly from the tree tops. The blue ground dove (*Claravis pretiosa*) prefers to forage in open or lightly wooded areas, picking up seeds and insects. Its voice is a persistent "boop " called from the tree tops. The grey-headed dove (*Leptotila plumbeiceps*) and the ruddy quail dove (*Geotrygon montana*) like to walk along the forest floor.

The pale-vented pigeon (*Columba cayennensis*) likes the forest and isolated trees, eating berries in flocks of 12 or more. Its voice is a pleasant, repetitive "cu-cu WOO." Less easily seen are the birds that prefer deep forests and shade, including the short-billed pigeon (*Columba nigrirostris*), which eats fruits and berries and the beautiful scaled pigeon (*Columba speciosa*) which usually forages alone.

Parrots, Parakeets, and Macaws (Family *Psittacidae*)

Seven species of this bird family live in the Cockscomb Basin. Parrots generally have short, square tails, while parakeets have long, pointed tails and wings. Macaws are larger, brilliantly coloured, and have long, pointed tails. The hooked bill of parrots is a well-adapted tool that can grind, clamp, and bite, crushing seeds so completely that the birds have no role in seed dispersal. The muscular claws can grab, climb, and even lift food to the mouth, which most birds cannot do. Many species are mostly green in colour but also have some yellow or red feathers. These colours blend in well with forest vegetation. Nevertheless, flocks of parrots are easy to spot, noisily flying in the canopy and stopping in the trees.

Parrots are monogamous. Male and female birds remain together and share in the raising of their young. The young hatch naked and helpless and must remain in the nest for several weeks or even a few months, depending on the species. The flock is important in the socialization of young birds. They are good imitators and are able to learn a variety of calls from other flock members. Humans like this trait, and spend hours teaching their parrot pets to talk. Yet, the capture of parrots for the pet trade has all but devastated some species. Habitat loss and hunting are also a problem.

The most magnificent of the parrot family, the scarlet macaw (*Ara macao*) is a large bird with a bright red back and tail, deep blue wings with yellow, and a blue rump. Macaws prefer high tree holes for nesting sites and lay one or two eggs.

The silhouette of the macaw is unmistakable. No other parrot is as large, flying with the long, pointed tail outstretched. With wide, strong wings, macaws can reach speeds of 35 miles per hour. Macaws fly in pairs or small family units and call to each other with voices more hoarse and deep than those of other parrots. Their raucous calls are so loud as to be almost ear-piercing at close range and give the birds away from further distances.

Macaws are known to have very large territories. The total population of the Basin is probably small but they move widely, following seasonally available fruiting trees through the year. Cockscomb's macaws may even cross the Maya Mountains to spend part of the year in the Chiquibul Forest to the west.

During January of 1986, scarlet macaws were frequently seen near Quam Bank. At that time the polewood (*Xylopia frutescens*) was bearing fruit on which the birds were feeding. A month later when there was no more fruit, the great parrots were harder to find. In recent years they have only been seen in the remote areas of the West Basin. However, in June, 1994, a flock of ten flew over Maya Center just after dark and four were seen 3 kilometers west of the CBWS Headquarters.

Macaws

Macaws are wary of humans and for good reason. Alan Rabinowitz reported that they were hunted during the days when Quam Bank stood as a logging camp. Several factors make this species susceptible to extinction: (1) its preference for tall trees which are not usually found in secondary growth and deforested areas, (2) the low numbers of its offspring, (3) the long infancy of its young, and (4) the hunting or capture of the birds by humans for feathers or the pet trade.

The aztec, or olive-throated parakeet (*Aratinga astec*) is mostly green in colour, with a dull olive chest and yellowish belly. These birds travel in small groups, and are seen feeding along the river or at trees such as the bucut tree in the CBWS Headquarters. For nesting the parakeet excavates a hole in an arboreal termite nest and lays 3 or 4 eggs.

The most common parrot in the CBWS is the white-crowned parrot (*Pionis senilis*), which has a dull blue head and neck, a white crown and throat, and wings of blue and green. White-crowned parrots form groups of as many as 50 birds which fly rapidly and erratically from tree to tree. When feeding, they are generally quiet, climbing from branch to branch.

The red-lored parrot (*Amazona autumnalis*) is medium-sized, about 30 cm from head to tail. It is mostly green, with red just above the bill and yellow cheeks. It frequents semi-cleared land and forest edges, eating palm nuts, seeds, and cultivated oranges where available. It nests in the hole of a dead tree.

The mealy parrot (*Amazona farinosa*) is a rather large bird, up to 40 cm long. It is green with red on the tail and a blue crown. The mealy parrot is sometimes difficult to spot, as it prefers the canopy of forested areas. Mealy parrots may travel in groups of 15-20, or in small family units. Unlike the red-lored parrot, this is a deep forest species which declines rapidly with deforestation. They are most frequently encountered several kilometers west of the CBWS Headquarters.

Goatsuckers (Family *Caprimulgidae*)

This bird family is called goatsucker because they were once falsely believed to drink the milk of goats. It includes nightjars, nighthawks, whip-poor-wills, and pauraques. The pauraque (*Nyctidromus albicollis*) is a common bird in the CBWS, locally called "whoyou." At night pauraques frequent forest edges, savannas and farmland. In the more dense forests, they inhabit gaps and small clearings where they can see their insect prey in the moonlight, such as the trails and open areas of the CBWS Headquarters. They fly up and snatch passing insects, particularly beetles and stink bugs. Their eyes are set high on their heads, making it easy for them to spot their prey overhead. Pauraques allow a hiker on a night walk to approach as closely as 3 meters and then flutter up, flashing the white bars on their wings. They land only a few yards ahead in the trail and repeat on the next approach. Visitors who have discovered the technique of holding their flashlight next to their eyes to catch reflections will easily see the bright orange eyeshine of the pauraque.

The bird has a pleasant call, which becomes especially loud and persistent during the full moon. It sounds something like "cu-WHEE-o," or "cucucu-WHEER." Pauraques lay two eggs under a shrub on bare ground, and both male and female birds incubate them. If disturbed at their nests, parent birds often attempt to distract the intruder by fluttering away or flopping as if injured. Although pauraques are easily approached, please do not disturb or attempt to handle them. This can interfere with their feeding and breeding habits.

Swifts (Family *Apodidae*)

Swifts are masters of the air, as they swoop and glide in pursuit of high-flying insects. Swifts even mate in the air, tumbling for a few seconds in the process. Swifts are monogamous, staying paired throughout life. At night they perch in groups, usually in rock crevices or other protected places. They build soft nests of plant matter or feathers and cement them with saliva.

The most common species in the CBWS is Vaux's swift (*Chaetura vauxi*), a small dark bird (less than 12 cm), which soars in small to medium flocks. The white-collared swift (*Streptoprocne zonaris*) is very large (20 cm) with a prominent white collar and square or slightly notched tail. It is more commonly seen in the West Basin. The lesser swallow-tailed swift (*Panyptila cayennensis*) has a white neck and upper breast and a deeply forked tail, although the fork is not always visible. They can be seen on cloudy or rainy days soaring low with a bouncy and erratic flight.

Hummingbirds (Family *Trochilidae*)

Hummingbirds are easily recognized by their small size, their glittering feathers, and their fascinating flying habits. There are fifteen species of hummingbirds recorded in the CBWS.

Hummingbirds have very strong chest muscles. Other birds have most of their strength in the downbeat of the wings, but hummingbirds are strong in the upbeat as well. They can fly backwards, up and down, and can even hover upside down. To support this powerful flight, hummingbirds have to eat a lot and digest their food quickly. For this reason, their main food is nectar, made up of easily digested sugar. When they collect this nectar they also play an important role in pollination. Many flowers with a tubular shape are adapted to hummingbird pollination, particularly red, pink, and orange ones. Some flowers grow in shapes perfectly suited to specific hummingbird species which defend their territories fiercely. Hummingbirds also eat insects, which provide them with the protein needed to maintain their flight muscles.

Female hummingbirds get no help from their mates in raising their young. They carefully select soft grass, flowers and moss for the nest, binding them all together with spider webs and concealing them with lichen camouflage. The nest can only hold two tiny eggs, which hatch after 2 or 3 weeks. The young birds flatten their nest completely as they grow.

Among the more common hummingbirds found at Cockscomb are the little hermit (*Phaethornis longuemareus*) and the larger long-tailed hermit (*P. superciliosus*). Both build their nests on the undersides of palm or heliconia leaves. Heliconia plants, which are related to the banana, rely on hummingbirds to pollinate their blossoms. Hermits have evolved to become the best at this task, because their long, curved bills have a perfect shape for sipping nectar and carrying pollen from flower to flower.

Little Hermit

The rufous-tailed hummingbird (*Amazilia tzacatl*) is found in nonforest habitats and along rivers. It feeds at a wide variety of flowers, and is extremely aggressive toward others.

The violet sabrewing (*Campylopterus hemileucurus*) is a large, beautiful hummingbird with a long, curved bill. It is dark purple with a green back, but looks quite black in the forest. The tail has white corners. It prefers forested areas and stream sides. The violet sabrewing is quite aggressive, defending particular flowers as its territory .

The white-bellied emerald (*Amazilia candida*) is small, with a light-coloured belly and green back. It feeds along the forest edge and open areas at shrubs or heliconia.

The white-necked jacobin (*Florisuga mellivora*) has a striking coloration with a deep blue throat and head, green back, and white on the back of the neck. This bird is often found feeding at bribri trees and heliconia along South Stann Creek.

Trogons (Family *Trogonidae*)
Other names: ramatutu

Trogons are beautiful, stately birds with glittering colours. They have compact bodies, short legs and necks, and are often seen perched below the canopy on a hanging liana or overhead branch. When spotted, they often sit still, allowing detailed observation. When feeding, trogons tend to pluck insects, fruits, and an occasional lizard from foliage. Both male and female birds participate in nest building, carving cavities from rotting tree trunks or termite nests. Both parents help in raising the young, which are born naked and helpless. There are four common species of trogons in the Cockscomb, two with red bellies and two with yellow bellies.

Violaceous Trogon

The slaty-tailed trogon (*Trogon massena*) is the largest trogon in the area. The male is glossy green on the upperparts, and has bright red on the belly. The tail is dull black with no white bars. The female is similar, but has a dull black upper breast, head, and neck. Slaty-tailed trogons have a slow, resonant call of "cuk cuk."

The less common collared trogon (*Trogon collaris*) is distinguished by its narrow, white collar separating the green chest from the red belly and narrow black and white bars interrupted by three wide white bars on the tail. The collared trogon is more likely to be encountered in the higher elevations of the West Basin.

The black-headed trogon (*Trogon melano-cephalus*) has a black head and upper chest, metallic green upper feathers, white breastband, and bright yellow belly. The tail has broad black and white bars. It has a repeated, accelerating call of "cow cow cow." The citreoline trogon is the same species as the black-headed trogon.

The violaceous trogon (*Trogon violaceus*) also has a yellow belly, but is smaller. It can be distinguished from the black-headed trogon by its narrowly barred tail. It has a soft, pleasant "cow-cow-cow" call.

Kingfishers (Family *Alcedinidae*)

Five species of kingfishers have been spotted at Cockscomb, and all live along the river and streams. As their name suggests, kingfishers eat mostly fish, with an occasional crab or insect. They generally have large heads and bills, with short necks. To catch their prey, kingfishers plunge from the air or an overhanging branch, grabbing the fish with their long, straight bills. Along South Stann Creek, kingfishers like to skim just above the water's surface and perch on nearby branches or rocks. To raise their young the male and female birds take turns excavating a 1-2 m long burrow in the mud of a river bank. Three to six eggs are laid directly on the mud at the end of the burrow. When the young hatch, they are helpless and blind. The parents do not clean out the nest and it becomes littered with droppings and fish bones. After three to five weeks, the young are able to fly but still expect food from their parents for a few more weeks.

The ringed kingfisher (*Ceryle torquata*) is a large (up to 40 cm), easily spotted bird. The male has a rufous (red) belly and blue-grey on head and back, with a white collar and throat. The female is similar, but has a blue-grey chest band. The burrow of the ringed kingfisher has a large entrance (about 15 cm across) a meter or more above the water surface during the dry season.

The belted kingfisher (*Ceryle alcyon*) is a migrant that nests in Canada and the United States, but spends the northern winter in the CBWS. It is quite similar in appearance to the ringed kingfisher, but smaller. The female has rufous on her underside.

Belted Kingfisher

The Amazon kingfisher (*Chloroceryle amazona*) is about the same size as the belted kingfisher. It is a bright green bird with a large crest and a white throat and collar. The male has a rufous breast and white belly spotted with green. The female has all white underparts, also spotted with green. This bird prefers fast-flowing rivers and streams.

The green kingfisher (*Chloroceryle americana*) has markings similar to the Amazon kingfisher, but it is small and does not have a noticeable crest. It often hides the entrance to its burrow behind hanging vines or roots.

The very small pygmy kingfisher (*Chloroceryle aenea*) has a green back and rufous belly and chest. The female also has a green breast band. This bird is less common than the other kingfishers, and fishes in small forest streams and puddles for small fish and aquatic insects.

Motmots (Family *Momotidae*)

There are three species of motmots in the CBWS. The beautiful blue-crowned motmot (*Momotus momota*) is the most common. It has a black crown bordered by bright blue, with a shiny green back and olive belly. It is about 40 cm long from head to tail and has a fairly long bill that curves slightly. Like most motmots, the blue-crowned motmot has curious racket-shaped tail feathers. There is some disagreement how the tail achieves that shape. Some suggest the bird plucks the shaft bare, but more likely the barbs are loose and fall off naturally.

The blue-crowned perches on lower branches, quite still except for the tail swinging from side to side. The motmot captures insects, spiders, and small reptiles from the ground and foliage, and eats fruit as well. The bird's low call, an owl-like "hoot-hoot," is often heard at dawn and dusk. To nest, the motmots dig a burrow up to 4 m long in a muddy hillside or riverbank. The female bird lays three or four eggs at the end of the tunnel on the bare ground.

The tody motmot (*Hylomanes momotula*) is a rare bird in Belize, but fairly common in the higher elevation forests of the CBWS. Unlike most motmots, it lacks the racket tail.

Jacamar (Family *Galbulidae*)

The rufous-tailed jacamar (*Galbula ruficauda*) is like a jewel, a slender, metallic green bird with a rufous breast and underside of tail and a white throat. The feet are very weak, most suitable for perching and not for walking or hopping. The jacamar sits without motion on branches just overhead, ready to snatch insects with a remarkably long, straight bill, sometimes knocking the prey against a tree to rid them of their wings. Jacamars often prefer glittering prey, like blue morpho butterflies and shiny beetles or wasps. Parents together dig a hole in a clay bank along a stream or under an uprooted tree. At the end they place the nest and lay two to four round, white eggs. Jacamars live together with their mates, even when they are not breeding. The voice of the jacamar is a high-pitched whistle or an ascending trill. It inhabits the borders of dense woods, especially along riverbanks.

Toucans (Family *Ramphastidae*)
Other names: billbird

Three species of these fantastic, colourful birds live at Cockscomb. They all have extremely large bills, which are light-weight and supported inside by many thin bony struts. Toucans eat mostly fruits from palms, cecropias, and other trees. They add an occasional insect or other small animal to their diet. Nests are built in tree holes, and both parents incubate and care for the young, which hatch naked and helpless.

The large and colourful keel-billed toucan (*Ramphastos sulfuratus*) is the National Bird of Belize. Its cheeks and chest are bright yellow, but the rest of the bird is black except for a bright red patch under the tail. The huge bill sports a beautiful pattern of green,

Keel-billed Toucan

red, orange, and blue. Keel-billed toucans fly in small groups from treetop to treetop, with two wingflaps and a swoop. The keel-billed toucan has a dry, scratchy call repeated monotonously, almost sounding like a frog croaking. It also makes a dry, rattling noise.

The collared aracari (*Pteroglossus torquatus*) is more slender than the keel-billed toucan. Its underside is mostly yellow and is streaked with red. There is a black spot and a broad black band on the belly also. The chest and head are dark black, and the back, wings, and tail are mostly olive. The even and level flight of the aracari can be easily distinguished from the more erratic flight of the keel-billed toucan. Flocks of six to fifteen birds follow each other through the mid and upper levels of the forest. They nest in old woodpecker holes or natural cavities, with as many as five or six birds sleeping in one hole. Sometimes several adults will attend the same nest.

The less common emerald toucanet (*Aulacorhynchus prasinus*) is quite small, and has a much shorter bill than the other species. It has a yellow-green belly and green or olive upper body. The tail has some reddish-brown markings. The emerald toucanet flies with rapid wingbeats in small flocks. The voice of this bird is a repetitive, scratchy croak.

Woodpeckers (Family *Picidae*)

Woodpeckers are a unique group of birds. As their name suggests, their bills are like chisels, adapted for pecking into wood in search of termites and other insects. Woodpecker skulls are well reinforced against constant hammering and digging. The toes have extremely sharp nails and are spread wide. With two toes facing forward and two backward, woodpeckers get an expert grip on the tree bark. Their stiff, spiny tails act as props. Woodpeckers carve nesting holes 100 feet up in dead trees, where the female bird lays about two eggs. Both parents incubate the eggs, but the male bird is more domestic and occupies the nest at night. His partner sleeps outside. There are seven woodpecker species in the Cockscomb Basin.

Two small forest woodpeckers are found in the CBWS. The black-cheeked woodpecker (*Melanerpes pucherani*) has a red crown, black cheeks, and a red belly patch, and black and white zebra stripes on its back. It gleans insects from the bark of trees, but also eats fruit and nectar. The small smoky-brown woodpecker (*Veniliornis fumigatus*) likes to forage high in the canopy or lower along streams and forest edges.

Two medium-sized woodpeckers include the golden-fronted woodpecker (*Melanerpes aurifrons*) which has a zebra-striped back, plain belly, and red at the nape of the neck and the golden-olive woodpecker (*Piculus rubiginosus*) which has an olive back, grey crown, two red stripes on its head and a chest barred with buff-yellow and olive.

Among the three crested woodpeckers, the most difficult to see is the beautiful but elusive chestnut-colored woodpecker *(Celeus castaneus)* which prefers dense forest. It has a golden-buff crest and deep chestnut back and belly with black markings. The male has a red face. The other two crested woodpeckers are frequently encountered anywhere in the Basin. The lineated woodpecker (*Dryocopus lineatus*) and the pale-billed woodpecker (*Campephilus guatemalensis*) are similar-looking large woodpeckers, both having red crests, black backs, and barred bellies. The pale-billed woodpecker is slightly larger and does not have the black ear patch of the lineated woodpecker.

Woodcreepers (Family *Dendrocolaptidae*)

Woodcreepers are birds that forage on the trunks and branches of trees for insects and other invertebrates. They probe under bark and in crevices, sometimes digging into soft or decaying wood. Woodcreeper toenails are extremely sharp, allowing them to creep up and down with little difficulty. Their tails are stiff and provide support and stability. Woodcreepers nest in tree holes that they line with bark, leaves, and moss. They usually lay two eggs. After hatching, the young begin to move out and about after only two weeks. Because their feathers blend in so well in the shady understory, woodcreepers are difficult to see and identify. Most are of reddish-brown colour. Some woodcreepers have beautiful barred cream markings on the head, neck and breast, like the tiny wedge-billed woodcreeper (*Glyphorhynchus spirurus*) and the larger ivory-billed woodcreeper (*Xiphorhynchus flavigaster*). Others have less distinct colour patterns, like the olivaceous woodcreeper (*Sittasomus griseicapillus*) and the ruddy woodcreeper (*Dendrocincla homochroa*). Of the seven species of woodcreepers, the ivory-billed is the most common. Its rapid, descending whistle is one of the distinctive jungle sounds heard in the CBWS.

Ovenbirds (Family *Furnariidae*)

Ovenbirds comprise a large family found only in the American tropics. Belize is near the northern limit of their range and only has four species, all of which occur in the Cockscomb Basin. Despite the similar name, the North American ovenbird is not a member of this family, but is, instead, a wood-warbler. Ovenbirds are drab skulkers which are elusive and difficult to see. Most species feed on insects and spiders and have slender, slightly curved bills. The rufous-breasted spinetail (*Synallax erythrothorax*) is quite common in the thickets near the CBWS Headquarters. Its four note "peet-peet-peechew" song is often the only thing that gives it away. The tiny plain xenops (*Xenops minutus*) has a wedge-shaped bill that appears upturned. The larger buff-throated foliage gleaner (*Automolus ochrolaemus*) forages discreetly among the vines and foliage of the understory.

Antbirds (Family *Formicariidae*)

Another large family found only in the American tropics is the antbirds, of which only six species are found in the Cockscomb Basin. The name, antbird, originates from the fact that some family members follow army ants to eat the insects that flee the invasion. But the family also includes members similar to other birds, called antwrens, antshrikes, antthrushes, or antvireos. Antbirds eat insects and other arthropods such as spiders and have strong, slightly hooked bills. They are elusive forest-dwellers given away mostly by their calls. They can sometimes be seen by sitting patiently in areas where the calls are heard. The black-faced antthrush (*Formicarius analis*) has a clear whistle given in a rapid series on the same pitch. The barred antshrike (*Thamnophilus doliatus*) calls with a rapid, accelerating rattle.

Manakins (Family *Pipridae*)

Manakins are small, fruit-eating birds. With patience they can be observed along the trails of the CBWS. Two of the three species found at Cockscomb have fascinating courtship habits. Making up for their relatively weak voices, male manakins make sharp snapping and rolling sounds with their wings, sounding like a very loud typewriter or finger-snapping. This attracts the quiet and dull green females, who choose mates from among the competitors. The females build their nests and raise two young by themselves.

The red-capped manakin (*Pipra mentalis*) is one common species. The male is unmistakable with a bright red cap, bright yellow trousers and black body. Males compete for females on high branches by sliding backward in a manner that reveals their yellow legs, and noisily leaving their perches with a loud snap.

The white-collared manakin (*Manacus candei*) is also common. The male has a broad white collar, bright yellow belly, black wings, and a green rump. During courtship, groups of male manakins clear the leaves and debris from an area of ground about 1 m in diameter to form a lek, or courtship ground. They leap back and forth between small, straight saplings on either side, wings snapping loudly. After mating, the female lays her eggs in a shallow nest decorated with green moss, fungus and even tiny flowers.

The thrushlike manakin (*Schiffornis turdinus*) is quite different from the other species, being larger with a longer bill and tail. It has more subdued courtship habits. In fact, it is so unlike the other manakins, some ornithologists consider it to be a flycatcher instead.

Cotingas (Family *Cotingidae*)

Seven members of the cotinga family are found in the CBWS. They are closely related to flycatchers and feed on insects and berries. The colourful lovely cotinga (*Cotinga amabilis*) male is a rich, glossy blue with purple patches on the belly and throat, while the female is a dappled grey-brown. Another dramatic member of this family is the masked tityra (*Tityra semifasciata*) which is white with a black mask, wings, legs, and a black bar on the tail. The bill is black at the tip with deep pink on the inside and continuing around the eyes. The black-crowned tityra (*Tityra inquisitor*) is similar but lacks the pink area and, as its name suggests, has a full black crown. Other members of this family are more modestly-coloured, such as the rose-throated becard (*Platypsaris aglaiae*), the cinnamon becard (*Pachyramphus cinnamomeus*), the white-winged becard (*Pachyramphus polychopterus*) and the rufous piha (*Lipaugus unirufus*).

Flycatchers (Family *Tyrannidae*)

With 38 species flycatchers comprise the largest family of birds in the CBWS. Typical members of this family perch patiently on branches and dart out after passing insects. Others eat small lizards or even fish.

Many small, retiring forest flycatchers are commonly found in the CBWS. They are a dull green, difficult to distinguish from one another and include the ochre-bellied flycatcher (*Mionectes oleagineus*), sulphur-rumped flycatcher (*Myiobius sulphureipygius*), the stub-tailed spadebill (*Platyrinchus cancrominus*) and the yellow-olive flycatcher (*Tolmomyias sulphurescens*).

Three tiny flycatchers, the size of hummingbirds, are the common tody-flycatcher (*Todirostrum cinereum*), the slate-headed tody-flycatcher (*Todirostrum sylvia*), and the yellow-bellied tyrannulet (*Ornithion semiflavum*). The common tody-flycatcher is frequently seen in the CBWS, especially near their woven nests hanging over the water. The slate-headed tody-flycatcher and the tyrannulet are rare in the CBWS.

The pileated flycatcher (*Aechmolophus mexicanus*), not known in the rest of Belize, can be seen nesting in the CBWS Headquarters area. This olive-green bird has a permanently erected crest.

Three easily identified open country flycatchers, all with yellow bellies, are found throughout Belize and, especially, in the CBWS Headquarters area.   The great kiskadee (*Pitangus sulphuratus*) is a large, noticeable flycatcher with a black and white head with a yellow crown. It is named after its call of "ki-kis-kadeer." This bird is large enough to include small vertebrates in its diet and will knock them repeatedly against a tree to crush them and make them easier to swallow. The great kiskadee's nest is a sloppy-looking roofed structure built on a strong branch. For building materials, the bird uses grass stems, trash, and even the entire nests of smaller birds that were abandoned.

The smaller social flycatcher (*Myiozetetes similis*) also has a black and white head, but no yellow crown. Social flycatchers live near open areas and along rivers, where they also like to hunt their insect prey. They sit quietly on exposed branches and then swoop after insects. They will also eat berries or seeds, and even tadpoles. Pairs stay together throughout the year and build a roofed nest in a shrub near water during the dry season.

The tropical kingbird (*Tyrannus melancholicus*) has a grey head, and deeply forked tail. It prefers forest borders and secondary growth and has expanded its range in recent years due to deforestation. It has a high-pitched, twittering call. Tropical kingbirds are very graceful in the air during insect-hunting forays, and return to a favorite exposed branch or dead limb. The nest is a sloppy assembly of vines, weeds and grasses, sometimes looking as if it can barely support the eggs. Groups of kingbirds have been known to mob larger predator birds and chase them away.

Jays (Family *Corvidae*)

The noisy cries of the brown jay (*Cyanocorax morio*), locally called "piam-piam," are common on the CBWS forests. It is a large bird, with a sooty-coloured back, wings and neck, with a lighter belly. Its voice is a loud "chaa," often repeated. Brown jays are omnivorous and forage in flocks or individually for insects, spiders, small vertebrates, fruits, and nectar. They poke under bark and leaf litter for insects, and even catch insects mid-air like flycatchers. They also eat a wide variety of fruits. Nests are made of sticks and are supported by flexible roots and vines. Brown jays sometimes appear to have cooperative nesting habits, with the oldest pair in the flock constructing most of the nests. Some females lay their eggs in others' nests, and divide brooding tasks. The flock usually chooses to nest in isolated trees in pastures and other cleared areas, perhaps to thwart predators.

The less common, but more beautiful green jay (*Cyanocorax yncas*) is found in the CBWS, near the southernmost edge of its range. It has a purple head with black throat, a green body, paler underneath, and a green tail with yellow edges.

Wood-Warblers (Family *Parulidae*)

Wood-warblers are small, delicate birds that eat mostly insects, catching them on the wing or plucking them from vegetation. Some wood-warblers eat seeds or berries as well. Wood-warbler pairs are monogamous and quite territorial. Almost 30 species of wood-warblers have been seen in the CBWS. Typical wood-warbler colours are yellow, grey, olive, and sometimes red or brown. Females generally have duller colours than males.

Most wood-warbler species travel thousands of miles each year to breed and nest in North America. When the cold winter months set in up north, wood-warblers return to the tropics. To survive, migrant wood-warblers must be able to find intact habitats in both winter and summer destinations.

Only four wood-warbler species remain in the Cockscomb to breed, the grey-crowned yellowthroat (*Geothlypis poliocephala*), the golden-crowned warbler (*Basileuterus culicivorus*), Grace's warbler (*Dendroica graciae*), and the rufous-capped warbler (*Basileuterus rufifrons*).

Blackbirds (Family *Icteridae*)

The blackbird family comprises 12 species in the CBWS, including members that are not all black, such as the oropendolas and orioles. Other birds at Cockscomb are certainly black, but do not belong in the blackbird family, such as the scarlet-rumped tanager. Many blackbirds build beautiful, intricately woven nests but some, like the cowbirds, make no nests at all.

The bronzed cowbird (*Molothrus aeneus*) is a small, glossy blue-black bird with red eyes. Females are similar, but more dull. This bird frequents the CBWS Headquarters in small flocks. It forages on the ground for seeds and insects. During courtship the male cowbird fluffs up his feathers, jumps and hovers above the female. Cowbirds are parasitic, and do not make their own nests. Instead, they deposit their eggs in the nests of other birds. The cowbird chick often hatches first and grows more quickly than the host bird chicks and is able to take much of the food.

The melodious blackbird (*Dives dives*) is difficult to miss. Its loud, melodic whistles are heard throughout the day in cleared or semi-cleared areas. Both males and females are all black, but the male's feathers are more glossy. The melodious blackbird eats mainly insects, which it plucks from foliage. The nest is deep and woven of coarse fiber.

The less obvious yellow-billed cacique (*Amblycercus holosericeus*), or "bamboo cracker," is all black with a bright yellow cone-shaped bill and yellow eyes. The yellow-billed cacique prefers dense secondary growth along rivers or creeks. It searches for insects between the thick, overlapping leaves of bromeliads and heliconias.

The males and females stay paired throughout the year and build a nest of vines and heliconia leaves in a dense thicket.

Although orioles belong to the blackbird family, they usually have bright orange or yellow colours, especially males. Oriole nests are finely woven cups that hang from slender branches. Two of the five oriole species are migratory and do not breed at Cockscomb, the orchard oriole (*Icterus spurius*) and the northern oriole (*Icterus galbula*). In the winter they join the yellow-tailed oriole (*Icterus mesomelas*) and the smaller black-cowled oriole (*Icterus prosthemelas*) in mixed flocks along forest edges and thickets near the river. The fifth species, the yellow-backed oriole (*Icterus chrysater*), is much less common.

Probably our most spectacular blackbird is the Montezuma oropendola (*Gymnostinops montezuma*), locally called yellowtail. Though related to the smaller orioles and blackbirds, it is very large, reaching 50 cm from head to tail. It has a black head, neck and chest, with a chestnut body. Males have a maroon tinge. The bill is black and tipped with orange.

Montezuma Oropendola

The bright yellow tail feathers are especially noticeable when the bird is flying. The male oropendola makes a loud, peculiar gurgling sound. In the morning and evening, several will call back and forth over some distance, sometimes later assembling in the same tree.

Oropendolas nest in colonies of up to 150 nests in a single large tree, such as the ceiba trees found along South Stann Creek near the picnic table at the end of the River Path. Each nest is a large, hanging basket, attached near the end of a branch. Parasitic botfly maggots often infest and kill young birds. In an interesting example of symbiosis, oropendolas tend to choose trees that are home to bees or wasps that defend their own nests against the botflies, and at the same time keep them away from the oropendolas.

Those that are not located near bee or wasp hives appear to tolerate the giant cowbird. The cowbird does not build its own nest, but lays its eggs in other birds' nests. Generally, the oropendola will toss out these unwanted eggs, but not when they need protection from botflies. When the chicks hatch, the cowbird chicks groom their oropendola nest-mates free of botfly larvae, thus increasing the chances of survival of the colony. In this type of situation, the relationship between cowbirds and oropendolas is more mutualistic than parasitic.

Tanagers (Family *Thraupidae*)

Tanagers are some of the most beautiful birds and have a wide variety of brilliant colours and patterns. Nineteen species are found in the CBWS. They are monogamous birds and many remain with their mates even when nesting season is over. When nesting, the female bird does most of the work but her mate is usually present and helps as well. Both parents help to feed the little nestlings. The young grow quickly and begin to move around in the tree after two weeks or less. Most tanagers have moderately thick bills that allow them to eat fruits, seeds, and some insects.

Several species can be observed around the CBWS Headquarters area, along the CBWS Access Road and the Victoria Peak Path. The blue-grey tanager (*Thraupis episcopus*) is blue with grey underparts. It has a slurred, squeaky voice. The crimson-collared tanager (*Phlogothraupis sanguinolenta*) has a bright red crown, back, breast, and rump, surrounded by black. The male scarlet-rumped tanager (*Ramphocelus passerinii*) is completely black except for a bright scarlet rump. The female is brownish with an olive-coloured breast. The male masked, or golden-hooded tanager (*Tangara larvata*) has a golden hood with black and blue mask, black back and chest, blue and black wings and blue rump. The yellow-winged tanager (*Thraupis abbas*) is large, with lavender head, blue-grey upper back and grey belly, and bright yellow wing patches.

The raspy call of the comparatively drab red-throated ant tanager (*Habia fuscicauda*) is a frequent sound in the thickets and forest understory. If you hear the call, look closely, for frequently they are associated with other birds in mixed species flocks. The grey-headed tanager (*Eucometis penicillata*) is another understory species. It is an ant specialist and frequently follows ant swarms.

References

Garcia, J., Matola, S., Meadows, M., Wright, C.1994. *A Checklist of the Birds of Belize*. World Wildlife Fund: Belize.

Peterson, R. T. & Chalif, E. L. 1973. *Field Guide to Mexican Birds*. Peterson's Field Guide Series. Houghton Mifflin Company: Boston, MA.

Russell, S.M. 1964. A distributional study of the birds of British Honduras. *Ornith. Monogr.* Vol. 1. Amer. Ornith. Union

Stiles, F. G. & Skutch, A. F. 1989. *A Guide to the Birds of Costa Rica*. Cornell University Press: Ithaca, NY.

Wood, D. S., Leberman, R. C., Weyer, D. 1986. *Checklist of the Birds of Belize*. Special Publication No. 12, Carnegie Museum of Natural History: Pittsburgh, PA.

Red-eyed Tree Frog

Marine Toad

CHAPTER 9

Amphibians and Reptiles
James Beveridge and
Katherine M. Emmons

Frogs (Order *Anura*)

In June the rainy season begins in the CBWS, often very dramatically, and the wildlife activity accelerates. Ants are flushed out by
the rising waters. Termites take to the air in swarms, settle, and then
discard their wings which drift down to blanket the bunks and tables
with a fine cover. Butterflies can be seen flocking around damp areas
on the CBWS Access Road, taking off in a frenzy of colour at a
person's approach.

The insect-eating birds seem to plan ahead for the rains. Nests
have been built; eggs have been laid; and chicks are already pushing
their way though eggshells, beak agape, waiting for mum or dad to
thrust a juicy bug into their mouths. As the sun sets, the bats come
out. For both the insect- and fruit-eating varieties, there is no
shortage of food. The abundance of insects and new plant growth
brought by the rain passes on up through the food chain. Birds and
smaller mammals benefit directly and larger predators feed on them,
to the advantage of all.

Even for the visitor the wet season is a time of plenty in the
rainforest. There is a much better chance of encountering most
organisms in the CBWS if you are willing to put on rubber boots and
plod through flooded forests and muddy trails. You may even be
rewarded with the music of the tree frogs!

With their gaping mouths, large eyes and serious expressions
frogs invite attention. They sing in the rain, make love in swamps
and gulp their food. There are approximately 3,500 species of
anurans found in the world, and they are found on all continents
except Antarctica. Approximately 75% of them live in tropical rain
forests.

The Family *Hylidae* includes the tree frogs. There are more
than 100 tree frog species found in Central America and close to 700
are known worldwide. They range in size from 1.5 to 13 cm long.
They are tan, brown, or green, or any combination of these and are
able to change shades or colours quite rapidly.

In the normal course of events a visitor to the rainforest may
never see a tree frog, for they normally stay high up in the forest

151

canopy. During daylight hours they conserve their body fluids by hiding in damp areas such as tree hollows, under loose bark or in the interior of tank bromeliads. Their legs are drawn up close to their flanks and their feet are positioned under their bodies which form an ovoid. In this manner they expose as little of their body surface as possible, thereby diminishing water loss.

As tree frogs are nocturnal, their active period starts with the coolness of the evening when they rouse themselves from their torpor, sing a little and check out the available insect life. Unlike other frogs, hylids have fixed tongues. So, rather than snaring their insect prey with a long sticky tongue, they catch their food by lunging and gulping it down whole.

In order for a frog to sing, he inhales, filling his lungs. The air is expelled through the vocal cords, causing them to vibrate, and into either one or two vocal sacs located on the underside of the throat before being vented. The result is a specific, highly amplified sound, the character of which depends on the species and whether the call is territorial or a love song.

My first experience (James Beveridge) with a full-blown frog concert was in June quite a few years ago. The first heavy rains of the season had already fallen and I was alone, the only visitor in the CBWS.

That night I was jarred awake surrounded by loud, electronic sounds. I stumbled across a blackened room and threw open the door, half expecting to see flashing coloured lights and a slowly descending luminous saucer-shaped craft. There was nothing but darkness and a constant drizzle, but the noise was all around me. As I moved toward the closest of the sounds, it stopped abruptly. As I moved on, the noise started up behind me. I flashed my light on the tree, but nothing was visible to the eye.

The next morning on the trail I followed a frog song and found myself in a low depression surrounded by high forest trees. There was a little standing water near the center, and it was damp and mossy underfoot with low, dense shrubs. I was aware of tiny shapes hurtling through the

Stauffer's (left) and Red-eyed Tree Frogs

bush in front of me, too fast for my eye to follow. So I stood still. Suddenly, I saw a tiny frog a little over 2 cm in length and light tan in colour. Then I saw another but this one was larger, perhaps 8 cm, green in colour with coppery blotches and it had beautiful golden eyes with horizonal slits. I noticed that one of the large leaves just above my head had a paler green oval on its underside - another frog, this one a uniform sherbet-lime green. I gently lifted the leaf for a closer look. Its large, bright red eyes opened quickly showing pupils that were narrow vertical slits. Suddenly there was a flash of blue and yellow, and he was 2 m away, climbing rapidly towards the canopy.

A few rainy days later this same temporary pond was hip deep and filled with tadpoles. Most were only a little bigger than mosquito larvae, but some were larger and a few had a light blue colouration. So began my fascination for the frogs!

The first of these three frogs was probably either the yellow tree frog (*Hyla microcephala)* or Stauffer's tree frog (*Scinax staufferi*). Male frogs are generally smaller than females. The females in these species seldom reach 6 cm in length. The yellow tree frog differs from Stauffer's in its call, and in the fact that it has a brown and white stripe running from each eye along the length of its flank. It also has two brown stripes on its back, which run in parallel, one on either side of the spine. Stauffer's tree frog has broken longitudinal brown markings on its otherwise tan body. Both of these small frogs congregate around temporary breeding ponds. Spawn is laid in the shallows where it is fertilized by the male.

The second frog was the Mexican tree frog (*Smilisca baudinii*), a large hylid reaching a maximum of 9 cm length. Its colours transform from a light golden brown with irregular darker brown blotches to vivid green with the same brown markings. Its eyes are golden with horizontal pupils. This is a common frog in Belize. The Mexican tree frog lays approximately 200-300 eggs directly into the water where they lie close to the surface of the pond.

The third frog, the red-eyed tree frog (*Agalychnis callidryas*), is the Cockscomb's most striking frog. During its quiescent or resting period it is a very pale green. Its flank colours are not visible in this inactive stage. However, at dusk it darkens to a vivid green and shows the deep blue and yellow sides when it jumps. Its large eyes are a startling deep red.

Tree frogs have many predators, including birds, snakes and mammals, such as coatimundis, kinkajous and fringe-lipped bats, which can actually locate the frogs by zeroing in on male calls. When tree frogs are threatened by a predator, they leap as far as thirty times their body length. As the red-eyed tree frog takes off, the predator is presented with a flash of its colourful flanks. But when the frog lands on a leaf with its legs are drawn in, only the leaf green colour shows, puzzling predators. This leaping defense is also

*Red-eyed tree frogs
in pectoral amplexus*

advantageous because it breaks the scent trail which is so important for frog-eating mammals and snakes.

After the first heavy rains of the season, tree frogs descend in mass from the high canopy to congregate around areas which later become temporary ponds. Very rarely do they gather near permanent ponds or running water, because the future spawn and tadpoles would be eaten by the small freshwater fish and other aquatic predators found there.

The male red-eyed tree frog sings from a point high above a temporary pond. At this point the call is probably territorial. At dusk he descends and changes to a mating call. The female answers by approaching close in front of him. The male then mounts her and clamps tightly with his forelegs. This is known as pectoral amplexus.

As one, they climb to the overhanging leaves. By this time, the female has filled her bladder with water by absorbing rain or pond water through her skin. At the critical time, she lays a small mass of eggs while releasing the stored water over them. The male then releases his sperm over the eggs.

The spawn adheres to the leaf, directly above the pond, a pale jelly enveloping about 40 pale-green eggs. Tadpole development is rapid and in five or six days, the miniature polywogs break through the rapidly disintegrating membrane and fall into the pond below.

However, the frogs' timing must be just right. In many cases the first rains are a false start and the pond is no longer there. So, rather than falling safely into the water, the fertilized eggs hit the soil and dehydrate. If the frogs wait too long, until the pond is deeper, water bugs and the naiads of damselflies and dragonflies will be well-established. So, rather that falling to a dusty death, the spawn would fall to the tearing maws of predatory insects.

If all goes well, the pale blue tadpoles will congregate in the warm waters. They will lead a vegetarian life for ten weeks before emerging as young froglets with the vestige of a tail. They slowly make their way up to the canopy, feeding on small insects. In time they will take on the colouration of their parents and, if they survive the dangers of the canopy, descend the next season to sing the song of the tree frog.

Developing tadpoles on a leaf above a temporary pond in the CBWS

Another common tree frog in the CBWS is the picta tree frog (*Hyla picta*), also called the yellow-line tree frog. This small, active frog is less than 3 cm long. It is easily identified by the two yellow lines starting at the eyes and moving back along the body.

The narrowmouth frog (*Gastrophryne elegans*) is also seen in the temporary breeding ponds where its spawn is laid and fertilized. It is about 6 cm. The upper back is a rich coppery brown that can change abruptly to a dark brown with white spots on the sides. The nose is sharp and the mouth noticeably small for a frog.

The variegated tree frog (*Hyla ebraccata*), also called clown frog, is found in the CBWS. It is about 5 cm long and has creamy blotches on a darker background.

Toads (Family *Bufonidae*)

Toads are closely related to frogs, but where frogs generally have a smooth, damp skin, toads have a dry and warty hide. In addition, toads are more inclined to crawl or hop in comparison to the long jumps of frogs. The Cockscomb Basin has three species of toads.

Marine toads in pectoral amplexus

Marine Toad (*Bufo marinus*)
Other name: spring chicken

The marine toad is the largest toad in the Western Hemisphere and can weigh well over a kg. A large one may be 23 cm long and 12 cm wide. This heavy-weight amphibian will eat anything it can overcome, but is primarily insectivorous and in a short period can consume an amazing number of insects. The young are voracious insectivores and grow rapidly, consuming any arthropod which comes within range. Adults have a distinctly toad-like appearance with a warty grey to brown skin and strongly developed bony ridges on the cranium.

Just behind the eyes on each side are huge paratoid glands, which combined are as large as its head. These glands exude a powerful toxin that can kill a predator as large as a dog. The toxin must have hallucinogenic properties, for it is said that the classic Mayan priests licked the toad to put themselves into a trance. The interpretations of the resulting visions were very important to the day-to-day life of the Maya. In the sixties and seventies, some North American hippies were known to wander southern Mexico and Central America seeking enlightenment by licking spring chickens.

The marine toad lays enormous numbers of eggs after dark in flooded areas alongside the CBWS Access Road. There the spawn is laid and fertilized by the male tightly mounted on the larger female in pectoral or pelvic amplexus. The spawn is toxic, so the only danger to the eggs is dehydration if the temporary ponds dry up. Small black tadpoles develop from the darkly pigmented eggs and quickly metamorphose into small toadlets, which are virtually identical to other toad species.

Gulf Coast Toad (*Bufo valliceps*)

The gulf coast toad favours coastal lowlands and can be identified by wide black stripes on its flanks with three light stripes centering along its spine. Like the marine toad, it also has pronounced cranial ridges. The male has a large yellow vocal sac, with which it makes a loud trilling call lasting from 4 to 6 seconds.

A new toad species (*B. campbelli)* very similar to the gulf coast toad has been discovered in the Maya Mountains and probably exists in the CBWS

Mexican Burrowing Toad (*Rhinophrynus dorsalis*)
Other names: burrowing cow toad

The Mexican burrowing toad is seldom seen, because it normally lives in a hole in a low, moist area. But more often this toad is heard, the mournful, lowing sound of a sick cow, which accounts for its local name. Only when torrential rains cause flooding does this elusive toad emerge. It is a flat-bodied creature with a rough reddish-brown skin.

Lizards (Order *Sauria*)

The popular impression of a lizard is that of an agile, scaled creature with front and hind legs, long tail, sharp teeth and well-developed eyes, complete with eyelids. The body of a lizard may be flattened or cylindrical, and scales may be soft and skin-like or hard and enlarged.

When attacked, many species of lizards distract the predator by separating from their tail, leaving it wriggling on its own. This function allows the lizard time to escape. This is made possible by the existence of a shearing plane within the vertebrae. That is, the vertebrae do not disconnect, but rather split into two parts. Special muscles then contract, closing the artery and preventing loss of blood. A new tail grows back, but vertebrae are replaced with a simple fibrous rod, and colouring and scales differ from the original. On rare occasions, the tail is not completely separated and a new tail also develops, resulting in a double tail.

Lizards bask in the sun to raise their body temperature to digest their food or creep into the shade to avoid overheating. Reptiles have no sweat glands, and, unless they get out of the sun, their bodies reach a threshold where movement becomes impossible and they will die.

Green Iguana (*Iguana iguana*)
Other name: common iguana, bamboo chicken

The green iguana is the largest iguana found in Belize and may approach 2 m in length. The bamboo chicken is much hunted for its flesh because it tastes like chicken. As a result, the common iguana is

Green Iguana Hatchling

no longer common in Central America. They can be seen from South Stann Creek, lying on tree limbs over the water. When danger approaches, they make spectacular dives into the water. Iguanas are excellent swimmers and can swim underwater for some distance to escape danger.

The female iguana digs a hole, usually in a sandy area close to a river, and lays 20 to 30 round, soft-shelled eggs. In about three months, the hatchlings dig themselves out of the sand. At this stage they are about 15 cm in length and bright green in colour. Their hue is their only defence from predators, so they quickly scatter to the luxuriant green of the forest. Young iguanas predominantly feed on insects, but as they grow, they begin to browse on the greenery. By the time they are adults they are almost completely herbivores.

An adult male iguana may be bright green, but they are capable of colour changes, so reddish or brown-grey specimens can be observed. They have a large spiny crest, high behind the head and running down the back to the upper tail. Under the chin and throat there is a large skin dewlap which they extend in a typical territorial display.

Casque-headed Iguana (*Laemanctus longipes*)

Casque-headed iguanas are rarely seen in Cockscomb. This is partially because of their excellent camouflage. They are much smaller than the green iguana, not longer than 1 m, of which three-quarters is tail, the body and head being only 21 cm.

This iguana is very slender and emerald-green in colour. The top of its head is flattened, sloping down towards the eyes. It is more like a chameleon in habit than an iguana, depending mostly on its excellent colouration.

> On one occasion I (James Beveridge) came across one on the Victoria Peak Path, high up in the tall cane. By slowly bending the stalk of cane down to within two meters of the trail, I was able to get several photographs of it. It patiently modeled for me as I focused 1 m from its head.

Spiny-tailed Iguana (*Ctenosaura similis*)
Other name: scaly-tailed iguana, wishwilly

The spiny-tailed iguana is very common on the cayes and coastal areas of Belize. They are not common in Cockscomb, but have been seen in the Headquarters area. The wishwilly is coloured in tones ranging from light grey to black. Like the green iguana, the male has a magnificent crest. It also feeds primarily on vegetation, but supplements its diet with insects and other animals. Large adults have been known to eat birds caught in mist nets before the ornithologists could release them.

Striped Basilisk (*Basiliscus vittatus*)
Other names: Jesus Christ lizard, cock maklala

The striped basilisk is a half-meter long lizard which is quite common in Cockscomb, especially along the Access Road and around the CBWS Headquarters, where it can often be seen basking in the sun.

Jesus Christ lizards are olive-green with a yellow stripe running from the eye down the flanks, tapering out at a point above the back legs. The underside of the jaw and throat is cream-coloured. It has a large, elongated oval crest starting above the eye and hanging over the back of the neck. On occasions, the end of the tail will have dull brick-red bands. These lizards have a varied diet of insects, other smaller lizards, fruit, and flowers.

The name "Jesus Christ lizard" derives from a particular behavior. When startled, it stands upright and runs on its two hind legs. If there happens to be a body of water in its path, the lizard runs right over it. This miracle of walking on water is made possible by an extremely swift gait and the positioning of large skin flaps between the toes. This strategy provides the means for them to escape large predators.

Striped Basilisk

Old Man Lizard

Old Man Lizard (*Corytophanes cristatus*)
Other name: helmeted basilisk

Helmeted basilisks are usually a dull brown or green, which allows them to blend in with dead vegetation. They are common, but rarely seen because they cling motionless to vegetation and depend on their excellent camouflage. Above the eyes are bony ridges that run back across the head to meet above the neck and connect to form a bony crest. A smaller comb-toothed crest is under the throat. Old man lizards feed on a variety of insects.

Anole lizards (*Anolis* spp)
Other name: maklala

Anyone who has been to the tropics has seen an anole, the small lizards that scurry along the ground or threaten from trees and bushes with territorial displays, nodding their heads and extending their colourful dewlap under their throats. Four species of anoles have been recorded in the CBWS. They are often seen from the trails or around the buildings in the Headquarters.

Anoles range in colour from black and brown, to tan and bright green. Several have light dorsal stripes or zigzag patterns. Some can change colour from a brilliant green to a dark brown within seconds.

They feed on in-sects which they catch by a combination of stealth and speed. They are capable of swallowing arthropods that are quite large in relation to their own size.

Anole

Geckos (Family *Gekkonidae*)

Geckos, unlike other lizards, can walk on inverted or vertical smooth surfaces. This is made possible by claws and enlarged pads on the underside of their feet. These pads are composed of plates covered with microscopic hair-like structures with spatula-like tips. Geckos have soft, flattened bodies which can range in colour from off-white to almost black.

Most geckos are nocturnal and have eyes with vertically elliptic pupils that are covered by a clear film formed from a fusion of the upper and lower lids. Only 2 species have been recorded in the CBWS, the boldly patterned banded gecko (*Coleonyx elegans*) and *Sphaerodactylus millepunctatus*, which has no English common name.

Geckos are vocal and gregarious. On still nights, usually prior to a storm, they can be heard croaking loudly, so they may be reacting to a low pressure weather system or the calls may be used to establish territorial limits.

Yellow-spotted Night Lizard (*Lepidophyma flavimaculatum*)

The yellow-spotted night lizard is the only species of night lizard reported in Belizean rainforests. Night lizards are similar to geckos except they have large plates on the head and squarish, granular scales on the belly. The eyes are large and pupils are vertically elliptical. Eyelids are lacking.

Night lizards are unusual in that they are live-bearing. The female is an active participant in the delivery, removing the embryonic membrane with her teeth. Normally this activates the young, but now and again the mother stimulates them by nipping them on the flanks. Only one or two are born at a time.

Skinks (Family *Scincidae*)
Other name: galliwasp

The CBWS has three species of skinks. Most commonly seen is Cherrie's skink (*Sphenomorphus cherriei*), locally known as the galliwasp. It grows to about 23 cm and is coppery on the back with a creamy yellow belly. Black and beige lines run along the flanks. Like many other lizards, the tail of the skink will break off if seized, letting the creature scurry to freedom. A new tail will then be grown. This lizard thrives in open areas where it forages for insects and their larvae.

Snakes (Superorder *Squamata*, Order *Serpentes*)

Snakes have fascinated humankind since history began, playing significant roles in many of man's religions, either vilified or venerated. For example, the Mayan plumed serpent Kukulcan was worshipped as the god of wind and air in the area now called Belize. Even in Judeo-Christian folklore the snake plays a major role in the story of Adam and Eve. The Greek god of healing, Aesculapius, was said to have tended serpents in his sanctuary. This connection of snakes with skill in healing persists today in the medical insignia, a snake coiled around a staff.

Belize has no shortage of snake stories. A commonly-heard story is that a pregnant woman can kill a snake by looking at it. Another story is that if a victim of a snake bite sees a pregnant woman, the victim will die. Some people also believe that snakes can inject poison through the tail. Sometimes the tail is whipped around in defense, but the tail itself is not dangerous. Some snake stories tell positive things about snakes. In some cultures, snakes represent givers of life and are considered sacred animals.

Snakes have neither eardrums, eyelids nor limbs. How do snakes move when they have no legs? The whole body of the snake is full of muscles and large scales (called ventral plates) on the snake's underside overlap toward the tail and allow it to move smoothly and keep from sliding backward. Some snakes brace their back end and push against the ground to propel the front forward.

The front then grips the ground allowing the back end to move forward, curving gracefully in a swimming motion. On other snakes, especially big ones, the muscles attached to the ventral plates move in groups to propel the snake forward in a fairly straight line.

Because of their narrow tubular body the internal organs are elongated, and where organs are paired, such as in testes or kidneys, the right and left organs are positioned at different levels. Snakes have a flexible backbone running their entire length with 200-400 vertebrae. Except for those in the tail most vertebrae are connected to movable ribs which allow enlargement of girth to provide room for bulky food items, or, in the case of females, eggs or young.

Snakes eat insects, frogs, lizards, other snakes, birds, and small mammals. They smell their prey by flickering their tongues in the air. Different snakes have different means to overcome their prey. Some inject venom into their prey. Others, such as the kingsnakes and boa constrictors, suffocate their prey by constriction. The majority of snakes, however, have no specific means of subduing their quarry except to swallow it alive and struggling. Many snakes use their muscles to spring and strike at their prey and then catch it with their teeth.

Green vine snake swallowing a red-eyed tree frog

The swallowing of food is made easier by the ability of snakes to totally disconnect the lower jaw from the upper and by the movable ribs. Thus, they are able to engulf creatures many times wider than their body. The strong muscles move the prey down the gullet. Snakes do not chew their food.

Snake venoms may be haemotoxic, if they attack the vascular or blood systems, or neurotoxic if they attack the nervous system, or a combination of both. Fortunately, antitoxins are available for most snake venoms. Anyone bitten by a snake should be taken immediately to a licensed doctor. More details of first aid are given in Chapter 13.

However, of the 58 different species of snakes in Belize, only 9 are dangerous to humans. Moreover, most of these dangerous snakes are not commonly seen. Many snakes help us by controlling the populations of rats that create unsanitary conditions near our homes and carry diseases. Venomous or not, snakes generally go about their business and have no interest in chasing or attacking people. Snakes are too small to eat humans and they would rather not have anything to do with us! Some people kill snakes simply because they fear them. Sadly, many very beautiful, harmless, and beneficial snakes are killed because of this fear.

At Cockscomb, ALL snakes are protected and must be left alone. Wear shoes and pants on the trails. If you see a snake of any kind, keep your distance, leave it alone and walk softly. The Cockscomb Basin has twenty-four species of snakes recorded thus far, but undoubtedly more species occur.

Boa Constrictor (*Boa constrictor*)
Other name: wowla

The boa constrictor is the largest snake found in both North and Central America. It can grow to over 4 m and 30-40 kg. In the entire world, only the South American anaconda and several of the Old World pythons are larger. Boas are found all over Belize and in Cockscomb they are in the lower, damper areas close to water.

Boa Constrictor

In spite of its size the wowla is not considered dangerous to humans. It would be feasible for a large wowla to kill a person, but it would need to be draped around the person's neck or chest.

Normally, after the initial capture, boas are quite gentle creatures. I (James Beveridge) have handled two boas in excess of 4 m straight from the wild. I would have to admit, though, that I required help getting the larger one unwrapped from my arm.

They feed on a variety of prey, lizards, birds and mammals. In Belize, it is uncommon to find a wowla over 3 m, but they can easily consume an animal as large as a curassow or a gibnut. Boa constrictors kill by constriction; that is, they throw two or three coils around their prey's thorax. As the animal exhales the snake tightens the coils, preventing the prey from inhaling. Soon the creature dies from suffocation. The boa does not break bones. After death the victim is swallowed whole, which may take 5 minutes to an hour, depending on the size of the meal.

The boa constrictor is a very handsome beast, especially soon after shedding, when its skin has an iridescent sheen that flashes blue. Most boas are predominantly tan with markings of silver, black and brown in a connected circular pattern. The head is small and, except for a dark slash from the eye to the hinge of the jaw, is light-coloured. The New World boa constrictors differ from the Old World pythons in that they are live-bearing.

Black-tailed Indigo (*Drymarchon corais*)
Other name: blacktail

The black-tailed indigo is one of Belize's largest and most common snakes. It is quite heavy-bodied and can reach over 3 m in length. It is neither venomous nor a constrictor, but beats its prey against the ground or a tree while holding it in its extremely powerful jaws. The barely conscious prey is then swallowed whole. The blacktail feeds on rodents and other snakes and has been witnessed in Cockscomb consuming a fer-de-lance.

Blacktail's upper body varies from dark olive to a golden tan with lighter underparts. Its long tail is tapered and always black. This snake is easily tamed and seldom bites after its initial capture. It is commonly seen in the Cockscomb Basin.

Speckled Racer (*Drymobius margaritiferus*)
Other names: guinea hen snake

The speckled racer is one of the most regularly seen snakes in the Basin, because it is diurnal and quite common. As its name suggests, it is an extremely fast snake which can grow to over 1.2 m in length. This slender, dark-speckled turquoise snake is found near water where it feeds on frogs. It is aggressive, but does not bite, as Judy Lumb reports in this encounter—

"I was walking in the early morning on the Wari Loop when suddenly I was hit three times on the leg before I had time to react. I only got a glimpse of a beautiful green and yellow snake rapidly retreating into the bush. I was in awe of its beauty and speed as it seemingly flew, head high and the rest of its body looped several times. The snake must have been sleeping among the yellow leaves in the trail.

"I continued walking calmly, but realized I'd just been hit three times by a snake. I did not feel anything, but thought maybe I was in shock. I pulled up my pant leg and saw no bite. Only when I told the story to Park Director Ernesto Saqui did I learn that it was a speckled racer and, though they are aggressive, they do not bite."

Tropical Kingsnake (*Lampropeltis triangulum*)
Other names: bead-and-coral snake

The tropical kingsnake is a coral snake look-a-like with the same colours and general body and head shape. As with the coral snakes, the local name is bead-and-coral. They can be distinguished by the sequence of the coloured bands. The sequence of the coral snakes is black, yellow, red, yellow, black. In contrast, the tropical kingsnake band order is yellow, black, red, black, yellow. In addition, the tropical kingsnake is larger, growing up to 1.8 m long.

This similarity between species is called Batesian mimicry. Hazardous species are often brightly coloured. Would-be predators are warned off by this bright colouring. Look-a-likes, or mimics, have evolved that enjoy the same protection as do their more dangerous counterparts.

Tropical kingsnakes are extremely docile, non-venomous and kill by constriction. They feed primarily on other snakes, including fer-de-lance and other pit vipers, and seem to be resistant to the effects of the pit viper venom. They also feed on rats and mice, which makes them welcome guests at most farm and grain storage areas. The tropical kingsnake is an extremely helpful and beautiful snake which should never be killed under any circumstances.

Cat-eyed Snakes (*Leptodeira septentrionalis and L. frenata*)
Other names: cohune ridge tommygoff

The pretty cat-eyed snakes have narrow necks, wide heads and, similar to many dangerous snakes, vertical pupils. However, although these snakes are venomous, they are rear-fanged and are dangerous only to their prey, anoles and frogs. They are gentle creatures and rarely make an attempt to bite. They are common in the CBWS, especially during the rains when frogs are abundant.

The smaller of the two, *L. frenata*, is usually no more than two-thirds of a meter in length with a slender body. Its belly is a deep rosy pink and the back a darker rose with large brown markings along the body. *L. septentrionalis* is larger, up to a meter. It is orange with rows of dark spots.

Green-headed Tree Snake

Green-headed Tree Snake (*Leptophis mexicanus*)

Green-headed tree snakes are very common in the CBWS. They are slender with long prehensile tails, which they use very effectively while stretching between branches. When threatened, they generally present a bold approach, opening their jaws wide while swaying back and forth. Usually, however, it is all a bluff, as seldom do they bite.

These snakes are small, barely 1 m in length, coppery above and white below with a green and black line separating the two prime colours. As the name suggests they have green heads with a dark eye stripe.

The green-headed tree snake is almost totally arboreal. It is found in tropical lowland moist rainforests where it feeds mostly on tree frogs which it subdues with a venom delivered by way of rear fangs. It is not considered dangerous to humans.

Coach Whip (*Masticophis mentovarius*)
Other name: tropical whipsnake

The coach whip is more common in coastal pine savannah areas, but occurs less commonly within the CBWS. It is extremely fast-moving and is sometimes seen crossing the CBWS Access Road. The coach whip is drab olive with an almost white belly. The underside of the chin and throat are off-white with dark yellow and grey markings. This is a long, slender snake reaching 3 m. It is non-venomous and feeds on rodents.

Red Coffee Snake *(Ninia sebae)*
Other name: bead-and-coral snake

The small red coffee snakes are pretty, harmless snakes that are often found after rains along the banks of streams but disappear into tiny holes as soon as they see you. Though they have the same local name as coral snakes, they are easily distinguished. The red coffee snakes are very small, seldom more than 30 cm. They have rings only near the head and the rings do not encircle the entire body.

Green Vine Snake (*Oxybelis fulgidus*) and
Grey Vine Snake (*Oxybelis aeneus*)

Both the green and grey vine snakes are exceptionally well-camouflaged. Unless threatened, vine snakes improve their camouflage by moving extremely slowly, swaying to and fro as if in a gentle breeze. Long and unusually slender, they can easily be mistaken for a hanging vine. The head is large, but compressed, giving an appearance of a leaf growing at the end of a stalk. Vine snakes can grow up to 2 m in length, but no more than 2 cm in width.

These rear-fanged snakes have 4 to 6 fixed fangs at the rear of their mouths. The venom is neurotoxic, but is surprisingly mild. Although it has little effect on man, it will paralyze its prey, small reptiles or amphibians. If an attempt is made to catch a vine snake, it will generally bite viciously.

The green vine snake is very beautiful. Its back is emerald green while the belly is a shade of lime green, sometimes varying to a greenish blue hue. Separating the upper and lower greens there is a prominent yellow stripe running the length of the body.

The grey vine snake is not as colourful. It is a pale grey, mottled with darker and lighter shades of the same colour, resembling a slender branch or woody liana.

Green Vine Snake

Spotted Rat Snake (*Spilotes pullatus*)
Other names: monkey snake, thunder-and-lightning snake

The spotted rat snake is a large rodent-eating snake commonly known in Belize as the thunder-and-lightning snake. This is quite a descriptive name for its dark colouration is broken with vivid streaky yellow markings like lightning flashes. The underbelly is bright yellow with variable black rings. Its yellow jaw often has it confused with the yellowjaw tommygoff.

Although this species may reach over 4 m further south, the Belizean subspecies, *S. pullatus mexicanus,* seldom reaches 3 m. This snake is non-venomous, but no attempt should be made to pick it up because it has a nasty disposition and will always attempt to bite. Unless you have had lots of experience with snake handling, it will generally be successful because of its great speed and strength. This is a common snake in the Cockscomb Basin.

Coral snakes (*Micrurus* spp.)
Other names: bead-and-coral snake

Coral snakes are only found in the New World. There are three coral snakes in Belize, and all have been reported within the Cockscomb Basin. *Micrurus diastema* is quite common while the other two are relatively rare.

Coral snakes are extremely attractive with alternating bands of bright red, yellow and black throughout the length of the snake. Generally they are small snakes, less then a meter in length. Separate species of coral snakes can be differentiated by the number of bands on the body, and the respective widths of the individual colour belts.

The local name for coral snakes, bead-and-coral, is also used for several other harmless snakes, such as the tropical kingsnake (*Lampropeltis triangulum*) and the red coffee snake (*Ninia sebae*), which have similar markings. But only the coral snakes have red bands next to yellow ones. A local rhyme, "Red touch yellow, deadly fellow; red touch black, venom lack," works well for the snakes found in Belize.

Coral snakes are extremely docile and inoffensive. During daylight hours they are normally concealed under leaves, in hollow logs or in ant hills. At dusk they generally come out to hunt but are quick to retreat. The slightest footfall is enough to send them back out of sight.

Coral snakes have small, fixed fangs in a little mouth and they do not normally strike as do other snakes. Venom is usually injected only when the snake is handled. Often the tail is suddenly raised prior to biting to distract the attention from the head. This action gave rise to an old wives' tale that the coral snake stings with its tail. However, there is no truth to it.

Coral snakes have the most lethal venom in the Americas, a specialized neurotoxin. Although there is little local tissue damage, the toxin affects the sympathetic nervous system, stopping heart and lung functions.

Many coral snake bites are dry bites, that is, no venom is injected. Of 20 reported in the US, only 6 suffered effects from the bite, but 4 of these died. In Cockscomb there has been only one coral snake bite, a dry bite.

Pit vipers (Family *Crotalidae*)

Pit vipers and true vipers differ from other snakes by having large hinged fangs which fold up against the roof of the mouth when not in use, ready to swing down to an erect position when the mouth is opened. There are only two fangs visible but, when a fang is broken, a replacement will quickly grow in. Venom is produced in special glands positioned at the upper part of the head, giving it the characteristic triangular shape. The pit viper venom has a largely haemotoxic effect. The toxicity levels of the *Crotalidae* differ between the species.

Pit vipers have an additional sense which other snakes lack. This is a deep pit located between the eyes and the nostrils. This sensory pit is a heat-sensing organ which allows them to perceive temperature differences of one degree centigrade or less. This enables the snake to fix on a warm-blooded animal and strike with precision in the forest in complete darkness.

All pit vipers are viviparous, that is, they bring forth their young alive. Even newly-born young are capable of inflicting a venomous bite.

Eyelash Viper (*Bothrops schlegeli*)

Although the eyelash viper has not been sighted in the Cockscomb Basin, it is most likely there. It has been recorded in the Chiquibul National Forest to the west and the Cockscomb Basin offers ideal habitat. Since it is exceptionally well-camouflaged and exclusively arboreal, it is easy to miss.

The eyelash viper differs from most other pit vipers in that it has a prehensile tail, and is relatively slender, seldom reaching half a meter in length. This snake, in spite of its size, is considered very dangerous because of its relatively large poison glands, extremely potent venom, especially long fangs, and habit of resting on shoulder-high heliconias. It feeds on hummingbirds attracted to the heliconias.

The eyelash viper may be banana yellow or an olive green with black, yellow or red, unlikely camouflage colours. But it is often found coiled around heliconia blossoms where it blends in exceptionally well. It has a distinctly triangular head and slender neck and, as its name implies, "eyelashes," three or four enlarged scales that protrude directly upwards right behind the eyes.

Jumping viper (*Porthidium nummifer*)
Other name: jumping tommygoff

The jumping viper is a small, but extremely heavy-bodied pit viper. The local name refers to its ability to throw its body forward, in some cases actually leaving the ground. It is a rather ugly, aggressive snake. For all this aggressiveness, the jumping viper has quite short fangs and its venom is only mildly toxic. Mostly they are dark brown in colour with or without a black zigzag pattern. Noticeable dark stripes run from the nostrils between the eyes to the back of the head.

Fer-de-lance (*Bothrops asper*)
Other name: yellowjaw tommygoff

The fer-de-lance is the most dangerous snake in Belize and also the most common of all our pit vipers. In South America fer-de-lance are known to exceed 4 m in length, but in Belize they are seldom seen greater than 2 m. But even at this size, it is formidable. It is dark brown with distinct

Fer-de-lance

triangular markings of yellow and a darker brown edging the yellow. The chin, lower sides of the head and throat are noticeably yellow, which gives rise to its local name.

The ability of the fer-de-lance to camouflage itself is legendary, as this story from Ernesto Saqui demonstrates —

"A female tourist reported the presence of a dangerous-looking snake, coiled close to a bench on the Rubbertree Trail, so I went to investigate. I searched the area for some time, but found nothing. I returned to the Headquarters and got the tourist so she could show me where it was.

"'There it is!' she exclaimed upon our arrival. Sure enough, a fer-de-lance was coiled not ten feet from the bench, as she had seen it three hours before. It was practically invisible on top of a dried cecropia leaf. Not only had I failed to spot it, but I had walked all around it. It was a miracle I had not stepped on it."

The fer-de-lance is thought to be an aggressive snake by many, but this story highlights its true nature. The fer-de-lance neither retreats nor advances on man's approach, but depends both on its excellent camouflage and lethal bite. Incidents happen when its protective colouring works so well that someone steps on it. Its natural reflex is to strike and a foot or leg is bitten with dire consequences.

Alan Rabinowitz wrote of several experiences with the yellow-jaw tommygoff while conducting his research in the Cockscomb Basin. He tells how one of his guides, a dog-handler named Guermo, was bitten on the ankle and died.

Several years ago, a British soldier was bitten by a fer-de-lance. The fangs penetrated right through his army boot. Fortunately, he was taken out by helicopter and treated, so he lived to tell the tale.

Fer-de-lance feed on rodents so they tend to be where rats are found. Unfortunately, rats are found where people and their food are found, so confrontations between fer-de-lance and people occur around farms, grain storage warehouses and barns.

Crocodiles (Family *Crocodylia*)

Morelet's crocodiles (*Crocodylus moreleti*) have not been seen in the Cockscomb Basin since 1984 when there was a single report of a sighting in the West Basin. Prior to the 1950s, they were reported regularly in the Cockscomb Basin. At that time they were hunted extensively for their hides throughout Belize. By 1981 when the Wildlife Protection Act was passed, their numbers had dwindled to only a few. Since then they have rebounded as a species, and can be found in most lowland interior rivers and ponds.

In light of the 1984 sighting, it seems likely that a small population remains within the Sanctuary boundaries. The species was first seen by wildlife collectors in 1851, but it was not until the 1930's that it was concluded this was a distinct species of crocodile.

The Morelet's crocodile is a small crocodile, seldom exceeding 3 m. However, occasional individuals have grown to nearly 4 m. Such beasts are so much heavier than their smaller brethren that they can be considered dangerous to humans.

Female Morelet's crocodiles make large nests of twigs and rotting vegetation in which they lay up to 3 dozen round, hard-shelled eggs and cover them well. The decomposing vegetation keeps the eggs warm for the 12-week incubation. The female protects and cares for the nest, often dripping water over it to keep a moist environment. She is never far away. If an intruder approaches, she will rise up out of the water and attack with a loud roar.

Morelet's Crocodile Hatchlings

When the hatchlings are close to emerging, they make a loud squeaky call. This attracts the mother who pulls apart the nest. Meanwhile the young break out of their shells using an egg tooth positioned at the end of the snout.

The young emerge with the egg sac still connected and this provides food for many weeks. Any egg slow in hatching is assisted by the mother, who lifts it up in her mouth and, by applying gentle pressure, breaks the egg, allowing the tardy youngster to escape the shell.

After the hatching is completed, the adult female gathers up her children in her mouth and carries them into the water. The hatchlings have been known to stay near their mother for up to 20 months. But even with a handy bodyguard, there is still a high predation rate by raccoons, coatimundis, herons and even male crocodiles. For the first year, they stay hidden in the water grasses, feeding on insect larvae, froglets and fish. They grow rapidly and, by the end of their first year, they may reach 75 cm and are then feeding on rodents, birds and amphibians. They can be very long-lived, reaching ages of 80 years or more.

Turtles
Mud turtles (*Kinosternon* spp.)
Two species of mud turtles are the most commonly seen turtles in the creeks of the CBWS. Mud turtles have a dull olive-brown upper shell and a creamy yellow under plate. They have a hinged outer shell so they can pull in their entire body and close the shell for protection. They grow to about 30 cm.

They are normally found in ponds or slow-moving sections of streams or rivers. On occasions they may be found making their way along a trail in the forest some distance from water.

"Several years ago I (James Beveridge) came across a mud turtle on the Antelope Trail. The nearest water was over two kilometers away and I judged that this turtle was in a vulnerable position. So, I picked it up and gave it a lift to the water. It showed its gratitude by biting me. Then, as I released it into a deep pool in the river, it took off without a backward glance."

Terrapins (Family *Emydidae*)
Two terrapins may be found in Cockscomb Basin. The smaller black-bellied turtle (*Rhinoclemys areolata*) is named for its black under shell. The upper shell is olive green with yellow marking bordering the individual plates.

The other species is the red-eared slider (*Trachemys scripta*), also known as the yellow-bellied turtle, the ornate terrapin and, locally, as the bocotora. The shells of the bocotora are used as percussion instruments by the Garifuna in Belize. The first musical group from Belize to participate in the New Orleans Jazz Festival was a Garifuna band called the Turtle Shell Band.

This is a handsome turtle with a green-black upper shell marked with yellow and a yellow under shell. In addition, its dark green head is streaked with bright yellow. Like the mud turtles, both the terrapins can be found in deep river pools and slow-moving tributaries.

References

Forsyth, A. and K. Miyata. 1984. *Tropical Nature: Life and Death in the Rain Forests of Central and South America.* Charles Scribner's Sons: New York, NY.

Campbell, J.A. and J.P. Vannini. 1989. Distribution of Amphibians and Reptiles in Guatemala and Belize. *Proc. Western Foundation of Vertebrate Zoology* 4 (1): 1-21.

Hartshorn, G. et al. 1984. *Belize: Country Environmental Profile,* Robert Nicolait & Associates Ltd: Belize City.

Leviton, A. *Reptiles and Amphibians of North America.*   Doubleday: New York, NY.

Meerman, J.C. (in press).   Checklist - Herpetology of Belize. Appendix, Belize Country Environmental Profile.

Saqui, E., et al. 1990.   The Cockscomb West Basin Expedition Report, June 11-18, 1990.

Weyer, D. 1990. *Snakes of Belize.* Belize Audubon Society: Belize.

CHAPTER 10

Insects and Other Arthropods
Katherine M. Emmons and Jan Meerman

The most numerous animals in the forest are arthropods, a broad group that includes insects. They are invertebrates, meaning they have no bones. Instead they have a protective outer layer called an exoskeleton. Insect bodies have three major parts: head, thorax, and abdomen. All insects have six pairs of legs attached to the thorax, and most have two pairs of wings as well. Insects are incredibly diverse. Some crawl, and others fly, jump, and even swim. Insects are an important component of nature and help keep everything else running smoothly. They pollinate over half of all flowering plants, including many of those that we rely on for our own diets, and they play important roles in the distribution of nutrients in the forest. In the natural forest environment, insects that would be considered pests on a farm serve important ecological functions. Humans and most other land organisms would quickly perish if insects were to suddenly disappear. Other arthropods that are not insects include scorpions, spiders, tarantulas and beetles.

Ants (Family *Formicidae*)

Ants are among the most numerous of all the insects. They are essential to the tropical forest ecosystem. According to ant expert and naturalist E. O. Wilson, if all the ants were to be removed from the earth, it would be catastrophic for us and the rest of life. Ants turn the soil and redistribute nutrients. They also clean the ecosystem by removing small dead or dying creatures which hastens decomposition. Leave any crumbs of food around and within minutes ants will emerge to eat them. Most ants live in elaborate nests and form complex societies. In a typical nest, most ants are sterile female workers or soldiers, all daughters of the one queen. When necessary for reproduction, each nest of ants will produce fertile, winged female and male ants. Most ants are scavengers, but they can also be predators like army ants, or specialized eaters like nectar feeders. Leafcutter (wee wee) ants even raise their own food by cultivating a fungus.

I (Katherine Emmons) once found a small dead coral snake and watched tiny ants consume it. Within days it had completely disappeared.

Army Ants (Subfamily *Ecitoninae*)

Army ants have a fascinating niche in the forest. They do not have permanent nests, but move from camp to camp. The queen stays in the camp with her eggs until the entire colony moves in what is called a bivouac. In the bivouac, the workers lock their legs together to form a huge, layered mass with the queen and eggs at the center. On hunting forays, the troops radiate out from the camp to catch their food by group predation, communicating with chemical signals. They surround their prey, which consists only of animals, anything from insects to baby birds and small lizards. They follow logs or climb trees and lianas all the way up to the canopy. If they enter your dwelling, just stay out of their way. They will leave shortly, and your house will be rid of unwanted pests. Be careful, though, as their powerful jaws are capable of a nasty bite.

Without the queen, the colony will die or merge with another. During the dry season or early rainy season, the colony produces fertile winged males and females for breeding. These fertile individuals are able to see better than their sister soldiers and workers, who are nearly blind. Army ants on the move provide a good opportunity for bird watching. In a remarkable example of symbiosis (commensalism), the ants flush up so many insects wherever they go, that many species of birds, especially antbirds of the *Formicariidae* family, make their living following army ants around. Making the procession even longer, some species of *Ithomiinae* butterflies follow the birds to feed off the bird droppings.

Azteca Ants (*Azteca* spp.)

Azteca ants tend mealy bugs and milk them for a fluid containing sugar and proteins. The main predators of Azteca ants are woodpeckers.

Azteca ants have a fascinating symbiotic relationship (mutualism) with cecropia trees. Cecropia trees have hollow sections in their trunks and branches that make perfect nests for the ants. A young queen starts a colony by first boring into a young tree where she lays her eggs. The colony expands as the tree grows. Cecropias have few natural defenses and their leaves, fruits, and flowers are enjoyed by many different species. The ants attack any predator perceived to be threatening the tree. The work the ants do in trimming unwanted vegetation from the tree is obvious because most cecropia trees are free of vines.

Ants of the genus *Pseudomyrmex* have a similar relationship with the bullhorn acacia (*Acacia sp*). In this case the ants live in hollow bullhorn spines of the plant. An even more remarkable aspect of this relationship is the tree's production of nodules that the ants use for food. Called Müllerian bodies, these nodules are high in glycogen, which is not usually found in plants, only in animals.

Leafcutter Ants (*Atta* spp.)
Other names: wee wee ants, parasol ants

Ants of the genus *Atta* form thick trails that lead to and from their collection sites. They live in large, underground nests that can be easily spotted by the mounds of excavated dirt. These nests are constructed to allow hot air out and cool air in. This sophisticated climate control is necessary for the ants to be able to practice their primary occupation, which is farming. Inside the nest chambers, the ants tend gardens of fungus that they eat and feed to their larvae.

Only one species of fungus is used by the *Atta* ants, and this species is found only in *Atta* colonies. They have a mutualistic relationship: ants and fungus are linked by co-evolution and are totally dependent on each other. The ants rely on the fungus for food and the fungus relies on the ants for its reproduction because it does not produce spores as other fungi do.

Leafcutter ants collect leaves of many different trees and shrubs, selecting leaves that are free of toxins that might harm the fungus. Some leaves have natural anti-fungal properties and these the ants must avoid. The ants carry rather large leaf pieces back to their nest to clean and cut into tiny pieces. They add saliva which is rich in enzymes to help the fungus break down proteins in the leaf.   A small piece of fungus is planted on the mixture and grows as it consumes energy from the leaf matter. The ants tend it until it is ready to be harvested for food.

In this way, the ants are able to make use of the energy in rainforest leaves that would otherwise be unavailable to them. In the process, they serve a valuable ecological function by breaking down nutrients and dispersing them throughout the forest system. Fungal refuse is disposed outside the nest and is fed on by insects and microorganisms.

When a young queen leaves the nest to form a colony of her own, she must take a sample of fungus with her. If it dies, she is unable to feed her first brood, and the colony will never be started. If the queen is successful, the new colony will grow to as many as five million individuals.

A colony consists of large soldier ants that protect the workers, medium sized workers that collect the leaves, and tiny minima ants that primarily chew up the leaves and tend the nest. Some of the smaller ants also patrol the trails. They ride on the backs of the leaf carriers or directly on the piece of leaf. They help fight off parasites that try to attack the workers. All of these ants are sisters, descendants of the one queen. Special chemicals produced by the ants determine the sexes of the young. Male ants hatch only during times of mating and die soon afterward.

Black Flies (*Simulium* spp.)
Other names: botlas flies
The black flies at Cockscomb are small (no more than 5 mm in length) and are very active in the daytime, especially around streams. They lay eggs in fast-moving water like South Stann Creek. After hatching, the larvae attach themselves with silk threads to rocks or vegetation in the water. Female black flies at Cockscomb deliver irritating bites to humans. Long-sleeved shirts and pants can easily thwart their efforts. The local name, botlas, is short for bottle-ass, for the appearance of the female full of blood from biting a mammal.

The male flies eat plant nectar. Other than their irritating bites, the black flies at Cockscomb are probably not seriously harmful. In other areas of the world, related species can carry viral or parasitic diseases like onchocerciasis.

Butterflies
Many different kinds of butterflies frequent the CBWS. Some species prefer open, sunny areas and others prefer the shade of the understory. Blue morpho butterflies (*Morpho peleides*) are magnificent insects that delight Cockscomb's lucky visitors. In flight, their blue wings are dazzling. They appear to fly deceptively slowly, but they are strong, quick, and elusive in the understory.

When perched, morphos fold their wings up and hide the blue colour, making them very difficult to spot. This flash and hide strategy might confuse predators, such as flycatchers and jacamars.

The large owl butterfly (*Caligo memnon*) prefers to fly at dusk and dawn, or in the forest shade as it seeks out rotting fruits. During the bright daylight hours, it sits without moving on tree trunks or under large leaves. The owl butterfly has an eyespot on the underside of each of the large wings The purpose of this large marking may be to distract predators or disguise its true identity as a butterfly.

Blue Morpho Butterfly

Several types of butterflies of the *Pieridae* family fly along the roadside and assemble at puddles and mud spots. These small- to medium-sized butterflies are yellow, orange, or white. They create a colourful flutter when disturbed, only to resettle immediately around a mud puddle or ditch. They are attracted by animal urine from which they derive important nutrients or chemicals that are essential for breeding.

Some of the most brightly coloured and conspicuous butterflies at Cockscomb are heliconids, or long-winged butterflies (*Heliconius* spp.). They are diverse, ranging in wing patterns from yellow and black stripes to bright red lightning bolts. They often fly lazily in light gaps and along forest edges, apparently unconcerned about predators.

Indeed, heliconids do not need to take cover. Their caterpillars feed on the leaves of passionflower vines, which contain high levels of toxic compounds. The caterpillars are able to digest and retain this poison, which in turn makes them poisonous to predators both as caterpillars and adult butterflies. Birds remember both the taste and warning coloration and stay away. This is such an effective strategy that some non-poisonous butterflies have adapted similar colours and avoid being eaten as well.

Passionflower vines are so tormented by the heliconid caterpillar pests that some species have developed ways to thwart them. Some passionflower leaves grow structures that resemble eggs, fooling prospective egg layers. This works because female butterflies will not lay eggs where another has already laid. Other passionflower leaves grow tendrils that appear to invite eggs, but they soon fall off, taking the eggs with them. Adult butterflies visit the flowers of several plants for pollen, from which they derive amino acids to aid reproduction.

Cicadas (Family *Cicadidae*)
Other names: dry weather cricket, chickeri

Cicadas are the loudest insects in the world. The males have sound-producing organs located at the base of the abdomen, and apparently create the sound to attract female cicadas. At dusk their high-pitched buzzing easily drowns out conversation. Cicadas are from 1.5 to 5 cm long, and have long clear wings folded over their fat bodies.

They are often mistakenly called crickets, but cicadas do not jump like true crickets or grasshoppers. Female cicadas deposit their eggs into slits they cut on tree branches.

Cicada

After hatching, the nymphs (juveniles) drop to the ground and burrow into the soil to tree roots where they feed and grow for several years. They eventually climb the tree and pass into the adult stage. Cicadas are often spotted on the trees by the river, emerging from their nymphal skins. Sometimes dozens of empty skins hang on nearby trees as testimony to a good season. These empty skins retain a reflective shine, looking like the eye of a little frog until they are investigated more closely.

Dragonflies and Damselflies (Order *Odonata*)

Adult dragonflies and damselflies are fast-flying insects that prey on smaller flying insects such as mosquitoes and black flies. The larvae are strictly aquatic and are equally carnivorous. Both suborders are closely related but there are some important differences.

Damselflies have hindwings which are virtually the same as the forewings and usually they close their wings vertically when at rest. Many species breed in streams and rivers. With all its streams, it is not surprising that damselflies are more numerous than dragonflies in Cockscomb.

Dragonflies are usually larger and have hind wings that are clearly different from the forewings. They always hold their wings horizontally expanded when at rest and breed mostly in ponds and other stagnant water bodies.

There are some families of dragonflies, however, that are adapted to flowing water. One of these families is *Gomphidae*. Gomphids are usually large dragonflies and many species have a conspicuously widened tip of the abdomen which gives them the popular name "clubtails." Gomphids are very seasonal and adults of most species are only seen during the end of the dry season and first part of the rainy season.

Gomphid larvae are carnivorous like all other dragonfly and damselfly larvae. In order not to be swept away by the fast current of the stream, they dig themselves into the sand or the mud of the stream bottom. Here they wait until a suitable prey comes within reach. Since they are not very active hunters, they don't get a lot to eat and, as a result, they grow very slowly. It is not unusual for Gomphid larvae, even in the tropics, to need three or more years to reach maturity.

This long lifecycle makes them very vulnerable to habitat changes and pollution and it is not surprising that the *Gomphidae* are the most threatened family of dragonflies worldwide. In Belize most *Gomphidae* are not threatened but increased deforestation may eventually lead to the drying up of many streams during the dry season, threatening all aquatic life in these streams. The stream needs to dry up only once in a three-year period to wipe out the entire local population!

Mosquitoes (Family *Culicidae*)

Female mosquitoes are not only bothersome to mammals, but also to birds and even reptiles. They have mouthparts that enable them to pierce skin and suck blood. Male mosquitoes eat plant juices. Some species carry diseases such as malaria and dengue fever. At Cockscomb it is best to avoid mosquito bites by covering the body with light cotton clothing and using insect repellent. Some species of birds and bats are important agents in mosquito control because they are adapted to catch and eat these insects on the wing.

Scorpions

When sleeping under a thatch roof, the sound of scorpions crawling around through the thatch is enough to keep many people awake, especially once they know what it is. Scorpions are quite common in Belize, especially the large *Centruroides gracilis*. Including extended tail and stinger, these entirely black animals may reach well over 10 cm.

Scorpions are insectivorous, that is, they eat insects. They may rid your house of many an unwanted cockroach. Female scorpions, like other members of the spider family, are very good mothers. It is not uncommon to come across a scorpion that appears to be covered with a dense mat of fur. On closer inspection, this fur consists of baby scorpions, riding on the back of their mother, waiting to be fed. With her claws, the mother tears tiny morsels from a prey and feeds them to her children on her back.

Scorpions are not aggressive towards humans. The biggest risk is that they might crawl between your clothes or in your shoes and sting you when you put them on. Shake out your clothes and shoes before putting them on and avoid reaching under piles of lumber, stones or coconut husks. If you should get stung, do not panic. More details on first aid are found in Chapter 13.

Spiders

Spiders abound in Cockscomb. Anyone who wants to get some idea of their numbers has only to go on a night walk and use a headlamp, or put their flashlight next to their eyes. All the greenish reflections on the forest floor are from the eyes of wolfspiders (*Lycosidae*). The reflections can be remarkably bright and many people are surprised that such small animals have such bright eyeshine.

Another conspicuous spider is the golden-orb spider (*Nephila clavipes*). Adult females of this species are about 2.5 cm in body length. Their web can be massive, often 60 cm in diameter, not including the anchoring threads. The orb, or concentric circles of the web, is often covered with a golden substance, hence the common name of the species. The silk of the web is tremendously strong, as anyone who has walked first on the trails can testify. In spite of their large size, golden-orb spiders do not specialize in large prey and are harmless to people, but they make excellent photographic subjects!

Tarantulas

Tarantulas are huge, hairy spiders that are a nightmare for anyone that fears creepy, crawly things in general. Actually, these spiders are quite harmless. They do not attack people and bite only when highly irritated. A threatened animal rears up on its back legs and holds out its front legs towards its tormenter. However, if left undisturbed, they are harmless insectivores.

The most common species, *Euathlus vagans*, may reach a span of 12 cm and can be recognized by the reddish hairs on the abdomen. They live in silk-lined holes which are commonly found along forest trails or in grassy areas. The females tend to be sedentary and do not wander far from their holes. They wait for a suitable-sized insect to wander by, dash out of their hole, and grab the unsuspecting prey. The smaller, more slender males live in holes, too, but tend to wander around in search of females, especially in the rainy season. The tarantulas seen at night crossing the road are usually males. Sometimes hunting tarantulas enter a house or wander around in thatch roofs, but they usually stick to the ground.

The biggest enemy of any tarantula is the tarantula wasp (*Pepsis sp.*). The female wasp bites the tarantula, paralyzing, but not killing it. She lays an egg on the live tarantula and then buries it. After the larva hatches, it consumes the fresh tarantula. You might see a tarantula being dragged by the tarantula wasp.

Termites

Arboreal termites are often seen at Cockscomb, with their large, brown nests clinging to tree trunks and branches. Their covered trails are also commonly seen leading up tree trunks and wooden structures. These insects fill an important niche in tropical ecosystems because they can break down the toughest plant material that most other animals cannot eat. In doing so they help transfer plant nutrients through the forest system.

Termites have an elaborate social system with infertile workers and soldiers, and fertile, reproductive individuals. The winged reproducers swarm until they find a mate, attracted by chemical signals called pheromones. Termites also use pheromones in defense and orientation. Soldiers emit a smelly, sticky matter that helps repel various predators. The workers are blind and lay a chemical trail that they can later follow to and from their collection sites.

Arboreal termite nests are made from wood that the insects have chewed into a carton-like material and cemented together with fecal matter. They are hard on the inside, but fairly soft on the outside.

When the nest is damaged or threatened, soldiers quickly rush out in defense. Almost immediately, the workers come and begin to patch the hole. Heavily damaged areas are sealed off.

Termites have several major predators. Tamanduas, or ant bears, like to eat termites, but generally only attack the nest when the defenses are low or when insects are especially abundant during times of swarming. Tamanduas prefer to hunt the workers along the trails or at the food source. Termites are also prey for several types of ants, other insects, and lizards. When swarming, the many winged insects become meals for birds, bats, and other predators. Some trogons and parakeets hollow out cavities in termite nest to build their nests. Some kinds of ants move into termite nests and may even drive out the original inhabitants.

Wasps
Fig Wasps (Family *Agaonidae*)
One of the most fascinating parts of the fig tree life-cycle is the pollination of its fruits, an amazing example of co-evolution. The immature fruits are in reality not fruits at all but are clusters of enclosed flowers (or florets) called synconia. Because the flowers are not exposed to the outside, pollination is difficult. To carry out the task, each species of fig relies on its own symbiotic species of tiny wasp.

A female wasp bores into the synconium with pollen held in pockets on her thorax. The entry weakens her and strips off her wings. She pollinates each floret in the synconium and lays an egg in many of them, then dies. After about a month, the wasps hatch. Males burrow out, find newly hatched female wasps still in their florets and inseminate them.

Still inside the synconium, the female wasps gather pollen to store in their thoraxes. The male wasps cut a hole through the fig, which allows the fertile female wasps to exit, each with a supply of pollen. The males then die. The ripened fig is eaten by animals and the mature seeds are dispersed. The female wasps fly off in search of immature synconia and the cycle continues.

If you are lucky enough to find ripe fig fruits you will see the tiny holes that the male wasps have dug for the females to crawl out. If your fig has a live wasp in it, this means that the males have not yet been successful in digging a burrow. More likely, you will find a parasitic weevil larva in your fig, quickly trying to wiggle away.

Tarantula Wasp (*Pepsis* spp)
Tarantula wasps are huge black wasps with a wingspan of up to 8 cm. They are often seen flying low over cleared areas looking for the holes of tarantulas. They may land and walk over the ground, nervously moving their antenna. When they locate a tarantula, they have to get near enough to sting the spider. This is not without risk

for the wasp, but usually the wasp is the victor. The sting does not kill the tarantula, only paralyzes it. The wasp then drags the inert tarantula, crossing considerable distances over the ground, to its own burrow. The wasp deposits the tarantula in the burrow and lays one egg on it. Once the maggot emerges from this egg, it eats the tarantula. Since the unfortunate tarantula is still alive, its flesh remains fresh until the maggot is full grown and pupates.

References

Art, H. W., ed. 1993. *The Dictionary of Ecology and Environmental Science.* Henry Holt: New York, NY.

Forsythe, A. & Miata, K. 1984. *Tropical Nature: Life and Death in the Rainforests of Central and South America.* Charles Scribners Sons: New York, NY.

Janzen, D.H. (ed) 1983. *Costa Rican Natural History.* University of Chicago Press: Chicago, IL.

Kricher, J. C. 1989. *A Neotropical Companion: An Introduction to the Animals, Plants and Ecosystems of the New World Tropics.* Princeton University Press: Princeton, NJ.

Wilson, E. O. 1990. *The Diversity of Life.* Belnap Press of Harvard University Press: Cambridge, MA.

PART II

Environmental Education

CHAPTER 11

Teacher's Guide to the Cockscomb Basin Wildlife Sanctuary
Katherine M. Emmons

Planning a Visit to the CBWS

Whether this is your first trip to CBWS with a group of students or a return visit, you probably have a desire to make it as meaningful to your students as possible. You may want to make use of this time outside the classroom for students to experience nature first hand and learn as much as possible. Students, on the other hand, expect the visit to be a lot of fun. No matter where they are from, your students will look forward to adventure, novelty, and enjoyable time in the company of others. The environment in the CBWS is actually an excellent place to combine these two agendas. Students can learn in ways that stretch far beyond the traditional classroom experience, and they will have fun while they are doing it. The key is for you, their leader, to guide them and to show them how learning these new things can be both enjoyable and rewarding.

Explore and Discover with your Students

You do not have to be an expert about the environment to help make the experience a meaningful one for students. In fact, if you investigate, question, and hypothesize along with your students about what you see and hear, you will find that they will start thinking and wondering themselves. Teachers are often used to having all the answers. But why come all the way to the Cockscomb if you want to make the experience just like school? Even if you do have the answer, sometimes it is useful to pretend that you do not. When you are out on the trail, pose questions in a "I wonder why" format, or redirect a student's question back to the entire group. Later, when you have assembled at the cabin to discuss the day's activities, you can talk about what you saw on the trails, and draw on other information sources to inform the group. Students might want to try to identify a bird, or to learn why it behaves a certain way. You can encourage students to team up with friends to look for information in a book or in the Visitor Center.

Above all, enjoy yourself! Lead students in new and exciting adventures. After all, you serve as their role model. If you are brave, enthusiastic, and interested, they will be more likely to follow your lead.

Establish Clear Goals

You will be more likely to have a successful visit if you and your students know why you are going. Ask yourself: "What do I want this visit to accomplish, and what do I need to do to achieve this?" If you have examined the purpose of the visit consciously in your own mind, you will also be better equipped for letting students know the objectives of the visit. When students know what your goals are, there will be no surprises. They will be able to adapt and work your goals in with their own. You can address a range of environmental education learning areas during your visit to CBWS. For example, your goals might be included under the following broad categories:

1. *Knowledge and grasp of environmental concepts*: Students can improve their basic conceptual grasp of the rainforest environment. This might include an understanding of some of the functions of the rainforest ecosystem, and problems and issues that surround forest conservation.

2. *Environmental sensitivity and attitudes*: You may want students to develop sensitivity and positive attitudes about the rainforest environment. They can also examine how these feelings tie in with their own concern for environmental protection.

3. *Action skills and procedures*: Students can learn the steps involved for implementing action strategies. They can identify environmental problems and issues and organize ways to address them. Working toward this goal would ideally include hands-on action projects that students are allowed to choose and plan themselves (an outline is included in the Advanced Activities section).

4. *Empowerment and ownership*: In this area, students can explore what it means to be personally involved in environmental protection. They can gain a sense of their own capacity to make a difference and explore a personal and group responsibility for environmental problems and actions.

5. *Recreation*: The visit to CBWS can be fun and enjoyable for students.

Your own goals may correspond with the above areas, or they may be quite different. Your goals may also be very specific, or deliberately broad. Of course, as you and your students learn and grow, your goals will probably change. With careful reflection and a built-in flexibility, these kinds of changes can improve your program.

You can evaluate your students' learning both during and after the program. This does not mean you must give students a test, although that is clearly an option. You can also accomplish evaluation through discussions, activities, and projects (see following activities for ideas). If you are staying only a day or a few hours, do not set your expectations too high. Instead, concentrate on a few basic things and follow up on them when you get back to school.

Use the Natural Environment For Experiential Learning

Make use of the Cockscomb Basin environment to do things that you cannot do in a regular classroom. The trails and the river are great for experiential learning (learning through experience). Get out there and look, smell, listen, and touch (tasting is not recommended!). Bring some binoculars and make sure all students have a turn looking through them at birds and at other interesting sights. Ideally, the adults in the group will participate in the activities as well. If you are unwilling to hike up Ben's Bluff or take a night walk, you are sending the message to students that these are not important or desirable activities. Above all, spend time — a lot of time — in the CBWS. Stay overnight, or better yet, a few days. This allows students to get used to the new environment and to overcome any fears or uncertainties they may have about being in the "bush." It must be made a fun and positive experience. Once this is accomplished, students will be more open to the beauty of nature and to novel experiences.

Be Flexible

If you allow your program to be flexible, you will be able to respond to feedback from students and to rapidly changing circumstances. Give students some choice in their activities and do not stick with a plan that is clearly not working. If you introduce students to action projects, let them make their own plans and decisions. Have nightly meetings with students to find out what they learned, and the high-points of the day as they perceive them. Students who help make the decisions will be more enthusiastic about the activity. Remember also that rain can easily drown out the most carefully planned program. Do not let it defeat you! Plan around it, do something else for a while, or go out in the rain.

Planning the Trip

There are a number of important things to consider when planning an educational visit to the CBWS. Below are some of the things that you might want to think about.

1. *How long will you stay?* You can accomplish a lot more in a five day program than in a program that lasts an afternoon or a day. You may not have a choice here, so think about ways to optimize your visit, no matter the length. If you have substantial educational goals but are only staying for a short time, consider an in-depth follow-up after you return to school.

2. *What are your goals?* Do you want the time in the CBWS to provide students with initial first hand experience with nature, or does it serve to follow up extensive academic lessons that you have been conducting in class? Perhaps the visit you are planning is to serve primarily recreational purposes. If you have an entire busload of students with limited adult supervision, you will certainly have to limit the educational offerings. Whatever the case, make sure that your goals are realistic for the circumstances.

3. *Where are your students now in terms of your educational goals?* You might want to hold some discussions in advance with students to find out what they know, their attitudes, and their general feelings about nature and the environment. This information can be helpful as you plan the activities, so that you do not make the activities too advanced or too basic for your students.

4. *When are you going?* Some times are better for scheduling educational visits to CBWS than others. The driest times of the year are from January to May. The Easter holidays are a popular visiting time during the dry season. If you are planning a visit during this time, book well in advance because accommodations are limited. During the rainy season the road can become soggy, the river flooded, and the insects more of a problem. On the other hand, when there is a lot of mud, it is easy to study tracks and other signs of wildlife.

5. *Make necessary arrangements.* You will need to reserve the cabin or tent-space ahead of time. Call the Belize Audubon Society office in Belize City and follow up the first call to make sure there is space available when you want to go. You will also need to obtain permission from the parents or guardians before students can participate. Transportation must also be arranged, as there is no bus service to and from the sanctuary. There are cooking facilities at the Headquarters (for those staying in cabins), but food is not available. Plan your menu carefully and bring everything you need. The nearest shop is in Maya Center, 6 miles from the CBWS Headquarters. If students are to carry out the cooking and cleaning up responsibilities, it is a good idea to have the duties organized ahead of time.

6. *Gather materials and equipment.* Make sure you have all that you need to carry out your planned activities. Do you need reference materials, paper, pencils, markers, or a chalk board or flip chart? If you have access to magnifying glasses, binoculars, and thermometers, bring them. You might find them useful on the trails.

7. *Prepare students.* Let the participants know what they can expect during their visit. You may want to tell them that the facilities are comfortable, but not well developed. Students need to have some idea what to bring, especially those who are not used to camping. In addition, familiarize students with the rules of the sanctuary, and with your own rules.

Rules

All wildlife is protected.

Please do not disturb, harm, or attempt to capture any animal or bird.

Please do not disturb, collect, or remove any plants or trees.

Stay on the trails when walking and hiking.

Please carry out all trash and rubbish. Do not litter!

Cook in designated areas only - on the stove provided in kitchens or in the fire hearths.

Do not light fires anywhere else, along the trails or in CBWS Headquarters.

Please do not destroy or vandalize any facilities.

Please leave the facilities cleaner than you found them.

Please be careful not to waste water.

What to bring on an overnight visit

strong shoes for walking
shoes to wear in the river (rocks are too rough
    for bare feet and slippers will fall off easily)
socks, underwear, pajamas
bathing suit or shorts
long-sleeved shirt (for girls, a man's shirt will do fine)
long pants
toothbrush, hairbrush, etc.
toilet paper
towel, soap
hat
pen or pencil
notebook
flashlight and batteries
insect repellent
plastic water bottle

Environmental Education

Outdoor Ideas

There are many attractions within easy reach of the CBWS Headquarters, and the trail guides in Chapter 15 of this book provide general information about what to see and do. Here are some additional tips for leading groups of young people. If you need more information about plants, animals, and general concepts, check the glossary (Chapter 12) and the other chapters of this book.)

Headquarters Area

The area holds much potential for nature study. Students might tell you excitedly about something they have seen while relaxing outside their cabin, and you can turn these observations into interesting learning experiences. The Visitor Center also has a lot of good information and students will enjoy exploring it. This is also a good place to locate CBWS staff, who will be happy to answer your questions.

Here you can discuss with students the human side of the CBWS. Managing the Sanctuary and dealing effectively with various problems can sometimes be a challenge. The wardens must deal with visitors, maintenance, and wildlife, and must sometimes take law enforcement roles as well. Show students the garbage pit (a new one must be dug every one to two years), examine the rain-water tanks, and other facilities for visitors. Discuss the responsibilities of visitors in this type of situation. Because the cabins are not hotels with modern facilities and services, visitors who waste the drinking water or leave trash and messes are a problem for the staff and other visitors.

The River Path and the River

Almost every visitor to CBWS will take the walk to the river because it is close by and easy to reach. The soft, grassy path is a good place for your students to practice walking quietly. Once at the river, students will have plenty to see both in and out of the water. There are many rocks on the river bed, so have students wear old shoes so you can lead them up and down the river. Bring clothing and repellent to ward off the mosquitoes and black flies. The picnic table is a good place for small group discussions, if you can keep your students out of the river long enough. If you like, assemble the students here for a few minutes to share their discoveries with one another before returning to Headquarters.

Rubber Tree and Curassow Trails

This is a good route for introducing some basic rainforest concepts to your students. You pass through several regrowth areas where you can teach about forest succession. On the Curassow Trail where several large trees can be found, you can also tell your students about the different forest layers, and related concepts. The river, a stream, and a pond all provide opportunities for students to learn about aquatic ecosystems and the role of the CBWS in watershed protection.

These trails have numbered markers for a self-guided tour which is printed in Chapter 15. This same trail guide is also available as a brochure. You can buy additional copies at the Visitor Center. If you have older students, you can split them into small groups and have them take turns guiding themselves along this route.

The Wari Loop and Victoria Peak Path

The Wari Loop is one of my favorites for educational hikes. It is one of the best places to look for jaguar tracks and other interesting plants and animal signs. In addition, there are also opportunities to talk about the importance of the rainy season or flooding on the vegetation. You will also have a chance to show students some of the difficulties of maintaining a logging operation in this environment. Victoria Peak Path was once a logging road. Notice how quickly it can become overgrown!

The Gibnut Loop and Tinamou Trail

A combination of these two trails is a good morning hike. If you have less time, choose the Gibnut Loop only. The many steps going up and down make it fun for students. A very pleasant place for a rest and discussion is at the bridge that connects the Gibnut Loop with the Antelope Trail. The bridge offers a beautiful view of the stream and surrounding vegetation. Here is another good opportunity to discuss with students the role that rivers and streams play in the forest ecosystem.

The Waterfall Trail

If you have time, a hike to the waterfall is a must. Students won't necessarily get excited about a hot, steep walk, but when they hear about the waterfall at the end, you won't be able to keep them away. Take water and a snack, and leave some time for swimming and relaxing. The water in this stream is much colder than the river water. If you have a thermometer, take the temperature of both and encourage students to think of an explanation for the temperature difference. Remind your students that the waterfall pool has some deep places to avoid if they can't swim. If they can swim, they may enjoy swimming under the spray. For older students, a high-point of the whole trip is to climb the waterfall. If you are going to allow your students to climb up, they must start on the other side of the pool. They will have to stretch their legs pretty far over some of the rocks, but there are some hand-holds. Students should take it slow and be careful because some of the rocks can be slippery. At the top are some small, pretty pools. They can return by crossing the stream at the top and returning to the main pool by way of the main path.

Ben's Bluff Trail

This is an excellent trail to show students the transition between the rainforest ecosystem and the pine forest ecosystem. In addition, students have a chance to see for themselves why the area is called the Cockscomb Basin. From this point of view, you can easily discuss the vegetation, the watershed, and the Cockscomb mountain range. Keep in mind that you will all be quite breathless on the way up, and the group may spread out along the trail. This will make lessons difficult, so plan to discuss important concepts at the top or the bottom, or during resting times.

When one group of my students heard me call Ben's Bluff a challenge, that was all they needed to motivate them, and we were on our way! It is really a tough hill, with many very steep sections. You might not notice them, but some switch-backs have been cut, and that helps. I like to wear work gloves when I climb Ben's Bluff, because it makes it easier to grab trees and rocks. They also protect the hands coming down, if I happen to slip on the loose gravel. Once we were caught in rain and by the time we got to the bottom we were wet and extremely muddy. So why make the climb? Because the view is fantastic! Take your cameras and binoculars.

The Antelope Trail

The Antelope Trail is a good, long hike if you are staying several days in the CBWS with your students. If you are in the area for a short time, however, you might be better off hiking on some of the other trails instead. Because the Antelope Trail is so long, students might get tired, and this will reduce the educational opportunities. On the other hand, about half way along the trail you will encounter a lovely stream. Not only is it a good place to relax and cool off, but there is a lot to see in the way of vegetation and aquatic life.

The Antelope Trail provides opportunities for students to experience an extensive area of secondary forest. In some places, sunlight filters though the canopy, and you can show students the differences between shady and sunny microclimates. There are many young, straight trees that form a rather low canopy over the trail.

River Float

The river float is lots of fun. The staff may have some old inner tubes for rent, or come prepared with your own. If you have no tubes, consider walking down the river instead. There are some deep spots, however, so swimming might be necessary. Whether you walk or float, there are some very important considerations that are repeated here from the Trail Guide Section:

1. Do not go if the river is high and swift. Check with staff to see if it is safe, especially during the rainy season.

2. This activity is not recommended for children under 15 years of ages unless they are good swimmers and are well supervised.

3. Wearing shoes in the river is very important. The water can be low at times, and walking in shallow areas is a necessity.

4. Wearing long-sleeved shirts will protect you against insects.

5. Do not take a group of students on the river if you have not made the trip recently yourself. Be familiar with the currents and difficult spots. It is important that you are able to inform students, and have them walk in certain places.

6. Supervising adults must be good swimmers, knowledgeable about tubing, and not afraid of the river.

7. Some students have never floated on inner tubes before, and are not sure how to sit on them and control them away from rocks and so on. Make sure you give a lesson on checking for depth and hanging on to the tube. Sometimes when students get scared, their first impulse is to try to get off the tube and walk. If they choose to do this in a deep or swift area, they may panic and let go of the tube. Remind them that the tube floats and that it will carry them to a more shallow spot, so at all costs, HANG ON! If you have a student who seems very nervous, tie your two tubes together with rope before floating so the student feels more secure.

8. Never take more that five or six students at one time. If your students are not good swimmers, it is preferable to have one supervising adult for every three students.

9. Remember that each tube will float at a different speed, depending on tube size, weight of person, and the currents that everyone happens to catch. Stop at various intervals and let everyone catch up. The teacher or leader should float first, and ideally another supervisor will bring up the rear.

Environmental Education

There is a lot to see and watch for on the river float. It is an excellent way to spot birds and an occasional mammal because one can keep very quiet while floating. However, your students will likely be very loud and excited if they are not used to this type of adventure. It is a good idea to talk with students before you start and to let them know what to watch for and what to expect. A float down the river can be a pleasant finale to a lesson on water cycles and watersheds, allowing students to actually take part in the Cockscomb Basin's water cycle. It is also a good time to reinforce a lesson on Cockscomb Basin history, since during times of high water the timber resources of the area were floated down the river all the way to the coast. Stop wherever appropriate for impromptu lessons. The strangler fig tree and other attractions make fantastic teaching tools.

A Night Walk

The best reason for staying overnight in the CBWS is being able to take a night walk. Really, if you do nothing else with your students during your visit, do this. If some students don't want to take a night walk, insist on it. You will find that most students will be ready to try it, and no one wants to be left alone!

Speaking from experience, one has to muster a fair amount of courage to go walking in the jungle at night for the first time. It seems like an alien place to us. We can sense life all around us, but we cannot quite give it a form. Yet when students venture out in the security of a group, they can overcome the fear quickly. The walk becomes a memorable and positive experience.

Why do it? A night walk helps students sense their surroundings in a completely different way. Plants and animals in the forest that students hardly notice in the day will receive their close inspection at night. Moreover, students will begin to feel more comfortable with their surroundings and you will see their fears of the forest diminish. Some students are afraid of the forest even in the daytime. Venturing out at night makes the daytime much more predictable, and therefore less frightening. Night walks are novel and adventuresome for students. This is something about their visit that they will remember. Take your time and enjoy it.

Where to go. A favorite route for a night walk is the River Path down to the river, then back up the Rubber Tree and Curassow Trails. The Tinamou Trail, the Gibnut Loop, and Wari Loop are just as good, however. Another option is to just walk down the entrance road. The Antelope Trail is really too long, and the Waterfall and Ben's Bluff Trails are too steep for night hikes.

Preparation. Organize students in groups of 4 to 6. As on any hike, larger groups are more difficult. Participants are also less likely to notice interesting things when a lot of people are around. Have students wear good shoes, long pants, and a long-sleeved shirt. Some of my students wanted to wear hats and gloves as well. The more flashlights you have to go around, the better, since batteries might go dead on the trail. Students do not have to use their flashlights all at once, however.

Starting Out. Try telling students in advance that there is no talking during the first part of the night walk. Students will often giggle anyway, and they will find plenty of things in just the first 50 yards to talk about. Try to have them use gestures. Remind students in front not to walk so fast that they leave the others behind. Those with the best flashlights are likely to see more, and will more easily be carried away with the adventure. If you only have a few flashlights, make sure that they get passed around.

Show students how to hold their flashlights along the sides of their faces near their eyes. This is the only way to see the eye reflections of night creatures. Many nocturnal animals have a reflective layer in their eyes that will shine the light right back at you. Of course, a headlamp is best, if one is available.

Lights out time. After you have walked some distance and students have had a chance to look around, it is time for an awareness exercise. Have students sit down on the ground or on a bench (the picnic table at the river is a good spot). Instruct students that there will be no talking for five minutes (or whatever you decide) and that they must turn their flashlights off. This will encourage them to focus on sounds and the few things that they can see. After a few minutes, proceed with students again along the trail, continuing silently for a few minutes with lights off. Once on a very dark, moonless night, a group of students found the trail by looking through the gap in the canopy over the trail and following the stars!

What to look for on a night walk. You will find that students will want to inspect the bark of a tree, some small fallen flowers, or a centipede. Whatever occupies their attention, go with it. Show students how to find the reflection of crawling night spiders. These amazing animals have a bright silver-blue eye reflection coming from a single eye at the top of the spider. It can be spotted from a fairly long distance when the flashlight is held close to the eyes. (See the trail guides in Chapter 15 for more details.)

Basic Activities for All Ages

These activities can be tried with any age group. You know the background and experience of your students best, so modify the activities wherever appropriate to fit your situation. If your students are young, provide extra supervision. Older students can participate more independently.

Six-Legged Friends

What you need: Pen or Pencil, Notebook, Magnifying glass
Reference: Chapter 11 Insects - Ants

Have you ever examined the behavior of ants? They are fascinating creatures. Ants are easy to find in the CBWS. Leafcutter ants are busy at the Headquarters and on the trails, and tiny ants roam around inside the cabins, hoping for a scrap to carry back to the nest. If you drop a crumb outside, watch how quickly the ants find it! (Note: this activity is easily modified. You can have students quietly observe and document any number of things, a tree and the life that surrounds it, all the sounds heard in a area, the life in and near a body of water, and so on.)

For this activity students will first chose partners (or if you want to strongly emphasize quiet observation, have them do this alone). Then they go off in search of a troop of ants with a pen and notebook. For about 15 or 20 minutes, students will quietly observe the ants and their behavior. Remind students not to harm the ants or interfere with them. Students can document their observations with notes, drawings, maps, and so on. As the teacher, you are encouraged to participate in the activity yourself. This will help you understand what the students are experiencing and you can share your findings as well. What do the ants look like? How big are they? How many are there? Where are they going? Are they collecting food? What kinds of food? Are the ants communicating? Do they show any competition or cooperation?

After the allotted time, gather with your students to share notes. To extend the activity, you can speculate and hypothesize about ant behavior, and even do some additional research about them.

Solo Safari

The word solo means alone, and safari means journey. On this journey, students do not venture too far from the Headquarters, but the solo experience is memorable. Students sit alone on the trail and allow their senses to take in the nature that surrounds them. This helps students overcome their fears and uncertainties of the forest, and they become more comfortable in the Cockscomb Basin environment. Students also have a chance to quietly observe animal life, and are more likely to see interesting things than if they are with a loud group.

Organize a group of no more than 10 students and first explain how the activity will be carried out. Have students take along their notebooks to document any observations, feelings, and so on. Some students may be nervous about doing this, but assure them that they will not be far from the others, and there is no worry of them getting lost. Begin by leading all the students together on one of the trails. The Gibnut loop is a good choice for this activity, because it is easy to reach and is not too long.

After you have walked a short distance on the trail, leave one student in a pleasant spot. Proceed some distance until the first student is out of sight and easy hearing, and then leave the next student. There may not be benches for all students to sit on, but they can also make use of steps, tree roots, or even the ground.

After you have dropped off all the students, continue along the trail in the same direction until you reach the Headquarters. By this time most of the students have been sitting alone for quite some time! Now you circle around a second time in the same direction as before and pick them up in the same order that you dropped them off.

After you return to the cabin, or later when you have assembled in the evening, ask students to describe their experiences. What did they see and hear? Was it frightening? Was is enjoyable? Did the experience cause students to change any feelings they had about the forest?

Variation for younger students: Keep students closer together on the trail, just out of sight from one another. Instead of leaving students by themselves for a long time, have another adult or older student follow the group after 10 or 15 minutes to collect everybody.

A Postcard Home

What you need: Nature Postcards (or Paper and Envelopes),
               Postage Stamps

This activity allows students to think about what they experienced during their visit. They can put their awareness of nature and attitudes about the forest into words. It is easy for students to push the experience into the hidden corners of the mind when they return to the usual routines of school and home life. When they receive their postcards in the mail after they have returned home, students are again reminded of what they felt at the time of the visit.

On the last day of the visit, tell students that you would like them to think about their time spent in the CBWS and their feelings about the experience. What did they learn? How has it changed them? Has any event or incident been particularly meaningful? Then allow each student to choose a postcard and write a short note to himself or herself about

these experiences. If postcards are not available, have students write and illustrate letters to themselves. Mail the letters or postcards one or two weeks after the program. You can conduct a follow-up activity in school after students receive the postcards. They can discuss what they wrote and even use the cards to make a classroom display about the trip.

Everything is Connected!

What you need: Ball of string or yarn
Glossary References: Deforestation, Ecosystem,
                    Habitat Loss, Pollution

This activity demonstrates to students that the interrelationships in nature are very complex and delicate. Students learn that changing one element of nature can effect the entire system

Students all stand in a circle. Begin by asking, "who can name a type of plant that grows in the forest?" A student might say "vine." The student then takes hold of the end of the string. You then continue by asking, "where does the vine grow?" When another student says, "the vine grows up a tree," you hand the string to her, which represents a relationship between the vine and the tree. Continue by asking the other students what kinds of species use the tree for food or shelter, and then the relationships of those species to yet other species (predators, prey, habitat components, symbiotic relationships, etc.) until you have expanded your ecosystem.

If students get stuck, prompt them. Don't forget the insects! You can add other elements, like microorganisms in the soil, reminding the students that all life eventually decomposes to be used again by plants. Each of these relationships is symbolized by a string connection, until all the students are connected to one another. (Hint: throw the ball of string over the web in the middle to keep it from getting tangled.) Remind students of the role they are playing.

When all the students have a role, the criss-cross of string will look like a spider web. You can now demonstrate the interrelationships in the "ecosystem" by removing some of its elements. For example, you can "chop down" the trees. All of the students who have roles as trees then tug their strings. Then, those students who feel a pull, tug their strings also, until most of the students are affected. You can also introduce an insecticide that "kills" all of the insects. All of the insects then tug their strings, because they are now "dead." All organisms that eats insects, or plants that are pollinated by insects, die also. Ask students if anyone remained unaffected by these changes in the environment. More likely you will need to ask them why all the components were affected. Discuss with students how real environmental disturbances can irreversibly effect entire ecosystems.

Food Pyramid

Glossary References: Food Chain, Food Web,
                       Primary Producer, Consumer

This fun activity demonstrates the idea of food chains, and particularly shows how larger numbers of primary producers and first order consumers are necessary to support a few top predators. It also demonstrates how all animals are directly or indirectly dependent on plants for survival. Make your pyramid outside on the grass, using a sheet or towel if you want.

The group will build a model of a food pyramid with their own bodies. Before you start this activity, you need to have an idea what your end result should look like. First of all, how many students do you have? You can use this activity with groups of 6 or 10, or if you are really ambitious, try a group of 15. It might be easiest to first demonstrate with a small group and have the others watch. Remember to include yourself if needed!

Assign the students the following plant or animal roles (or make up your own, as long as you have the correct numbers of primary producers and consumers)

6 Students:	10 Students:	15 Students:
fruits	grass	flowers
seeds	tree	twigs
leaves	shrub	grass
red brocket deer	vine	leaves
collared peccary	caterpillar	wood
jaguar	beetle	caterpillar
	termite	beetle
	old man lizard	worm
	speckled racer snake	termite
	white hawk	tarantula
		lizard
		frog
		great tinamou
		blacktail snake
		ocelot

Environmental Education

The students who have the roles as plants are the primary producers. They should be the biggest students. They get on their hands and knees. Be sure to check the grass first for biting ants! The first order consumers are the animals that eat the plants. They climb on top of the first row. If there are second order consumers (animals that eat other animals) they go next. Finally its time for your top predator to scramble to the top.

After you are done making your pyramids, discuss with students what would happen if there were more consumers than primary producers. If you want, reassign roles and see if you can make a pyramid with these new roles. Of course, it won't work! This shows us that all animals rely on plants for their survival, even those that eat meat.

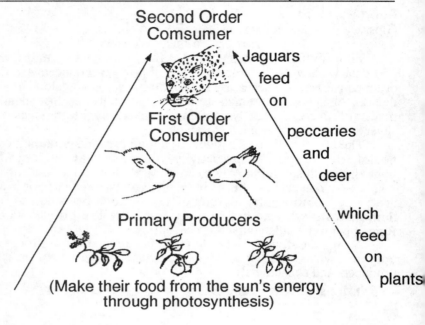

Second Order
Comsumer

Jaguars
feed
on

First Order
Consumer

peccaries
and
deer

Primary Producers

which
feed
on

plants

(Make their food from the sun's energy
through photosynthesis)

Do You Want to See a Jaguar?

What you need: Pen or Pencil, Paper, Tape, Chalkboard,
                    Large   Cardboard (or use wall of cabin)
Glossary Reference: Food Chain, Food Web

Everybody has an idea of kinds of wild species they would like
to see most. Many of us also have strong negative feelings about
other types of species, and there are others we don't really think about
at all! But what would happen if there was an abundance of the
species we wanted to see and fewer of the species that we try to
avoid? Through the modeling of a food web, this activity will give
students a good idea of the imbalance that would occur. For an
ecosystem to function properly, all components are necessary.

Cut paper into pieces about four inches across. With markers,
write the name of one of these species on each piece of paper:

vines	worms	lizards
wood	cockroaches	turtles
fruit	spiders	peccaries (waris)
roots	caterpillars	armadillos
seeds	ants	snowy egrets (gaulins)
leaves	flies	great tinamous
flowers	beetles	jaguars
termites	frogs	

Assemble your group of students and ask them which of the species they would like to see. Use pictures or describe the animal if students are not sure what it is. Hold up each paper, and ask students to show thumbs up if they would like to see the species, and thumbs down if they would rather not (these gestures will help eliminate the chaos of everyone talking at once).

Have one student make a quick count of the votes (100 percent accuracy is not important) and place papers in two heaps: one of species that the group generally would like to see, and one the group generally would like to avoid.

When you are all done, ask students to let you know if there are any other species they would like to include. Write them down, take a vote, and place the papers in the appropriate heaps. Don't include too many more or it will get confusing.

The next step is to take the heap with the names of the favorite species and have students assist you verbally as you tape them on your board or wall. The lower species, such as primary producers (plants) and first order consumers should be near the bottom, and the higher order consumers near the top. Use the following illustration for reference.

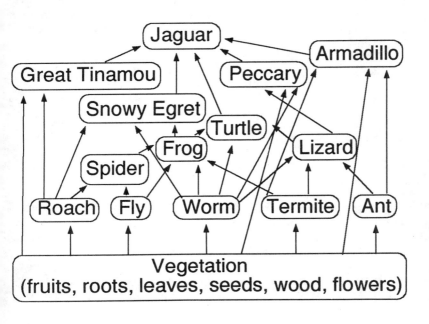

Environmental Education

Now it is time to look critically at the species that have been included in our model ecosystem. There are probably several species at the top of the board, the ones students would like to see. But if this were to actually represent nature, is there enough for them to eat? Maybe students have included jaguars as a species they would like to see. But jaguars eat armadillos, turtles, peccaries, and any birds that they can catch. All of these prey enjoy small animals like worms, lizards, frogs, and insects. Did the students include them? Those smaller animals in turn rely on even smaller animals or plants for food. If these are not all in place, there will be no chance of seeing a jaguar at all!

Now go through the remaining species and discuss with students the crucial roles that each plays in nature. Ask students to think about how an intact ecosystem is very different from a zoo, where relatively few animals are kept in an artificial environment where they do not have to look for their own food. If people want to see certain animals in their native habitat, not in a zoo, these animals must be part of an intact natural system where they can survive and reproduce in the wild.

Finally, discuss with students why people have these positive and negative attitudes about certain animals. Encourage students to share stories about experiences that may have formed some of these attitudes. If students are reluctant, start by sharing some of your own. For example —

> "I like snakes, but grew up wondering why other people did not share my sentiments. Eventually, I remembered an incident when I was a child of about two years old. At that early age, I had not internalized the fear of snakes that many adults had. When a visitor placed a young boa constrictor around my neck, I was not afraid. Since that time, I have always been fascinated by snakes."

Let's Communicate
What you need: Pen or Pencil, Paper
      Glossary Reference: Any terms needed

This activity draws on students' creative abilities to get a message across by acting. Students also demonstrate their understanding of various ecological concepts by trying to piece together the visual hints given by the other students. The activity can be conducted either inside or outside. It has a fun quality and may even fit in well with games planned for the evening. Don't be afraid to participate yourself. The teacher can team up with other adults or join a student group.

Form teams of about four students. Assign each group a concept term from the list below. Write it down for the group so that the other groups do not find out what it is, and so the students know how to spell it. The groups meet privately for about ten minutes to plan how they will act out their concept. They may need to do a little research first, which can be quickly accomplished by looking it up in the glossary (the following chapter). Then they take turns acting out their concept to the other students in the form of a mini-skit. No talking during the skit, only actions and gestures are allowed! Can the other groups guess what is being demonstrated? This may depend on the audience's familiarity with the concept, and on the group's ability to act it out. You may need to post an easy-to-see listing of all the terms on the wall so that the audience can use it for reference.

predator/ prey	omnivore	extinction
deforestation	arboreal	migration
erosion	nocturnal	photosynthesis
mutualism	diurnal epiphyte	poaching
parasitism	habitat	pollination
commensalism	canopy	scavenger
food chain	decomposition	seed dispersal
carnivore	water cycle	territoriality
herbivore		competition

After the audience has guessed the concept being acted out by the group, the group must briefly define and explain it to make sure it is understood by all. Then conduct a second round of this activity. As long as students are enjoying themselves, you can really take advantage of the situation and encourage them to learn more important terms.

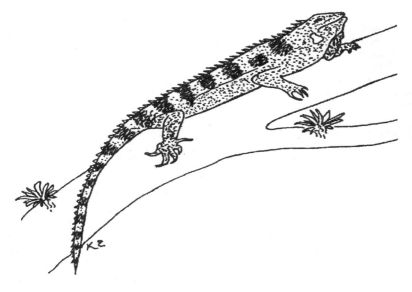

Cockscomb Basin Search and Draw

What you need: Pens or Pencils, Notebook, Large Paper or Chalkboard, Reference books

This educational activity is so much fun that students will think it is a game. You can use it either to teach students concepts that they do not know, or to help you informally evaluate what they have already learned. Students work in teams of two, fostering co-operation and teamwork.

The basic idea is for students to find and draw various items listed for them. On the chalkboard or a large paper, write down the list of things you want students to find and allow them to copy it. Include items that relate to concepts you have taught students, or to concepts you want them to learn (direct them to information sources such as this book or the Visitor Center during the hunt). Some of your requests may be broad. For example, if you ask students to find "something important in nature" they can draw virtually anything because everything is important in nature. Emphasize the fact that CBWS is a sanctuary and nothing is to be disturbed. That's why they are asked to draw each item instead of collecting it.

You can use this activity also to teach the students how to take scientific data accurately. Ask them to keep a notebook in which they write down exactly where they found each item, which trail, where on the trail, how far and which direction from a given landmark such as the numbered posts, numbers on trees, bridges, etc. You can use the following list, or create your own:

A drip tip
Something important in nature
A seed that is dispersed by wind
Something you found in a forest gap
Something a bird will like
A partially eaten leaf
Evidence of decomposition
A crawling insect
Part of a primary producer
A component of the water cycle
A cohune nut
Evidence of mutualism or parasitism
Three pieces of man-made litter that are in a place they do not belong
Something strong in nature

Let students know the criteria for being the winning team. There are two variations for selecting the winner, depending on the amount of time you have and the age of your students: (1) the first team to correctly finish the entire list is the winning team; or (2) the team that has the most correct items after a specific time (i.e. one hour) is the winning team. You may also wish to give the winners a small prize. Before you begin, students need to know the following rules:

1 Teams must stick together.
2. Everybody must stay on the trails.
3. No disturbing of plants or animals.

Now you are ready to go! When all teams have returned, you go down the list and check off the items for each group. This is also an excellent opportunity to have students explain why they chose those items as examples, and to reinforce the concepts involved. You will also have some teams who will get one or two items wrong, and they lose a point for each of these. Correct the team, but be gentle! It will be more fun for students if you try to preserve its game-like quality. After you have added up all the points you can determine the winning team.

Take a Stand
What you need: Markers, Paper
People have different opinions on a variety of subjects, and it is these differing opinions and interests that make many environmental problems and issues controversial. This activity is not so much intended for you to find out the attitudes and values of your students, but for students to think about them and to express them in a relatively safe manner. You can also use this activity as a precursor to "We CAN Make a Difference!" which is a more advanced activity.

For this activity you start by marking off five equal segments on the ground, on the side of a building, or on a wall. Use rocks, string, chalk, or other such materials to show the boundary for each section, which should be about five feet long or more, depending on the number of students you have. Then attach to each segment a label, one each with the following: STRONGLY AGREE, AGREE, NEUTRAL, DISAGREE, STRONGLY DISAGREE.

As you read a variety of statements relating to the environment, students position themselves in the section where the label most closely resembles their opinion. Some students may want to verbally clarify or expand their positions, but ask them to do so at the end. Otherwise, other students might become confused by the new input, and they will be less likely to know how to choose.

The make-up of your student audience will largely dictate what kinds of statements are appropriate to use in this activity. Student ages, grade levels, background, and levels of experience must all be considered. For example, you do not want to use a statement about global warming if your students have never heard of that theory. Define terms and explain concepts wherever necessary. The following is a list of possible statements. Select from it or create your own to suit your needs.

1. Conservation is not really my problem, so it does not really matter what I think about it.
2. If the forests in the CBWS were all cut, most of the animals could probably go somewhere else.
3. If the government makes any more protected nature areas, there won't be enough farmland in Belize.
4. Humans are meant to be the rulers of nature.
5. It is a good idea to remove bothersome plants and animals from places people like to visit.
6. It is more dangerous to walk in the forest than in a town or a city.
7. The world is severely overpopulated.
8. There should be a law that people are only allowed to have two children.
9. Belize has a serious deforestation problem.
10. All of us are responsible for environmental problems.
11. The zoo is the best place for wild animals to live.
12. Protecting natural resources is more important than getting rich.
13. All creatures on earth deserve respect, even mosquitoes and snakes.
14. I would like to have a jaguar skin in my house for decoration.
15. If I saw a snake in my yard, it would be best to have someone kill it.
16. Most environmentalists make a big deal about nothing.
17. Current rates of species extinction on Earth threaten the survival of humans.
18. Over-consumption in developed countries is the cause of most environmental problems.

After you are all finished, allow students to comment or clarify their choices. As an extension, you can have a team of recorders count and chart the positions of the other students on each statement. Students can later look at the data and discuss the general trends of the group. Ask the students what might have been behind the obvious trends. Were these trends due to honestly expressed attitudes and opinions or were they partly due to peer pressure? Allow students to explain why they chose as they did without judgment. You can also try the same activity again after a few weeks or months to see if there have been any changes. If so, discuss them with students.

Advanced Activities

Many times when students first learn about environmental problems and issues, they become very concerned. This is natural, but there are ways to help tap this concern and turn it in into productive energy and action. In order to do this, students must feel empowered that they indeed **can** make a difference if they feel something is important to them. This is not to say you should tell students that they **must** feel this way, but to show them that they can choose to take action if they wish. Moreover, if they do believe sincerely in something, then they have a responsibility to take ownership of it and to not merely sit back and watch.

We CAN Make a Difference!

What you need: Pens or Pencils, Notebooks, Chalkboard or Large Paper

Most of your time in the CBWS will probably be spent hiking and doing other outdoor activities. But it will be worth your while if you also find the time for this important discussion about environmental problems and ways of dealing with them. If you like, you can also save this activity for after you return to school. "We CAN Make a Difference!" has three parts. The first part helps provoke thought and sparks discussion; the second part encourages students to reflect on their own lives; and the third part asks students to think about taking action. This activity can also be used as an introduction to the next activity, the Action Project.

Students can learn to recognize how they themselves connect with environmental problems. They can start to recognize their own possible roles both in creating the problems and in helping alleviate them. Please remember, however, that people have differing opinions and values. Allow participants to express their views, regardless of where they stand on the issues.

Part 1: The Stories

Start by telling your students some stories or anecdotes about taking action. The following four passages might be useful:

Whose Job Is It?

This is a story about four people named Everybody, Somebody, Anybody, and Nobody. There was an important job to be done, and Everybody was asked to do it. Everybody was sure Somebody would do it. Anybody could have done it, but Nobody did it. Somebody got angry at them, because it was Everybody's job. Everybody thought Anybody could do it, but Nobody realized that Everybody wouldn't do it. It ended up that Everybody blamed Somebody when Nobody did what Anybody could have done. What's Everybody's excuse, anyway?

Babies in the River

Some time ago some women went down to the stream to wash their clothes. As they were washing, they suddenly saw something floating down the river. When they saw it move, they stopped what they were doing to look at it, and realized that it was a baby.

One of the women looked at the other women and said, "What do we do? There is a baby floating there."

Another woman said, "What should we do? We should save the baby, of course!" So they picked the baby up out of the water and took it home to take care of it.

The next day, they went to do more laundry. Before long, they saw something else floating on the river – two more babies!

One woman said, "What do we do about these two babies?"

Another woman answered, "We save them, of course!" And they took the two babies home.

On the third day there were more babies. Three of them. And on the fourth day, there were four babies. And so it continued.

By now the women were getting tired of saving all these babies, and they were not getting any washing done.

Finally, one of the women said, "My friends, there could not be babies floating down this river unless somebody was putting them in the water upstream. We should go up the river and find out who is putting the babies in the water and make them stop."

Another woman said, "But it is not any of our business what the people do up there. Whoever owns that property upstream can do what they want and it's not our problem."

The women discussed this for some time, all the while they were saving babies.

Finally the wisest women said, "But look! It is our problem! This is our river too, and we can't even use it any more with all these babies floating down it. And once we take the babies out, we need to feed them and care for them. I am an old woman, and I don't have energy for that. But I do have the energy to walk upstream right now and find out where these babies are coming from!"

What would you do? Whose responsibility is it, anyway?

Students Take Action

A young environmentalist told the following story about successful student action against erosion in a pasture on the Belize River:

"For the past two years, the government has lost at least eight acres of land there, just from erosion. The river kept coming and eating the soil away. When they were making the pasture, they thought that a pasture should have no trees in it . . . so they cut down all the trees and planted grass. But grass does not send down big roots into the soil like trees do. And now the river keeps coming in . . . and there is mass erosion . . . So we took bamboo and tied ourselves to ropes to go down and plant bamboo on the cliffs. Now, during the last rainy season, there wasn't as much erosion . . . It is still going to continue, but we managed to control most of it . . .

"We had gone to the Ministry of Natural Resources, to the Minister himself, and explained to him about the problem . . . that we wanted money to propagate the bamboo . . . Then we went back a second time, with more students and with more explanation. That time we went with pictures also.

"And then he said, 'OK, I'm going to give you five hundred dollars.'

"Just to do that was a big step for us . . . the satisfaction is there that we solved a problem and helped a lot of people."

The Earth Pledge

At the United Nations Earth Summit in Rio de Janeiro, Brazil, 1992 an Earth Pledge was signed by heads of state and government officials from all over the world. Belize's Deputy Prime Minister and Minister of Natural Resources Hon. Florencio Marin joined thousands of important people who signed the document, which read as follows:

Earth Pledge

Recognizing that peoples' actions towards nature and each other are the source of growing damage to the environment and resources needed to meet human needs and to ensure survival and development,
I pledge to act in the best of my ability to help make Earth a secure and hospitable home for present and future generations.

Part 2: Reflection

After you have read the preceding passages, students have hopefully begun to have an idea that to some people, making a difference is very important. This part of the activity helps students think about how to relate these notions to their own lives.

First, ask students to get out their pencils and notebooks and to write down a quick response to the following questions. Use a chalkboard or write the questions on large paper and hang it on the wall.

1. What have you seen in your lives – at home, at school, or in the community – that you felt was wrong? This can be anything, not just related to the environment.
2. Did you speak out or did you stay silent?
3. What else did you do, if anything?
4. Why did you do as you did?
5. Would you do something different now, or do you believe you did the right thing?

Let students know that the incident they describe need not necessarily be significant, but perhaps even something that happens from day to day. It is also a good idea to tell students that they will not be required to share their stories unless they want to. This may encourage students to be more honest with their feelings. If students get stuck, provide them with some ideas. Most students have seen things like litter, pollution, deforestation, drugs, violence, prejudice, domestic abuse, cruelty to animals, and so on. Here is an example written by a student:

"Last weekend I was walking along the beach with my little brother when I saw him throw trash from his food onto the sand. I didn't say anything to him, even though I thought it looked ugly. When I think about it, I should have showed him how ugly it looked and we could have picked it up and put it in the bin."

Ask for volunteers to share their stories to start the discussion. As the teacher, you should have answered the questions for yourself as well. That way, if your students are reluctant to share their stories, you will have your own story to help spark discussion. As students share their stories, ask some questions of the group. Is there another way this situation could have been dealt with? If action was taken, was it successful? Why or why not? What are some of the things that can make action successful? Perhaps more input was needed, like planning, facts or hard evidence, money, or people to help.

Part 3: Planning for Action.
    With this final part of the activity, students practice thinking critically about environmental problems and issues. Students form groups of three or four. They choose a problem or issue to discuss, preferably related to the natural or social environment. Be flexible to allow for differing interests and values. Each group then spends about 15 minutes on the following:

1. What is the problem or issue?
2. Why do you feel that it is a problem or issue?
3. What is something you can do to help deal with this problem?
4. What are some of the things you would need to make your action successful?

Then each group is to write up a draft plan for dealing with the problem or issue. A spokesperson from each group then briefly presents the problem and outlines the group's plan to the others. Have students save their plans. They may elect to return to them if they later decide to carry out an Action Project activity (below). Remember that these are only draft plans, and that in the time allotted, you can't expect students to come up with highly sophisticated strategies, especially if the concepts are brand new to them.

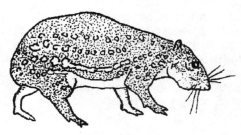

Action Project

What you need: Pen or Pencil, Paper, Reference Books, Chalkboard, Flip Chart or Large Paper, other materials depending on the nature of the project.

In this activity, participants plan and implement a strategy on an environmental problem or issue that they find important. The project allows students to practice planning, cooperating with others, and clarification of their norms and values. Students can also gain senses of empowerment and ownership if they feel their actions can influence an important problem or issue. Before this type of project can be successful, students must be motivated from the heart and be committed to seeing their project to the end. To help inspire empowerment and motivation, conduct the "We CAN Make a Difference" activity first.

For the Action Project to really have meaning for the students, it must be carried out as their choice and decision. The students will never really "own" their action if it is controlled or required by the teacher. Naturally, the teacher can help students learn the important skills and strategies involved, and provide background and guidance as needed. The outline below provides suggestions for this kind of assistance.

A Project to Educate Others

Action projects can take any number of forms, and can be large or small. Students may elect to undertake a project that can be completed during the program at CBWS, or one that must be implemented later. If your students come from different schools and are together only for the duration of the program in the CBWS, you will probably want them to select a project that can be completed during the visit. Otherwise they can choose a more lengthy project, provided you are willing to assist or advise them later if needed. A good option is a community education or public awareness project like the one outlined here. Of course, if students have their hearts set on another kind of activity, go with it.

Students may instead decide to carry out a clean-up day or a tree-planting campaign at their school or community, or to help in some way with CBWS's maintenance. Students may also elect to act on a problem that does not directly relate to environmental issues. If they are sincere about it, they should be allowed to go ahead with it. Most of the basic steps will be the same.

An Action Project for community education or public awareness has five phases: (1) Introduction, (2) Decisions, (3) Planning, (4), Implementation, and (5) Reflection.

Environmental Education

Phase 1: Introduction

Explain to students that an Action Project is a strategy that gives students an opportunity to take action on a problem or issue that they think is important. If you previously conducted the "We CAN Make a Difference!" activity, students may already be thinking ahead about a project. Let students know that the project is voluntary. Required projects may not inspire students as much as projects that they carry out as their own choosing. If students elect not to carry out a project, it should be a group decision. They can together decide on an alternative activity. If you have a large group of students, students may form smaller groups and work on different projects.

Discuss goals with students. If the outcome students desire for their project is unrealistic and out of grasp, students will become quickly discouraged and lose their motivation. Project goals should never be considered as fixed and unchangeable. They serve as targets to be reviewed as often as needed. Goals are adapted and changed as new information is acquired.

Explain to students that the first things they must decide are the **who, what, where, when,** and **how** of their educational project. Write this on the board.

Who refers to the participants in an educational program. Ask students to brainstorm about different kinds of participant groups. Students may come up with primary school children, visitors to CBWS, the community, classmates, a church congregation, government officials, and so on. Write their suggestions on the board.

What refers to the issue or topic that students want to tell others about. There are many different topics to choose from, depending on what students think are important issues or interesting topics. For example, suggestions might include "Problems with Garbage," "The Importance of Trees," or "The Need to Support the CBWS." Suggestions may also include ideas to spark general awareness and appreciation of the environment, such as "What To See On A Night Walk," or "How CBWS Became a Wildlife Sanctuary." Write down all suggestions for future reference.

When, where, and **how** involves the actual plan for implementing the project, or sharing what they have learned with others. When you ask students for suggestions, they will probably come up with ideas such as a skit, a poster, a radio show, a lecture or speech, a newsletter article, and so on. Later, a more detailed plan sets a date and venue for this sharing. Some students may get excited about writing and rehearsing a type of public performance or program, but will be reluctant to become actively involved. Help students understand that they must feel comfortable with all aspects of the implementation. Otherwise, they must choose a new strategy.

Phase 2: Decisions

Allow students to meet privately to make their first decisions:

1. Students decide if they want to do a project at all. If they decide not to do one, they then select an alternative activity. If students have split into smaller groups, the members of each group must make the decisions for themselves.
2. Students discuss and choose a realistic goal. What do they want this project to achieve? Remind students that goals are not fixed, and that no one can decide their goals for them. It is up to them to review and reflect upon their goals at each step to determine how realistic they are.
3. Students make a general plan of action, making decisions on the participants, the topic, and the method they will use to share information. Remind students that the parts of their plan must match. For instance, if students decide they want to involve primary school children, they need to realize that hanging a poster in the Visitor Center to inform people about the importance of donations is probably not an effective way of sharing that inform-ation with primary school children.

Phase 3: Planning

Students reconvene and announce their decisions. Help them review these decisions and summarize them on the board.

Help students list the steps involved in the project. They need to think about each of the tasks, the order in which they must be com-pleted, and whether or not they should be divided among individuals or completed by the entire group. Make sure they include details about the implementation. Do they need to get permission or make any special arrangements? What equipment or materials are needed?

Phase 4: Implementation

The project is implemented as planned. Students may need to be flexible and allow for on- the-spot changes.

Phase 5: Reflection

Students think critically about both the process and the final outcome of the action project. It might be difficult for students to actually evaluate the success of the program in terms of the goal, especially when environmental problems and issues are difficult to tackle. As an alternative, reflection allows students to take a more open, critical look at the project. Where and when did things go well? What aspects can be improved? Where must the goals be adapted and changed? Do the students think the project was success-ful? Why or why not? What has been learned? Where has it led them? Where can they go from here? The completion of a project need not signal the end of action. Students can continue to work on issues that they feel are important.

TAKE A LOOK!!

Welcome One And All to the beautiful And Interesting Cockscomb Basin.

Cockscomb is an enjoyable Sanctuary. In Order for it to stay that way, We Should protect animals and trees. Please be careful NOT to pollute the area.

The Sanctuary has Many facinating places to viset Such as: the river, trail tracks, water fall. You can take a look at the Victoria Peak, Walk through the forest and do some bird Watching.

NOTE: To vistors We should all stand and help to preserve the sanctuary by giving a little DONATION for its betterments

A poster made by students during an Action Project

Games

Now that you have spent a full day exploring and learning about the environment and the Cockscomb Basin, your group is ready for some fun and games to fill the evening. Here are some ideas to get things going. Although these games may sound a bit silly and childish to some, they are almost guaranteed to put the group in a playful mood, no matter the age level. Much of it depends on the leader's enthusiasm. It is important that the leader plays the game, too, so gather some energy and have fun!

The Tiger Hunt (a song)

We start by telling the students a story that has been circulating around Belize for some time. A young visitor to the country searched far and wide for an opportunity to see and photograph a jaguar in the wild. She spent several weeks camping and hiking in the forest, but to her great disappointment, saw only a few tracks. On her last evening in jaguar country, this visitor took one last half-hearted walk. On her way back to the cabin, nature called and she realized she couldn't reach the camp in time. So she stepped behind some underbrush near the path. Suddenly, a muscular, black and tawny animal leapt from the shadows and landed a few yards away! She could barely get herself together before she shouted and jumped back onto the trail. She dropped her camera and binoculars as she ran and didn't stop until she got back to the camp. And so she went back home, without her photographs, but with a great story.

Now we will start our own tiger hunt. This is to be done in one place, acting out the adventure rather than going out on the trail. The expedition leader leads the rest of the group, and we start out hiking by slapping our hands to our thighs like footsteps. This sets the rhythm. We hike slowly at first, and the leader calls out each line while the rest of us repeat:

Leader: *Going on a tiger hunt!*
Group: *Going on a tiger hunt!*
Leader: *I'm not afraid*
Group: *I'm not afraid*
Leader: *I've got my camera round my neck (act out the motion of putting the camera around the neck)*
Group repeats
Leader: *Let's have fun!*
Group repeats

As we continue through the forest, we will encounter of number of different obstacles. We pick up the pace as we cross a bridge, a stand of dumb cane, a swamp, and Victoria Peak (and whatever else we can think of). With each obstacle, we chant the following, again with the leader saying it first and the rest of us responding:

> *There's a bridge up ahead! (Or dumb cane, a swamp, or Victoria Peak*
> *up ahead. Act as if looking through binoculars.)*
> *Can't go under it,*
> *Can't go around it,*
> *Gotta go over (or through) it!*
> *(Stomp the feet on the floor as if crossing a bridge)*

Repeat the first lines after each verse:
> *Going on a tiger hunt!*
> *I'm not afraid*
> *I've got my camera round my neck*
> *Let's have fun!*

With each obstacle, appropriate motions are made as we pass through the dumb cane (make swishing sounds by rubbing the hands), through the swamp (act as if squishing through the mud), and over Victoria Peak (climbing motions). Finally, we come to a cave, and we hike more slowly because we can't see what is inside:

> *There's a cave up ahead!*
> *Can't go under it*
> *Can't go around it*
> *Gotta go in it! It's dark inside (slowly)*
> *Here's something furry (reach our with the hand) OUCH! (Pull hand*
> *back quickly) With BIG sharp teeth! A TIGER!*

With this discovery we have to run back as quickly as we can, exactly the way we came, passing the mountain, swamp, dumb cane, and bridge (and anything else you added), with plenty of running in between. Our footsteps (thigh slapping) are super-quick now:

> *Let's get out of here!*
> *Over the mountain (climbing motions)*
> *Through the swamp (squish, squish)*
> *Through the dumb cane (swishing with hands)*
> *Over the bridge (stomp with feet)*
> *Safe at last!*

As we collapse safely in our cabin, we consider going bird watching tomorrow instead!

Army Ants Tangle-Up

Army ants have the ability to lock their legs together to form a living, protective nest around their queen. They also build living bridges for the other ants to cross.

To play this game, we split up into smaller groups of 8 or 10 and stand together, facing inward in a loose circle. We count to three and shout "Army Ants Tangle Up!" We close our eyes and reach out with our hands and grab the hands of other people. Once we are all holding the hands of two other people, we do not let go.

When we all open our eyes, we see we're in quite a mess! Can we untangle without letting go? (If anyone has both hands of the same person, or the hand of a person next to them, switch now). As we take a few moments to study our predicament, we see some strategies to untie the knot. Is it possible? Some people step over, some step under, until eventually (hopefully) we have a neat, circular nest. If that doesn't work, we allow two hands to disconnect and make an army ant bridge instead. Remember: Don't twist the arms of other people! Loosen your grip just enough to move easily.

Night-time Neighbors

Diurnal creatures go about their business during the day. When night falls, they want to be snug in their nests or burrows, protected from any nocturnal predators that might be roaming about. Our diurnal animals seem to be somewhat young and inexperienced. When the sun went down, they were far from home. Only two made it back in time and they lie in their nest, camouflaged by the night. Can the rest of the troop find the nest in the dark? Unlike nocturnal animals, our creatures do not have eyes adapted for the night. They must be very observant and combine senses of hearing, touch, and sight to find the nest! *This game will help make students more confident and less fearful of the night-time environment.*

We play this game outside in the darkness, without the benefit of flashlights. First, appropriate boundaries are set. The size of the play area might depend on the size of the group. If our group is large, we may want to include the entire Headquarters area and the parking lot. It is probably wisest to exclude the cabins from the playing area, so other visitors will not be disturbed. Next, we all choose partners.

The game starts when one pair of creatures goes off to hide in a nest of its choice. After waiting about five minutes, the rest of us search with our partners throughout the area for the nest. If we find it, we don't say a word! We simply snuggle into the nest with our friends and sit quietly. Eventually, our hiding place becomes crowded, but we are not allowed to move to a new area. We must all try to fit without making any noise. How long will it take before everyone comes straggling in? The last pair to arrive become the first pair to hide for the next round.

Environmental Education

Babes in the Woods

Many baby animals learn how to behave from their parents and relatives. As they learn and grow, sometimes they make silly mistakes! Our young animals did not pay close enough attention to the parents, and they still have a lot of learning to do. They try to make up for it by learning from the older brothers and sisters. When they all catch up with the parent again, no one can believe how everyone got so confused!

We start this silly game by standing in a circle, facing outward so we can't see what the others are doing. The mother or father animal (leader) shows its first child an important animal behavior, without the others looking. For example, the parent can show the child how to flap its wings, shake its leg, and make a funny face to scare a predator. (Let's be creative: simple movements are not as fun as silly ones!) This movement gets passed secretly on from one young animal to the next, all around the circle. If we are not directly teaching or learning the movement, we must turn again to face outward, without looking at the others. Finally, the youngest animal learns the movement from its sibling. Then we all turn around to watch this baby show us what he or she learned. Now we need our parent to demonstrate to all of us how to do it again. We can't help laughing when we see how the original behavior differs from the one the youngest animal learned! Choose a new parent and play the game again.

Jungle Noises

When we hike through the forest, sometimes we hear a multitude of noises coming from insects, birds, frogs, and who knows what else! Where exactly are these noises coming from and who is making them? Let's see if we can find out.

We all stand in a circle and one person volunteers to be the hiker. The hiker leaves the circle and turns around so that he or she cannot see the others. Our teacher then silently chooses a leader to lead the others in making creative noises. This leader may clap the hands, stomp the feet, rub the hands, snap the fingers, make hissing noises, or something similar. The rest of us do what the leader does, and we begin making the noises. The hiker is called to the middle of the group. About every fifteen seconds or so the leader changes the sound or action and the rest of the group follows. The hiker must try to determine who the leader is! Careful observation and listening will give away the leader's general direction. Can the hiker figure it out? Once this is accomplished, the leader becomes the next hiker and we play the game again.

Suggestions for Further Reading

More environmental education ideas and activities can be found in the following publications:

Tropical Forests and Their Conservation: An Educational Manual for Standards IV, V and VI by Kerrien Redington can be obtained from the Belize Audubon Society, 12 Fort Street, P.O.Box 1001, Belize City.

This book is written for children and works well as a companion to this teacher's guide to the Cockscomb. It is intended for use in the classroon to prepare for a visit to the Cockscomb Basin Wildlife Sanctuary.

The Curriculum Development Unit of the Ministry of Education has produced several environmental education manuals for primary schools. They are full of information and ideas about important local topics such as Pollution, Land Use, and others. They can be obtained from the Curriculum Development Unit at the University College of Belize, Princess Margaret Drive, Belize City.

Sharing Nature With Children, and *Sharing the Joy of Nature* are two useful books by Joseph Cornell that emphasize positive learning experiences in nature. They can be obtained from Dawn Publications, 14618 Tyler Foote Rd., Nevada City, CA 95959, USA.

Environmental Education in the Schools: Creating a Program that Works! By Judy A. Braus and David Wood. This inexpensive, information-packed book can be ordered from the North American Association of Environmental Education, Box 400, Troy, OH 45373, USA.

Environmental Education

CHAPTER 12

Glossary
Katherine M. Emmons

Adaptation

Populations of living organisms adapt when they make evolutionary adjustments over time to their environment. Adaptations help secure the survival and reproduction of living things and help them expand to new areas. These adaptations occur slowly over more than one generation, and can be changes in how species look, function, or behave. For example, the red brocket deer (also known as the antelope) is adapted for moving through thick brush with its low shoulders and small antlers. Another example of adaptation is the root systems of many tropical trees. When the soil contains few nutrients, roots sometimes spread laterally just under the surface where they are able to quickly recycle nutrients from the leaf litter above.

Amphibians

Amphibians are a class of animals that includes frogs, toads, and salamanders. They are ecothermal (sometimes called cold-blooded) which means their body temperatures reflect the temperatures of the surrounding environment. When it is cold, amphibians are slow and sluggish. They have a moist skin with glands that allow water and gases to directly enter the body. Amphibians need only sit in a puddle of water to drink by absorbing it through the skin. This characteristic also allows poisonous or harmful substances to easily enter their bodies. Amphibians are thus very susceptible to pollution.

Another fascinating characteristic of these animals is their growth, or metamorphosis, from infants to adults. Most spend the larval stage as tadpoles in water. Eventually the tail is absorbed into the body, the legs grow, and the animal can explore the land. Many amphibians live entirely on the land after reaching the adult stage and return to the water only for breeding. They do need to keep their eggs moist, so they lay them in or near water and cover them with a protective jelly or foam. In the moist rainforest environment, this coating is often enough to allow the tadpoles to hatch and slip into nearby water. Due to their sensitivity to the environment, many populations of amphibians have disappeared in recent years. A variety of factors have probably contributed to their demise, including pollution, ozone layer depletion, and habitat destruction.

Antifungal

An antifungal is a chemical compound that can destroy or inhibit the growth of fungi. In a warm, moist environment, fungi grow quickly and accelerate decomposition. Many rainforest trees make antifungal chemicals, which help protect their leaves from rotting and against leafcutter (weewee) ants. Because the ants rely on a special fungus grown on the leaves of plants, they cannot select leaves that contain antifungals. Antifungal compounds derived from plants can treat skin infections like athlete's foot.

Arboreal

The word arboreal means tree-dwelling. Some arboreal animal species live entirely in trees, coming only rarely to the ground, such as black howler monkeys. Other arboreal species, such as the margay (tigercat) will leave the treetops when necessary. Arboreal termites build large nests in trees. Plants can also be arboreal. Many bromeliads and orchids are arboreal and live on trees as epiphytes.

Biodiversity

The various kinds of life on earth are what make up biological diversity, or biodiversity. The communities of millions of plants, animals, and other life forms on the planet create unique ecosystems, which together contribute to the entire richness of life. Much of this diversity is still undiscovered by scientists. Yet, environmental destruction is reducing diversity even before scientists have a chance to study it. In the tropics, deforestation is the biggest threat to biodiversity.

Camouflage

Camouflage is cryptic coloration and patterning. It is a useful adaptation of many animals to blend in with their surroundings to avoid the watchful eye of predators. Some insects have shapes and colours like the leaves, bark, or twigs of their habitats, fooling bird or reptile predators. Some moths, for example, sit on tree trunks with wings outspread and flat against the bark. Only a close examination will reveal their true identities. Katydids and leaf-hoppers often look just like leaves in shape and colour. Some even have markings and blotches that make them look like insect-damaged leaves. Other animals also use camouflage. Tree frogs tuck in their legs, close their eyes and lie flat and still. Even the brilliant colours of birds and butterflies can act as camouflage. In the shade under the canopy, the colours are subdued and blend in well with the vegetation.

Camouflage also allows many predatory animals to lie in wait or sneak unnoticed upon their prey. The yellowjaw tommygoff, for example, is very difficult to see as it lies quietly on the leaf litter waiting for its prey. Its crisscross pattern of gray and brown looks just like the forest floor. The jaguar, with its tawny colour and black spots, is also difficult to spot in shadowy vegetation.

Canopy

The canopy is the foliage and other life that form a loose roof over the forest. In moist tropical forests the trees that make up the canopy are all tall. Their leaves make a continuous, closed layer 20-50 m over the forest floor and overlap in a thick layer to break rainfall and sunlight like a tall umbrella. Many canopy trees must tolerate the shady understory when young, but when they eventually reach maturity they are able to take full advantage of the sunlight at the top. Vines and lianas drape from tree to tree and all the way from the ground. The branches of the canopy support an entire world of life to which epiphytic plants and arboreal animals are well adapted. The canopy has many more different animal species than does the forest floor. Many birds, insects, and mammals (such as the kinkajou or nightwalker) spend their entire lives in the upper or lower canopy. (see Forest Layers)

Carbon Cycle

Carbon is a natural element found in all organic matter. It circulates through nature in chemical reactions, moving from the atmosphere to plants and other life forms, and then back into the atmosphere. Through photosynthesis, plants fix carbon dioxide from the air. They produce carbohydrates (starches and sugars) to produce new living tissue. Animal consumers also use these carbohydrates by eating and metabolizing them for energy. In this process, carbon dioxide is released back into the air as the animal breathes and in the production of waste. In addition, carbon dioxide is released as dead organic matter decays. Carbon dioxide is also released from the burning of fossil fuels (oil, coal, gas, etc.) and living organic matter (wood). Humans are burning more and more forests and fossil fuels, and this increasingly distorts the natural carbon cycle. The resulting increased atmospheric carbon dioxide has caused much pollution and may also cause a greenhouse effect or a rise in global temperatures.

Environmental Education

Carnivore

A carnivore is an animal that obtains most of its nutrients from eating other animals. Mammalian meat-eaters of the order *Carnivora* often have sharp teeth adapted for killing prey and tearing meat. Jaguars and other cats are typical carnivorous mammals. Other animals may also be meat-eaters, including other mammals and many species of reptiles, insects, and fish.

Commensalism

Commensalism is a symbiotic relationship in which one type of organism lives on or in another organism, but does not harm or benefit its host in any way. Many epiphytes, such as orchids, live in trees, for example, but do not extract nutrients or water from them directly, nor do they provide a direct benefit to the host tree. (see Symbiosis, Mutualism, Parasitism)

Competition

When two or more species occupy the same environment and depend on the same limited resources, the interaction between them is called competition. One example is when various species of animals compete for the limited food at a particular fruit tree. Some species develop specific adaptations that give them a competitive edge over others. For instance, plants all need light to grow, but in the shady forest, light is limited. Some plants are able to grow very quickly up into the canopy to dominate the light source, thus denying sunlight to the plants around them. In some cases, competition between two species may be so intense that one of the two competing species may die. When a vine drapes over a tree it can use most of the available water and nutrients and block the sunlight so that the tree cannot survive. Eventually the vine covers what has become a rotting stump.

Conservation

Conservation is the wise use of natural resources, including their long-term management. Conservation also includes the preservation of wildlife and natural areas, as well as the reduction of waste and the recycling of materials. (see Natural Resources, Preservation)

Consumer

A consumer is an organism that eats other organisms. All animals are consumers, because they eat either plants or animals. Herbivores consume plants, making them first order consumers. Carnivores consume other animals, and are second order or third order consumers. Parasites may consume plants or animals, depending on their specific niche. (see Producer, Decomposer, Food Chain)

Cryptic

Cryptic markings on animals are those that allow the animals to remain hidden in their environment. (see Camouflage)

Crepuscular

Crepuscular animal behavior is when the animal hunts or forages at dusk and dawn in the twilight. These animals are neither nocturnal, active at night, nor diurnal, active in the day. (see Nocturnal, Diurnal).

Decomposer

A decomposer eats or absorbs dead plants and animals. It breaks down organic matter into simple molecules so that its nutrients can be used by the primary producers, the plants. Decomposers include many microorganisms, fungi, and some animals. (see Decomposition)

Decomposition

Decomposition occurs when plant and animal matter breaks down into microscopic components. The nutrients from this organic matter are able to pass from the living to the non-living parts of the ecosystem, then back to the living again. Bacteria and fungi play important roles in decomposition. By feeding on dead organic matter they pass nitrogen, calcium, magnesium, potassium, and phosphorus through their systems, breaking them down and allowing them to be quickly reused by plants, the primary producers. This amazing rate of decomposition allows luxuriant green tropical forests to grow on relatively poor soils.

Deforestation

Deforestation is the permanent removal of forest, generally to clear the land for another use, such as pasture, agriculture, or development. Deforestation can also occur from logging. Tropical deforestation has been accelerating over the last few decades, causing many local and global environmental problems. Tropical forests have already disappeared from much of their original area. According to noted biologist E. O. Wilson, if destruction of the world's remaining rainforests continues at the present rate until the year 2022, half of what now remains will be gone. In this process of deforestation, as many as one-tenth to one-quarter of the resident species will disappear. This equals as many as ten percent of the species in the entire world. With this destruction, opportunities to discover new and useful species will be lost forever. Many yet undiscovered species could potentially provide medical remedies, other useful products, or boost agriculture.

Deforestation also affects the climate. Natural ecosystems regulate the gases in the atmosphere that affect the winds, temperatures, and rainfall. Tropical rainforests create much of their own rainfall through their cycling of water. When they are cut, rainfall eventually decreases in the area because there are no longer trees to transpire large amounts of water into the atmosphere. With a change in climate, the area becomes a permanent scrubland or grassland, and conversion back into closed canopy forest is impossible. In addition, the burning of vast areas of rainforest, particularly in the Amazon Basin, has polluting effects world wide. It may even contribute to a global warming, or the greenhouse effect. Deforestation also results in increased erosion and severe damage to watersheds.

Agriculture is the main cause of deforestation. Traditional milpa agriculture (slash and burn) allowed ample time for the forest to regenerate before reusing a given plot of land, but the increase in human population has put pressure on the available land. Less and less fallow time is allowed and the forest cannot regenerate. In Belize large-scale agriculture of citrus and other crops causes much deforestation, as does conversion of forest into pasture. Some of these practices can be carried out in a sustainable manner that allows the forest to regenerate. New conservation strategies must be implemented to save the remaining tropical forests as human populations and agriculture expand.

Delayed Implantation
In mammals, the embryo must implant into the wall of the uterus in order for further development to occur. In some mammals, such as armadillos, implantation does not occur immediately after conception (the joining of the sperm and the egg). Instead, the embryo remains in an inactive state for a period of time, sometimes several months, before implantation and development occur.

Diurnal
Diurnal species are those that are active during the day. A diurnal animal carries out most of its hunting, feeding and breeding activities during the daylight hours. A diurnal flower is one that blooms during the day. (see Crepuscular, Nocturnal)

Drip Tip
Many rainforest leaves end in a narrow, pointed tip. This drip tip helps to slow erosion by allowing rainwater to run to the bottom of the leaf, where it accumulates and drips off. In this manner, the plant does not have to rely entirely on evaporation to dry the leaf. Most of these leaves also slope downward, and have a very smooth, shiny surface that also encourages the shedding of water.

Ecology
As a specialized branch of biology, ecology is the study of the relationships between living organisms, and between the organisms and the environment in which they live. The word ecology is derived from the Greek word (OIKOS), which means "house."

Ecosystem
An ecosystem is a unit of nature that includes living and non-living elements. Organisms within an ecosystem are connected by food chains, food webs, and nutrient cycling. Ecosystems vary greatly in size and characteristics, and often overlap. A change in one part or element of an ecosystem, such as the removal of organisms or water, or the introduction of non-native species, can impact and damage the entire system.

Ecotourism
Ecotourism is travel and tourism to natural areas to observe and learn about them. Ideally, ecotourism has minimal impact on the natural environment, yet provides maximum benefit to local people. This does not always happen, and any ecotourism endeavors should be carefully planned and closely monitored by governments, local communities, and environmental organizations.

Endangered Species

An endangered species is any species of animal or plant whose population has been reduced to the point where it is threatened with extinction over much or all of its range. (see Extinction)

Environment

The environment is the total surroundings within which an organism or a community of organisms lives and functions.

Emergent Trees

Emergent trees are the huge, tall trees that extend above the forest canopy in a mature rainforest. They are easiest to spot from the air. Since the crowns do not have to compete for space with neighboring trees, they spread out flat in the open sun and wind. Usually, a mature forest has only one or two emergent trees per acre. (see Forest Layers.)

Erosion

Erosion is the removal of soil or rock by running water or wind. Human activity can greatly increase the rate of erosion in an area. When vegetation is removed from the land, the exposed soil can become loose and dry and is more easily dislodged.

Evapotranspiration

Evapotranspiration is the loss of water through the combined processes of (a) evaporation from the soil and water bodies like rivers, lakes, and the sea, and (b) the transpiration of plants. The water lost through this process condenses in the atmosphere and returns to the earth as rain. As much as 75 percent of the rainfall in very wet rainforests is caused by evapotranspiration from the forest itself. Each canopy tree can transpire as much as 200 gallons of water in the atmosphere per year.

Evolution

Evolution is the process of change in all organisms over time. All currently existing plants and animals have evolved or developed from earlier plants and animals, and inherited new characteristics and adaptations over many generations. Through evolution, organisms react to their environments and neighboring species and develop adaptations that help them change and survive. Many species show a co-evolution with other species. Although separate species, they have evolved to interact specifically with each other. (see Adaptation, Symbiosis)

Environmental Education

Extinction

Extinction is the dying out of an entire species. Extinction of a species may be local to a specific area, or general to the whole planet.

Extinction occurs from a variety of natural factors, but humans are the driving force behind most extinctions today. Increasing human population disturbs wildlife in a variety of ways. The destruction of habitats, particularly in the tropics, is having a profound, irreversible impact on species diversity. Other factors, including pollution and hunting, can also cause extinctions. Some plants and animals are more prone to extinction than others. Species that have one or more of the following characteristics probably need some kind of protection:

1.   It has trouble adapting to environmental change.
2.   It interferes in some way with humans, like killing livestock or eating crops.
3.   It has specific food or breeding requirements, like the scarlet macaw, which needs tall trees for nesting.
4.   It migrates on a regular basis, like many warbler species.
5.   It is naturally low in numbers, as many rainforest species are.
6.   It has few offspring, or a long gestation or youth period, like scarlet macaws.
7.   It has value when collected or hunted by humans, like cat skins, parrots for pets, and orchids. (see Endangered Species)

Food Chain

In an ecosystem, each organism is linked to other organisms at other trophic levels (feeding levels), forming a food chain. The plants are at the lowest trophic level because they are primary producers and create their own food through photosynthesis. Plants are eaten and digested by animals (first-order consumers) at the second trophic level, as when a bird eats a fruit, or when a caterpillar eats a leaf. At the next trophic level, a snake might consume the bird, or a lizard the caterpillar (second-order consumers). A white hawk may consume the snake or the lizard (third-order consumer). Finally, decomposers will ultimately consume all components.

A food chain can be pictured as a pyramid, with many primary producers making a broad base. The first order consumers make up the next level, and so on until a single top consumer forms the peak (the hawk). This means that to support higher level consumers, the habitat requires larger quantities of lower level organisms. (see Food Web, Primary Producer)

Food Web

Ecosystems always contain more than one food chain, and these all overlap. The network of interacting food chains is called a food web. (see Food Chain)

Forest Floor

The forest floor is the bottom layer of the forest. Very little light penetrates the canopy, so only shade-tolerant species such as ferns, herbs, and fungi flourish on the moist forest floor. Mammals such as tapirs, jaguars, pacas, and peccaries inhabit the forest floor, as do the chicken-like tinamous, the coral snakes, and many insects and other arthropods. (see Forest Layers)

Forest Gap

When one or more trees fall, a gap is created in the forest canopy, creating a new set of conditions throughout the forest strata. A small or intermediate disturbance of this sort is important for maintaining forest diversity. In these new forest gaps, sunlight reaches the forest floor and creates a different microclimate. Sun-loving plants and animals flourish. Tree species that do not grow well in shade are able to compete. Some seeds lie dormant for years in the soil, waiting for a gap in the canopy to occur. Stumps will also sprout anew in the sunshine.

Other species, which have grown only to sapling size in the shady undergrowth, are poised to take advantage of a new canopy opening. Once they have successfully occupied a gap, these trees attract different species of insects, birds and other animals, bringing higher diversity into the immediate area. In the Cockscomb Basin, larger gaps were formed by Hurricane Hattie, logging, and slash and burn agriculture. In such cases regeneration is much more difficult than in small gaps, which close up quickly. If the area is disturbed repeatedly, the soil can no longer support forest life and regeneration becomes impossible. (see Succession)

Forest Layers

Undisturbed rainforests have four layers, each with their characteristics. They are the emergents, the canopy, the understory, and the forest floor. Each layer has a microclimate that forms a habitat for different life forms. Sometimes the layers are not distinct, particularly where the forest has been disturbed. Because the Cockscomb Basin was affected a great deal by Hurricane Hattie (1961) and continued selective logging, a well-preserved forest structure is found in only a few very remote places. The Visitor Center has an informative display that shows the structure of CBWS forests along a time line. (see Emergent, Canopy, Understory, and Forest Floor)

Gestation

Gestation is the time required for an embryo to develop into an animal which can survive outside the mother's body, that is, the length of a pregnancy in mammals, including humans. It begins with conception, the joining of the egg and sperm, and ends when the baby is born. In mammals that develop a placenta within the uterus for the nourishment of the embryo (placental mammals), gestation can take several months. But marsupial mammals do not develop a placenta, so gestation is very short. Instead, the marsupial mammal is born as a tiny, undeveloped embryo which then attaches itself to one of its mother's nipples for nourishment and remains there for several months as it develops. (see Delayed Implantation)

Global Warming (see Greenhouse Effect)

Greenhouse Effect
The greenhouse effect is caused by increasing the level of carbon dioxide in the earth's atmosphere. Since carbon dioxide traps the heat of the sun, similar to the effect of the glass on a greenhouse, increasing its level in the atmosphere can cause an increase in the average temperature of the earth, also called "global warming." Carbon dioxide levels are being increased due to the burning of fossil fuels, those that are derived from oil or coal.

Habitat
A habitat is the home of any particular species and the native area where it lives and grows. Habitats must provide food, water, shelter and living space, and all of these must be arranged in a manner that the species can use. A microhabitat is the part of the habitat occupied by a specific organism. For example, the larger habitat of the southern otter is the rainforest, but its microhabitat is the river area. (see Niche)

Habitat Loss
Habitat loss is the destruction of the places where plants and animals live. Usually, it refers to human activity such as deforestation. Most rainforest species are adapted specifically for that habitat and cannot survive once the land has been cleared. (see Deforestation, Habitat)

Herbivore
A herbivore is an animal that eats any part of a living plant, including its leaves, stems, wood, roots, fruits, seeds, and flowers.

Litter
The term litter has three different meanings: (1) Litter is dead and partly decomposed plant material, such as leaves, twigs, or flowers, which forms a layer on the forest floor. In the rainforest, this layer remains fairly thin, due to the fast rate of decomposition in the warm, humid environment. (2) Litter is trash or rubbish discarded by humans in an inappropriate place. In the CBWS there are cans and pits for discarding trash, and it does not belong in the outhouse, in the barbecue, or on the ground. (3) A litter is a group of offspring born at one time to one mammal. For example, the armadillo usually has a litter of four young.

Mammal

A mammal is an animal that belongs to the *Mammalia* class of animals. All are warm-blooded vertebrates, which means the body regulates its own temperature and uses energy from food to keep warm. Mammals have hair and claws or nails, and are able to nurse their young from mammary glands. Humans are mammals, along with dogs, peccaries, monkeys, and jaguars, to name just a few.

Microclimate

A microclimate is a narrow variation of the general climate patterns in an area. Microclimates are often caused by local physical characteristics, such as a rocky overhang beneath which the air remains still and cool. They can also be defined by the nature of the vegetation, such as in a forest gap where it is more sunny and warm than in the surrounding forest.

Migration

Migration is the seasonal movement of certain animals from one place to another. Many animals that can fly or swim, such as birds, butterflies, whales, and sea turtles, migrate thousands of miles every year. Many birds in the CBWS are migratory species. They nest in areas of the United States and Canada to take advantage of the warm summer weather and abundant food supplies there. They then fly south to Belize and neighboring countries to spend the rest of the year, many of them returning to territories they had previously established.

The migrating birds found in the CBWS include flycatchers, orioles, and twenty or more warblers. The plumbeous kite migrates to the CBWS from South America instead of North America. Weather conditions and the birds' own biological clocks stimulate the onset of migrations. The birds' ability to navigate, or find where they are going, is not completely understood by scientists. Birds are very sensitive to their environments and are able to detect changes in weather, earth magnetism, and directions of the sun and stars. They also probably learn routes by following their parents or the flock. Different species of birds follow different routes. The journey is very difficult, and over half of the population can die every year.

Habitat destruction has created a crisis for migratory species. In particular, many species of warblers have been declining in the last thirty to forty years. Flocks of birds may arrive freshly from the North only to discover their rainforest territories have disappeared. Remaining forested areas cannot support all animals and many will perish. Pollution and habitat destruction in North America also reduce the ability of birds to nest and reproduce. As a result, birds arrive in the tropics in increasingly fewer numbers.

Environmental Education

Milpa Agriculture (Slash and Burn)

Slash and burn agriculture, or milpa farming, is a sustainable method of farming practiced for hundreds or even thousands of years by the Maya and other indigenous groups in Central America. A section of forest is cut and burned to make room for crops. Newly burned vegetation provides immediate nutrients for the new crop. After two seasons, each plot is allowed to regenerate for at least 15 years. A new section of forest is then cut, creating a continuing cycle of shifting agriculture. In recent years, however, the pressure of increasing human population has caused the fallow period to be reduced, resulting in permanent deforestation because the forest is never allowed to regenerate.

Mimicry

Batesian mimicry is when a non-poisonous animal evolves an appearance similar to a poisonous one. Hazardous species are often brightly coloured, which is a warning to potential predators. Non-poisonous look-a-likes mimic this appearance and take advantage of the protection it provides.

Mutualism

Mutualism is a symbiotic relationship in which both organisms benefit. For example, a lichen is a mutualistic combination between an algae that provides energy from photosynthesis, and a fungus that provides the structure within which the algae lives. (see Commensalism, Parasitism, and Symbiosis

Natural Resources

Natural resources are materials found in nature that humans use in some way, such as minerals or timber. Rainforest resources include wild species that can improve domestic agriculture and human diets, chemical substances for medicines, and intact habitats that protect water and soil resources. In addition, intact ecosystems like forests are natural resources that have intrinsic value to humans who want to visit and enjoy their flora, fauna, and scenery.

Niche

An ecological niche is a combination of the function and physical location of a living organism. A niche is composed of all resources used or needed by that organism. It includes the place it lives, what it eats, where it gets its water, how it reproduces, the role it plays in the reproduction of other species (i.e. pollination), and the food it provides as prey to other organisms. In this sense, a niche is the "occupation" of the organism.

For exampie, an epiphytic bromeliad fills a niche in the branches of a large canopy tree, where it interacts with various systems and other species. It obtains its food and water resources from runoff and from the many small species that live in or on it and deposit their wastes. The flowers produced by the bromeliad are pollinated by insects and birds. All of this comprises the bromeliad's niche. (see Habitat)

Nitrogen Cycle

Other nutrients cycle through the ecosystem, too. One of the greatest limits to the growth of plants is the amount of nitrogen available, the main component of most fertilizers. Ironically, nitrogen occurs in the most abundant gas in the atmosphere, nitrogen dioxide, but in that form it can be used by only a few bacterial species, most notably those of the genus *Rhizobium.*

Nocturnal

Nocturnal life forms are active at night, carrying out most of their functions after dark. Bats, armadillos, most cats, and pauraques are typical nocturnal animals in the CBWS. Nocturnal flowers are those that bloom at night. (see Crepuscular, Diurnal)

Old-Growth Forest

Old-growth forest is a mature forest with large trees that have not been harvested for generations. In Belize, it is sometimes referred to as high bush. All species in these forests live and grow naturally, and some huge trees are a hundred years old or more. (see Primary Forest, Secondary Forest)

Omnivore

An omnivore is an animal that eats a variety of things, feeding at different levels of the food chain at the same time. For instance, the coati eats fruits, seeds, and any small animal or insect it can find. It does not feed like the howler money, which is a herbivore and eats only plants. Nor does it feed like carnivores, such as the jaguar, that eat only meat. The distinction between omnivores and carnivores is not always that distinct, however. Many carnivorous animals are somewhat omnivorous in the rainforest and take advantage of the plentiful fruits and nuts (see Carnivore, Herbivore).

Oxygen Cycle

One product of photosynthesis is oxygen, which is produced by plants and needed by animals to metabolize plant carbohydrates. Thus, plants give off oxygen which is then used by animals. The oxygen cycle is linked with the water and carbon cycles. There is some concern that these natural cycles are being thrown out of balance by extensive cutting of rainforests, the main producer of oxygen, and by burning of fossil fuels which uses oxygen and produces carbon dioxide and could cause what is know as the "greenhouse effect," or "global warming." (see Greenhouse Effect)

Environmental Education

Parasites and Parasitism

Parasitism is a type of symbiotic relationship that occurs in animals, plants, and microorganisms. A parasite is an organism that lives on or in another species and derives its nutrients from that host. Parasites generally benefit from this relationship at the expense of their host. A good example of a parasite is the botfly, whose eggs are deposited in the flesh of birds and mammals. The larva grows underneath the skin, feeding off the tissues. It remains there until it passes into its next life stage. Botfly larvae are very painful to their hosts. They can severely weaken young animals and can interfere with the daily functions of adults. Parasitism should not be confused with competition. (see Symbiosis, Mutualism, Commensalism, Competition)

Phenology

Phenology is the study of how climate effects periodic natural occurrences, such as leaf production, leaf shedding, fruiting, and flowering in plants, and migration in animals.

Photosynthesis

Photosynthesis is the chemical process whereby plants transform light energy (solar energy from the sun) into chemical energy. All living things need energy to grow and carry out their life functions and the sun is the ultimate source of this energy. Photosynthesis allows plants containing chlorophyll, the primary producers, to convert carbon dioxide and water into simple starches and sugars. These are stored in the plant material or used by the plant to grow. Photosynthesis normally occurs in the leaves of a plant. From there, the sap distributes the food energy throughout the plant. In the process, they make food for the first-order consumers, the animals that eat the plants. A by-product of photosynthesis is oxygen, a gas that is essential for life on earth. (see Primary Producer)

Pioneer Species

Pioneer species are colonizers. They are plants, animals, and microorganisms that become established and grow well in newly disturbed areas. Often, pioneer species are not able to thrive as succession or regrowth continues because there is too much competition from other species. For example, the seedlings of a tree species that first colonized an area may not be able to compete with other seedlings that are better adapted to the shade created by the pioneers. (see Succession, Secondary Forest)

Poaching

To poach is to illegally hunt, kill, collect, or capture a plant or animal. Poaching can take several forms. It is illegal to kill or collect any species protected by law, such as endangered species. It is also illegal to hunt or remove any plant or animal in protected areas like the CBWS. Laws protect some species during certain times of the year, and capturing them during this time is illegal. Animals are breeding or raising their young during "no hunting" seasons and should not be disturbed. The hunting of certain sizes or quantities of species is also sometimes illegal. For instance, hunters may be allowed to kill deer, but they are not allowed to kill as many as they want. In many cases, hunters and fishermen must purchase special licenses for their activities.

Pollination
Pollination is a necessary step in the reproduction of flowering plants. The plants are fertilized when pollen from the anthers of a flower is transferred to the pistils of either the same flower or another flower. This allows the male reproductive cells in the pollen to combine with female reproductive cells. Fruit and seeds develop after pollination and if suitable environmental conditions exist, new plants will grow. Pollen is tiny grains or spores that look like fine, yellow dust. Insects, birds, and bats are very important in the pollination of plants, as they transfer the pollen from flower to flower as they browse for nectar or pollen. Other plants are adapted for wind pollination. (see Pollinator)

Pollinator
A pollinator is an animal or other agent that moves pollen from flower to flower, aiding the reproduction of flowering plants. (see Pollination)

Pollution
Pollution is change in the environment that causes undesirable conditions. Pollution usually occurs from the human introduction of hazardous substances, but it can also result from natural occurrences such as volcanic eruptions. Substances that are not naturally occurring or do not decompose upset the balances in nature. Although some pollution is simply ugly to look at, much is deadly, affecting humans and severely disrupting natural processes. The most common sources of pollution are automobile emissions, industrial waste, human and animal waste, and agricultural chemicals.

Environmental Education

Predator
A predator is an animal that hunts and kills other animals (the prey) for food. Predation is the term given to the ecological relationship between two species where one hunts and kills the other. (see Prey)

Prehensile Tail

A prehensile tail is the tail of an animal that is equipped with the necessary muscles and reflexes to wrap around a tree branch. Animals that live in the trees often have prehensile tails, including the kinkajou, the hairy porcupine, and the howler monkey. True prehensile tails can support the animal's entire weight, allowing it to swing its body below a branch in search of food. The tail also provides animals with an extra grip so they can free their hands or feet for eating. The strong tail makes up a relatively high proportion of the body weight and is just as important to the animal as are the legs.

Preservation

Preservation is the maintenance or conservation of the natural environment. It can mean "hands off" protection for a specific area, where extraction of resources is not allowed. (see Conservation)

Prey

Prey is an animal that is hunted and killed by another animal for food. (see Predator)

Primary Forest

A primary forest is an ancient forest that has not been disturbed by any human activities such as logging or agriculture. Primary forests remain in very remote areas of Belize. However, it is difficult to determine their true nature because the ancient Maya civilizations occupied much of what is now modern-day Belize. Their activities likely had some role in the composition of the old-growth forests that remain today. (see Old-Growth Forest)

Primary Producer

Primary producers are organisms that are at the lowest trophic level, or the bottom of the food chain. Plants are primary producers that create their own food as well as food for consumers through photosynthesis. (see Consumer, Food Chain, Photosynthesis)

Rare Species

A rare species is one that is not commonly found or does not occur in large numbers. Many rare species occur in small, localized populations. Rare species are not necessarily threatened with extinction, but in many cases they are very vulnerable. Because of their small distribution, they can be easily wiped out by human disturbance. (see Endangered Species, Extinction)

Reforestation

Reforestation is the planting of trees and vegetation in areas where trees have been cut. As a conservation strategy, reforestation creates and protects wildlife habitat, prevents or halts erosion, and provides natural materials for people. The conversion of former forest area into citrus trees does not constitute reforestation because it is a permanent land use change, not an attempt to return the area to a more natural condition.

Reptiles

Reptiles are vertebrates that have dry, scaly skin. Snakes, lizards, crocodiles, and turtles are all reptiles. Reptiles originally evolved from amphibians about 300 million years ago. Unlike amphibians, reptiles are not dependent upon water to incubate and support their young. Instead, they lay tough leathery eggs that keep moisture in but also allow oxygen to reach the embryo. Some reptiles bear live young. All present-day reptiles are cold-blooded or exothermic. They require the heat of the sun to activate their bodily functions. For this reason, more types of reptiles are found in tropical areas than in cooler climates.

Sap

Sap is a liquid that carries water and nutrients through the vascular systems of plants. Water carries minerals upward from the soil into the rest of the plant, and sugars and starches created through photosynthesis are carried down from the leaves. Some saps provide food to insects and other animals; others repel them. Sticky sap oozes from the wounds of many plants to protect them from invasion by insects and microbes. Sap in some leaves is sticky enough to gum up the mouthparts of leafcutter ants. Humans have long used sap for rubber, copal, chewing gum, varnish, glue, and medicines. Sap from the water vine can quench the thirst deep in the forest.

Scavenger

A scavenger is an animal that feeds on dead animals or on refuse. Vultures are common scavengers in the CBWS. They do not kill their food but instead feed on animals that have died by other means. Many ants are also scavengers. All scavengers serve an important function in nature because they accelerate decomposition and do not allow dead animals to pollute the environment.

Environmental Education

Secondary Forest

When a forest has been cleared or otherwise disturbed, it undergoes a period of regeneration (succession) which results in a young stand of trees. Secondary forests differ in species composition from the original old-growth forests, and generally have less species diversity. After a period of hundreds of years, the forest may be close to its original state. Due to previous logging and slash and burn agriculture, some of the forest in the Cockscomb Basin is secondary forest. (see Old Growth Forest, Primary Forest, Succession)

Seed Dispersal

Plants grow seeds for the purpose of reproduction. To ensure the survival of their species, they need to disperse their seeds as widely as possible. Different plants have adapted different strategies of doing this: by wind, by water, by animals, and even by mechanical means. Seeds dispersed by wind are lightweight and often have fluffy hairs, like those of the ceiba or cotton tree, that allow them to float and glide to new locations. Others have thin, papery wings (mahogany) or flat pods (quamwood) that easily catch the breeze. Other wind-dispersed seeds are so tiny that they blow around like dust, such as orchid seeds.

Water dispersed seeds are tough or spongy and are very buoyant. Many plants that live near swamps, rivers, or other bodies of water disperse their seeds this way. One example is the water vine seed, an excellent floater. Coconuts can survive long sea journeys, a characteristic that has aided their dispersal throughout the coastal tropics. Some seeds, like those from the provision fruit, fall into a stream or river and germinate immediately. When they wash ashore, their roots are ready to take hold.

In the rainforest, animals also play a very important role in seed dispersal. The primary reason many plants produce such luscious fruits is to seduce animals into taking the seeds. Many of these plants are otherwise unpalatable or even poisonous! The animal eats the fruit and then moves away from the immediate area to disperse the seed elsewhere. Fruits with small seeds are eaten whole and the seeds are dispersed when the animal defecates. Large-seeded fruits are sometimes carried from the area. The animal finishes off the edible part and discards the seed. Animals bury some seeds for later meals but instead forget them. If the conditions are right, they can germinate and grow. Other seeds are sticky or prickly and stick to the fur of animals as they walk by, to be discarded later when the animal cleans itself. The sensitive plant is one common example. Its seeds often stick to our socks and pant legs.

Some plants have unique mechanical strategies for ensuring the survival of their offspring. Some legumes and other plants have pod fruit that burst open when ripe, allowing the seeds to scatter over a wider range than if they had simply dropped to the ground.

Slash and Burn Agriculture (see Milpa Agriculture)

Succession

Succession is a natural process of change in a community or ecosystem. After a disturbance, the species composition of an area gradually transforms and different conditions allow for different species and populations to succeed each other. Over time the area will eventually return to forest. Succession will occur after small human and natural disturbances create gaps in the canopy, such as the collapse of an old tree or the clearing of a milpa.

The first plants to colonize bare ground are small weeds like sensitive plant and grasses from seeds dispersed by animals entering the area. Taking over next are pioneer tree and shrub species like cecropia and piper that take advantage of the plentiful sunlight by growing very quickly. Other sun-loving plants are heliconia and prickly vines. Eventually other shrubs and trees grow, with many accompanying animal species. In the earlier stages epiphytes are not as common as in the surrounding forest, but become more prominent as the years go by. Diversity of species will continue to increase for many decades as the forest regenerates. If the area is not disturbed again, it will eventually become what is called a climax community, or a stable environment. This may take hundreds of years. (see Secondary Forest, Old-Growth Forest)

Symbiosis

Symbiosis is a permanent, close relationship between two organisms that belong to different species. The term symbiosis is commonly used to describe mutualistic relationships, or those that benefit both species involved. Symbiotic relationships also include commensalism, which benefits one species and has no effect upon the other, and parasitism, where one species is harmed and the other is benefited. (see Mutualism, Commensalism, Parasitism)

Territoriality

Animals practice territorial behavior when they defend a specific area, a territory, against intruders of the same species or other species. Many types of birds and mammals defend territories. Often this is accomplished by markings. Cats leave scratches and urine to show territoriality. Territories are also defended through overt aggression, such as when a hummingbird dives and swoops at other birds to drive them away from its favorite feeding areas.

Tropical Rainforest

The term tropical rainforest is often used to describe the forests of Belize. Technically the term refers to only those broadleaf, closed-canopy forests that receive immense amounts of rainfall all year round (over 500 cm a year). The forest in the CBWS has a period of drier weather from about February until May, and is thus more appropriately classified as a tropical moist forest. Precise rainfall data is not available, but the area most likely receives from 250-300 cm a year, with more rain near the mountains. Nevertheless, the species and types of ecosystems found in the CBWS are very similar to those found in true rainforests, and the entire area is commonly referred to as a rainforest area.

Understory

The understory is the layer in a mature forest that is below the canopy. It includes tree trunks, shrubs, and lower branches that provide habitat for epiphytes, shade-tolerant vines, and a wide variety of insects, birds, and small mammals, especially various rodents. In the dimly lit understory, one might meet a morpho butterfly, a thunder-and-lightning snake hunting a squirrel or a rat, or a margay searching for its dinner. Sun-loving species gain a foothold only when a gap in the canopy occurs and allows light to enter. (see Forest Layers)

Water Cycle

The water cycle involves evaporation, transpiration, respiration, condensation, precipitation and runoff. Driven by the sun's energy, water transpires from the earth's vegetation and evaporates from bodies of water, especially lakes, seas and oceans. Respiration (breathing of animals) gives off water vapor.

In the atmosphere, the water vapor condenses to form clouds. Growing heavy with tiny water droplets, the clouds eventually precipitate, returning the moisture to the earth as rain.

Some of the rain enters the soil to be used by plants; some is used by animals drinking from the streams; much is used by all the other components of the ecosystem such as insects, fungi and bacteria; and the rest soaks into ground water or runs off into creeks and rivers and into the ocean. Plants combine atmospheric carbon dioxide with water through the process of photosynthesis to make carbohydrates which are used as energy by animals and other life forms.

The water used by plants, animals and microorganisms is eventually returned to the atmosphere through transpiration, respiration and decomposition, beginning the cycle all over again.

Watershed

A watershed, or catchment, is the total area of land that feeds water into a specific river system or aquifer. Most of the hundreds of streams in the Cockscomb Basin feed into one of two river systems. Streams in the East Basin drain into South Stann Creek; streams in the West Basin drain into the Swasey Branch of the Monkey River, and a few streams in the north drain into the Sittee River. The forested areas of the Cockscomb Basin help protect these important watersheds. Acting like a sponge, the forest in the Cockscomb Basin absorbs and holds water.

Without proper management of the land upstream, a watershed can deteriorate and affect all systems downstream, including forests, agriculture, towns and villages, coastline, reef, and sea. When forest cover has been cleared, runoff from rain does not soak properly into the soil, but instead rushes into the streams and rivers, taking the soil with it. The rivers become flooded and the water becomes heavy with silt. Eventually, streams and rivers in the watershed may even dry completely. Because of the lack of vegetation, transpiration decreases and the water cycle is interrupted. The long-term result is less rainfall in the local area. In addition, development such as dams, agriculture, and mining can contaminate watersheds. Chemicals and pollutants entering the water upstream can damage both the immediate ecosystem and the systems downstream. (see Deforestation)

Wildlife
Wildlife includes any animals that are living independently of human interference. Wild animals, either captured or born in captivity, are generally not suitable for pets. The capture of some species for the pet trade (such as parrots and monkeys) has decimated wild populations. Many of these animals have a low birth rate and take a long time to recover from any kind of hunting. In some cases, parent animals are killed so that their babies can be captured. This is not fair! Keep in mind that capture of many types of animals for pets is illegal. Collection of wild plants can also threaten native populations and otherwise interfere with forest ecology.

References

Art, H. W., ed. 1993. *The Dictionary of Ecology and Environmental Science.* Henry Holt: New York, NY.

Forsythe, A. & Miata, K. 1984. *Tropical Nature: Life and Death in the Rainforests of Central and South America.* Charles Scribners Sons: New York, NY.

Hartshorn, G. et al. 1984. *Belize: Country Environmental Profile.* Robert Nicolait & Associates Ltd: Belize City.

Horwich, R. H, & Lyon. J. 1990. *A Belizean Rain Forest: The Community Baboon Sanctuary.* Orang-utan Press: Gays Mills, WI.

Janzen, D.H. (ed) 1983. *Costa Rican Natural History.* University of Chicago Press: Chicago, IL.

Kamstra, J. 1987. *An Ecological Survey of the Cockscomb Basin, Belize.* Master's Thesis. York University: Ontario, Canada.

Kricher, J. C. 1989. *A Neotropical Companion: An Introduction to the Animals, Plants and Ecosystems of the New World Tropics.* Princeton University Press: Princeton, NJ.

Newman, A. 1990. *Tropical Rainforest: A World Survey of our Most Valuable And Endangered Habitat with a Blueprint for its Survival.* Facts on File: New York, NY.

Wilson, E. O. 1990. *The Diversity of Life.* Belnap Press of Harvard University Press: Cambridge MA.

PART III

Practical Information

The original bunkhouses in the CBWS

CHAPTER 13

Tips for Visitors
Judy Lumb, Ernesto Saqui,
Katherine M. Emmons and Jan Meerman

Whether you come for a few hours, overnight, or an extended time, the Cockscomb Basin Wildlife Sanctuary (CBWS) is a wonderful place to visit. This chapter is intended to provide you with the practical information you need to make your stay an enjoyable one.

Transportation

Tours
Several reputable, licensed tour guides provide day trips or overnight tours. They provide transportation, food, and guiding services. From Dangriga contact the Pelican Beach Resort (05-22044) or from Placencia contact David Vernon (05-23207) or Wade Bevier at Rum Point Inn (05-23239). From Hopkins, contact the Jaguar Reef Lodge.

4-wheel Drive Rental
For those renting vehicles, 4-wheel drive is recommended and necessary in wet weather. Follow the Southern Highway south of Dangriga to the village of Maya Center. Stop at the gate to sign in and don't forget to look around the Craft Shop which sells the work of local artists from Maya Center and surrounding villages. Inquire about road conditions and water levels in Maya Center.

Julio Saqui's shop is just beyond the Craft Shop, your last chance to buy groceries and other supplies. Remember, there is no food in the Park! Follow the CBWS Access Road to the Headquarters. Please park in the parking lot provided.

Taxi from Dangriga
Tino's Taxi Service (05-22438) in Dangriga will, at a reasonable cost, either drop passengers in the CBWS, or he will wait for them to visit the park.

Bus Service
For the vigorous budget traveler, several public buses pass Maya Center on the Southern Highway. The daily bus service from Belize City to Punta Gorda is via Z-Line. The market buses for Placencia and Independence leave from Dangriga around midday.

There is no regular transportation from Maya Center to the CBWS, but there are several vehicles in the village. Check in Julio's shop to see if someone is available to provide transportation. You might be able to catch a ride with another visitor with a vehicle. Otherwise, be prepared to walk to the CBWS Headquarters or make other arrangements in Dangriga or Placencia.

From Maya Center it is a 10 km (6 mile) hike on the CBWS Access Road up and over the ridge and into the Cockscomb Basin. The elevation of the CBWS Headquarters is not much higher than the Southern Highway, but, as the name implies, it is a basin surrounded by higher ridges and peaks. Thus, the walk, either into the Sanctuary or back out again, includes considerable uphill stretches.

Fees

A fee of $10 BZ for international visitors and $2.50 BZ for Belizeans residents is charged for entrance into the CBWS. Tickets are sold by the Women's Craft Group at the gate in Maya Center.

Services in Maya Center

In Maya Center there are bed and breakfast accommodations and camping at the home of Aurora Garcia Saqui on the right side of the CBWS Access Road half a kilometer beyond the entrance gate. New services are being developed all the time. Inquire in the Women's Craft Shop or in Julio's shop.

Accommodations in CBWS

You must make reservations for overnight accommodations at the Belize Audubon Society (BAS) office in Belize City, 12 Fort Street (Address: P.O. Box 1001, Belize City BELIZE, Central America; Tel: 02-34987, FAX: 02-34985).

There are often large groups staying overnight during the tourist season, so you should check back to make sure there is room for your group. Remember, no food is available in the park — You must bring your own food!

If you want to request guide service and are not coming on a tour, you should make that request as a part of your reservation. Guides must be arranged for in advance.

The original overnight accommodations in the CBWS were in the buildings left from the logging camp. In 1996 the new, environmentally friendly Outlier View Dormitory was added with composting toilets, solar-powered lights and water system for washing and bathing. Rainwater is available for drinking except in the dry season. Inquire about prices with the BAS.

Cooking facilities are provided in shared kitchens, and a fire hearth for barbeques. Each kitchen has a gas stove and minimal equipment – pots and pans, utensils, plates, and cups. You must bring your own food and do your own cooking.

Camping

One hundred meters west of the CBWS Headquarters, off the Victoria Peak Path, is the main campground. It is one of the best places for bird watching in the entire area. Thatched palapas are provided for shade and rain protection. Tent platforms, picnic tables, a rainwater vat, an outdoor toilet, and a fire hearth are provided. Please do not light fires anywhere in the Sanctuary except in a fire hearth. Bring your own fuel – gathering of firewood is prohibited.

Two campgrounds are available for backpackers. Special permission is required for use of either of these campgrounds. One beautiful option is Tiger Fern Campground in the open pine ridge area of the eastern CBWS about an hour's walk from the Headquarters. Here in the open pine forest with grass and beautiful tiger ferns there is space for three tents.

The Outlier Campground is 6 km west of the CBWS Headquarters in the rolling hills on the Outlier Trail. Water is available from the creek, but must be treated before drinking. There is space for five tents. From this campsite it is only a hour's hike to the Outlier ridge.

Main CBWS Campground

Food

Most supplies can be purchased at Julio Saqui's shop just inside the gate in Maya Center. If you are staying for an extended time, you will need containers for storage of staples (rice, flour, beans, etc) that are mouse-proof and cockroach-proof. The clever CBWS mice can eat through some plastic containers. Old dry milk cans work well. Hang your food if you can, but don't be surprised if the mice win the contest.

What to bring

Food
Candles
Flashlight and batteries
Insect repellent
Mosquito net or mosquito coils
Hand lotion or other anti-itch product
Cortisone cream (for treatment of insect bites)
Triple antibiotic cream (for treatment of any open wound)
Fingernail polish (for treatment of botfly larva)
Unseasoned meat tenderizer (for treatment of stings)
Lightweight cotton long pants
Lightweight cotton long-sleeved shirt
Good hiking boots (water-proof, if possible. Some rubber boots are available for rent.)
River shoes - a pair to wear when floating the river on an inner tube or wading in the creeks

Guides

If this is your first time in a rainforest, or you find yourself wandering the trails without seeing much, it would enhance your experience tremendously to have a guide. The guides have an excellent knowledge of all aspects of the forest, including vegetation and animals, especially birds. They will point out things that you would never see. Fees range from $25 - $30 BZ.

Sanctuary wardens are fulltime employees and are not allowed to guide while on duty. However, guides are available from Maya Center. You can request a guide when you make your reservation with the BAS office; you can inquire in Julio's shop as you arrive in Maya Center; or you can ask the wardens in the Sanctuary to help you arrange for a guide. Since the guides will be coming from Maya Center especially to perform this service, they must be booked a day in advance.

Two trails require guides, the trail to the top of Victoria Peak and the one to the Outlier. Both are spectacular multi-day excursions which require advanced planning.

Insects and Other Hazards

There are a number of biting insects in the CBWS. Most are worse in wet weather and less abundant during dry weather. A few precautions will minimize your association with them. Insects are attracted by bare skin. The more you have showing, the more attractive you are to them. Wear light cotton long pants and long-sleeved shirts, and apply insect repellent to the remaining surfaces when you are on the trails. Be careful putting repellent on your face – it may sting and should not get near your eyes.

As strange as it may look, you can minimize insect bites by putting your pant legs inside your socks and keeping your shirt-tail tucked inside your pants. Another way to discourage insect bites is to use a mosquito net or to burn mosquito coils at night.

If you do get bit and start to itch, first apply lotion to sooth the area affected so you do not want to scratch. If there are blisters, swelling, or severe, persistent itching, apply cortisone cream. If the site forms an open sore, such as a popped blister, also apply antibiotic cream to avoid infection. This is not intended as medical advice, but first aid until you can get to a doctor if needed.

Mosquitoes

Mosquitoes are found near streams and peak around dusk and dawn. Although rare, malaria and dengue fever have been reported, so it is best to avoid mosquito bites. Wear long-sleeved shirts and long pants when hiking on the trails and use insect repellent. Use a mosquito net or burn mosquito coils if they are bad in the CBWS Headquarters.

Sandflies and Doctorflies

Sandflies (*Phlebotomus* species, also called "no-seeums") are tiny biting flies that are often found in the coastal areas and the cayes, but less often in the forest except in the heavy rainy season. Their bite is fierce in proportion to their size, but usually the itching goes away in a little while. In people who are sensitive to them, sandfly bites may cause a reddened area and persist for several days. They are small enough to get through screens and mosquito nets, but are repelled by burning mosquito coils.

Though it is rare, sandflies do carry a parasitic disease called cutaneous leishmaniasis, locally called "bay sore," caused by trypanosome (*Leishmania mexicana).* It has a variable incubation period from several days to a few months and is characterized by ulcerated sores.

Doctorflies are about the size of houseflies except they are flatter, longer, and have a deep yellow back. They bite softer than a horsefly, and may cause an itchy, swollen area in people who are sensitive to them.

Black Flies (botlas)

Black flies are locally called "botlas" (short for bottle-ass) because of the shape of their bodies when they are filled with blood drawn from biting. They hatch out in rushing streams, so they are increased during rainy periods. They look like harmless gnats and their bite is not felt at the time. But later you may notice small red dots of blood in the center of bites. Some people react to these bites with local swelling. Cortisone cream helps to minimize the swelling.

Ticks

Ticks can largely be avoided by staying on the trails and not wandering off into the thick vegetation. There are at least two kinds of ticks. One is black and big enough to be noticed and picked off. The other tick is called the white tick and is too small to see. They like warm places, so they crawl up your socks, under your pants and bite your legs. These itchy bites are small blisters with an area of red around them. Eventually they crust over, but often do not heal for several days. They can be mostly avoided by simply putting your pants inside your socks and keeping your shirt-tail tucked in. Cortisone cream helps to minimize the reaction.

Contact Dermatitis

A few plants cause contact dermatitis in sensitive people, like poison ivy and poison oak in the temperate zones. In the tropics there are trees called poisonwood that cause the same reaction, blisters and severe itching, but no redness. While these trees are not found in the Sanctuary, other plants may cause this reaction.

The chemical agent that initiates the reaction acts in very small amounts and, as with poison ivy and poison oak, it is possible to spread the reaction by scratching the lesion and touching your skin elsewhere. Cortisone cream is the best treatment, but apply it with care not to spread the reaction.

Botfly Larvae (Beef Worm)

The most unusual of the insect bites encountered in the CBWS is the botfly (*Dermotobia hominis,* locally called beef worm). The female botfly lays her eggs on the abdomen of a mosquito. Since mosquitoes bite warm-blooded animals, an egg may be deposited on warm skin, which triggers the hatching of the egg into a larva. The larva then burrows under the skin and grows right there. For a few days it seems like a persistent old mosquito bite until the larva contacts a nerve causing a twinge.

The larva can be killed by cutting off its oxygen with multiple layers of fingernail polish over the lesion. The first layer may begin to bubble up after a couple of minutes and should be reinforced with more layers and tape to seal it off. If you continue to feel twinges, reapply the fingernail polish. Give it a day or so and then the dead larva should be removed to avoid infection.

Bees, Wasps, Scorpions and Tarantulas

A number of kinds of stinging insects, scorpions and tarantulas all inhabit the CBWS Headquarters. However, none of these are aggressive and stings are rare. Tarantulas are harmless to humans. They are large, fuzzy spiders that are intimidating only because of their size.

First aid for any sting involves removing or destroying the toxic protein which is causing the pain. Bee sting kits are available which have a suction device to apply to the lesion. Even if you do not see anything come out, a microscopic amount of fluid may be removed which reduces the problem. You can destroy what remains with an enzyme which breaks down proteins found in meat tenderizer. Make a paste of unseasonized meat tenderizer and a small amount of water. Any sting may become much more serious if the person is allergic to the toxin. Symptoms of shock include sudden swelling and itching all over the body. This person needs immediate medical attention.

Scorpions may sting if one comes in direct contact with them. Usually this happens when the scorpion curls up in a nice warm shoe for the night and an unsuspecting human puts his or her foot inside the next morning. Shake your shoes or knock them against the floor to startle any unwanted inhabitants before putting them on!

In the unlikely event one gets stung, there is no need to panic. Unless one is allergic to them, a scorpion sting is no more serious than a bee or wasp sting. In general, the only medication needed is some antihistamine tablets. A typical sting results in the following symptoms: the sting itself is very painful, but the worst pain lasts for only a few seconds. A single stingmark may be visible and may bleed a little. The affected body part may throb, swell a little, or turn red. But the most curious effects do not show for one-half to one hour later. The mucus tissue in the mouth starts feeling numb, a sensation very similar to having novocaine in a dentist's office. Speech may be difficult and, in severe cases, there may be some difficulty walking. Although disconcerting, these symptoms subside after a couple of hours and the patient is left with another story to tell the folks back home.

Snakes

Snakes are probably the most feared thing in the forest, but actual snake attacks on people are very rare. If you follow the rules and stay on the trails, your risk of snake bite is very low. But still, you should know what to do if you see one.

When you see any snake, whether you can identify it or not, give it plenty of room. Under no circumstances should you molest the snake in any way. If you try to scare it away, it might attack you. Wait for the snake to move and, if it doesn't, change your route.

The two most poisonous snakes in the CBWS are the coral snake and the fer-de-lance. The coral snake has the most deadly venom, but is shy and only bites when handled. It is a beautiful snake with a variable number of red, yellow and black rings.

The fer-de-lance is the most dangerous snake found in the CBWS, not because it is the most poisonous, but because it is the most aggressive, the most likely to bite. It accounts for most of the deaths due to snakebites in Belize. It is light brown with black stripes forming a crossing pattern and yellow under the neck, thus the local name "yellowjaw tommygoff."

Snake bites can be a serious, life-threatening matter. If someone has been bitten, take the victim to a licensed doctor immediately. Antitoxins are available for most snake venoms.

Try not to get excited. Do not allow the person to walk. Do not cut or suck the wound, or apply a tourniquet. The person may go into shock after a bite, and should lie down with the feet slightly higher than the head, covered with a light blanket. If the victim wants water, give lukewarm, not cold, water. Watch breathing closely and give artificial respiration if necessary.

Some people are affected more severely by snake bites than others, especially small people and children. Sometimes a venomous snake injects little or no poison when it bites. Bites of some rear-fanged snakes cause only numbness or aching that subsides within an hour. However, it is best to assume any snake bite is serious and seek medical attention.

According to the Belize Audubon Society publication, *Snakes of Belize,* no swelling or darkening of the tissue occurs at the site of a coral snake bite. Coral snake venom is a neurotoxin. Possible symptoms include: irregular heartbeat and pulse rate, severe head-ache, dizziness, blurred vision, blindness, irregular breathing, difficulty in breathing, incoherent speech, stupor, mental confusion, unconsciousness, poor coordination, muscle spasms and twitching, tingling of the skin, numbness, heavy perspiration, drooling, fever, chills, vomiting, and diarrhea.

Venom from pit vipers, such as fer-de-lance or rattlesnake, is a hemorrhagic toxin that causes blackened tissue and swelling at the site of the bite almost immediately. Other symptoms include bloodshot eyes, bleeding from bite area, lips, or gums, severe pain at the site of the bite, severe headache, extreme thirst, dizziness, and nausea. Blood in urine may indicate internal bleeding.

CHAPTER 14

Tracks And Other Signs
Ernesto Saqui and Judy Lumb

Tracks

Most of the mammals that live in the Cockscomb Basin are rather elusive and difficult for the visitor to see, but tracks and other signs provide ample evidence of their presence.

Tracks are easiest to see in wet weather, but the majority of visitors come during the dry season from February to May. Even then, tracks are often visible along creeks or rivers and in the dust along the roadside. The Wari Loop with its kaway swamp is the last to dry out, so tracks may be seen there. Look in muddy sections of the trail before barging on through. The stumps on the low sections of the trails are very helpful. Stand on them and examine the soft ground. Just downstream from the picnic table at the end of the River Path there is a sand bar that many animals use. Old tracks can be seen in the water because the depressions in the lighter sand are filled with darker silt, highlighting the impressions of animals' feet.

Some other things might be confused with animal tracks. Impressions left by leaves in soft ground sometimes resemble rodent tracks. Impressions of nuts in soft ground or water drops in dust might look like impressions of the toes of wild cats. After a little experience they can easily be distinguished.

When you do see tracks, see if you can determine whether you are seeing right or left feet, forefeet or hind feet. Check the direction the animal is going and look for other tracks. You might be able to follow the animal backwards or forwards.

Sometimes animals step in their own tracks. For example, tapir tracks usually show fore and hind feet shaped the same, with three toes each. When the hind foot steps in the track of the forefoot, it gives the impression of one foot with six toes. Similarly. the hind paw tracks of running cats are often just in front of the front paw tracks, sometimes obliterating part of the front paw track.

But not all toes touch the ground. The tapir's forefeet and hind feet are not the same. The forefeet have four toes, one of which does not appear in tracks except on very soft ground, while the hind feet have only three toes.

You can also tell the age of a track. Fresh tracks have sharp edges, but as tracks age, the edges become rounded and less distinct until the track is no longer visible.

Other Signs

Other signs include feces, scratch marks and nests. The size and character of feces make it possible to identify the animal leaving it. Feces of herbivores such as deer or rodents tend to be in the form of hard pellets while those of carnivores are softer. Birds perch in the same place day after day, leaving feces on the ground below.

Jaguars leave feces to mark territory. Feces found on the road are left uncovered, but in the bush, feces are covered with leaf litter and soil, like a domestic cat's litterbox.

Jaguars and other cats leave scratch marks on trees. They may be marking territory or sharpening their claws. Tapirs leave marks on the buttresses of trees where they rub their trunks. Rodents leave scratch marks on cohune nuts when eating them.

Where they rest, jaguars and tapirs leave nests of smashed vegetation, which are especially noticeable because of their large size. Jaguars also leave areas of beaten bush where they have been rolling over, or where they have killed their prey.

Bird nests are often visible. The cups woven of twigs are seen in trees, especially around the CBWS Headquarters. Oropendola nests are large groups of hanging baskets found in tall trees along the river,

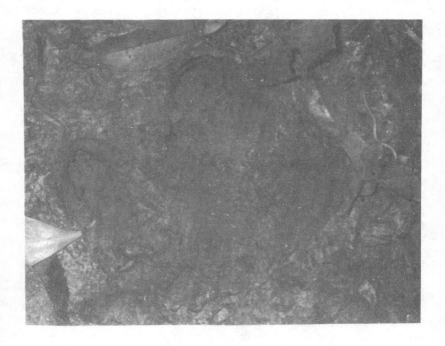

Tapir track on the Curassow Trail

usually visible from the River Path and Rubber Tree Trail. Motmots, jacamars, and other birds nest in burrows seen as holes in the banks of streams above the water line. Trogons make holes in termite nests for their own nests. Woodpecker holes in trees are often obvious. Parrots of all kinds nest in holes carved out of standing dead trees. This is yet another example showing that everything in the forest depends on everything else. Suppose campers removed these dead trees for firewood. The parrots would have no place to nest.

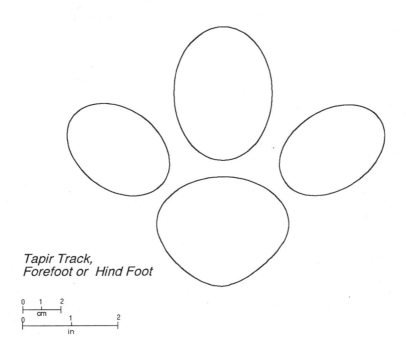

Tapir Track,
Forefoot or Hind Foot

Tapir Tracks

   The tapir tracks are the largest and easy to spot. Both forefoot and hind foot tracks show three broad toes with the entire track being 20 cm across (shown here at one-half the actual size).
   Tapirs are shy, but occasionally wander on the trails at night. This photograph (facing page) was taken on November 10, 1994, on the Curassow Trail. The tracks showed that a tapir had come from the west, walked on the River Path, through the bush to the Curassow Trail, and then along the trail for some distance, into the stream, back on the Curassow Trail, and, finally, through the bush across the River Path to the west.

Wild Cat Tracks

The tracks of cats are identified by the combination of four round toes and the foot pad. The forefeet are bigger than the hind feet and males are bigger than females of all five species. After considerable experience in the field, Alan Rabinowitz was able to determine the sex and even distinguish the tracks of individual jaguars.

The species are generally distinguished by size. Although jaguar and puma tracks are both from 8-12 cm across, they can be distinguished by shape. The jaguar track is wider than it is long, the toes of the forefeet are more widely spread than the hind ones, and the outside toe is further back than the others. Shown here are the right fore and hind feet at their actual size.

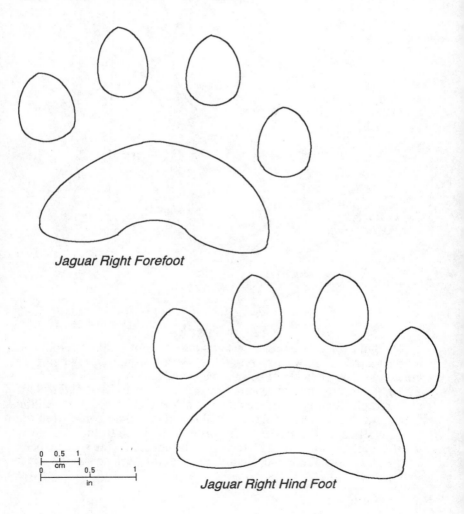

Jaguar Right Forefoot

Jaguar Right Hind Foot

The hind puma track is longer than it is wide and the toes are more spread out than on the forefeet In addition, the puma walks with its claws extended which can be seen in front of each toe. All other cats walk with claws retracted, and, therefore, not visible in the track. Ocelot tracks are 5-6 cm wide. Margay and jaguarundi tracks are 2.5-3 cm wide, distinguishable only by experts.

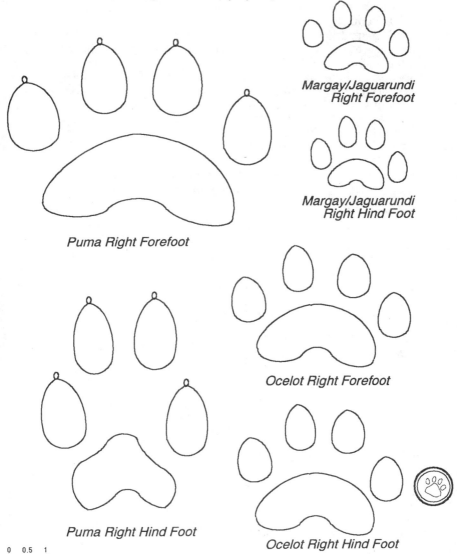

Margay/Jaguarundi Right Forefoot

Margay/Jaguarundi Right Hind Foot

Puma Right Forefoot

Ocelot Right Forefoot

Puma Right Hind Foot

Ocelot Right Hind Foot

```
0   0.5   1
|—————|
   cm
0           0.5        1
|——————————|
      in
```

Deer and Peccary Tracks

Deer and peccary all have tracks showing two toes. They are distinguishable because deer toes are parallel and closer together and the deer track is longer and narrower than the peccary's. The Central American white-tailed deer is larger than the red brocket deer, but not as large as the North American white-tailed deer. The red brocket deer is the most commonly seen on the CBWS trails. Their tracks are 2.5 x 5 cm.

Peccary tracks can be distinguished from deer tracks because the peccary toes form a "V" and are farther apart, making the tracks nearly square. The hind feet are larger than the forefeet in both species and the outside toes lead the inside toes. The two species of peccary can be distinguished both by size and form. The smaller (3-3.5 cm wide, shown here at actual size) collared peccary toes form only a slight "V" and the outside toes are only slightly ahead of the inside toes. The white-lipped peccary (wari) tracks are considerably larger (5-7 cm wide, also actual size) with an exaggerated "V" and the outside toes are quite a bit ahead of the inside toes. White-lipped peccaries are less common and generally travel in very large herds, so their presence is obvious from the trampled vegetation.

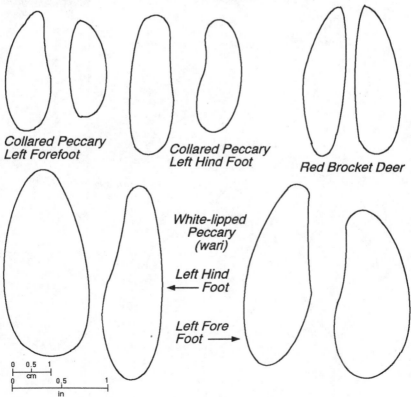

Collared Peccary Left Forefoot

Collared Peccary Left Hind Foot

Red Brocket Deer

White-lipped Peccary (wari)

Left Hind ← Foot

Left Fore Foot →

Rodent Tracks

Rodent tracks are shaped like oddly asymmetric leaves in a full impression, or show foot pads with long, pointed toes, easily distinguished from small cat tracks with their round toes. Rodents have four toes, but the outer toe does not appear on the hind foot track because it is too high to touch the ground. So, the animal will appear to have four toes on the forefeet and three on the hind feet. The two species of large rodents are distinguishable because agouti tracks are narrower (2.5 x 5 cm) while paca (gibnut) tracks are nearly 5 cm square (shown here at actual size).

*Agouti
Left Forefoot*

*Agouti
Left Hind Foot*

*Gibnut
Left Forefoot*

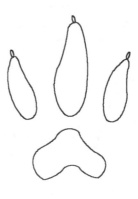

*Gibnut
Left Hind Foot*

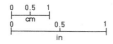

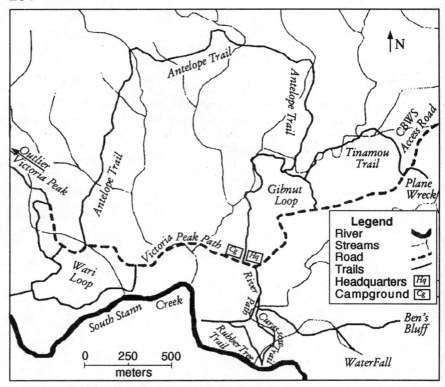

Trail System of the Cockscomb Basin Wildlife Sanctuary

Trail	Length (in km)	Difficulty	Time (est)
River Path	1.4*	Easy	30 min
Rubber Tree Trail	0.4	Easy	
Curassow Trail	0.5	Easy	
Self-Guided Loop	1.6*	Easy	1 hour
Wari Loop /Victoria Peak Path	3.7*	Easy	1.5 hours
Gibnut Loop	2.5	Moderate	
Tinamou Trail	1.0	Moderate	
Plane Wreck Trail	0.5	Moderate	
Gibnut/Tinamou Trail	4.0*	Moderate	1.5 hours
Antelope Trail	5.5*	Moderate	2.5 hours
Waterfall Trail	3.0*	Strenuous	1.2 hours
Ben's Bluff Trail	3.2*	Strenuous	1.5 hours
Outlier Trail	14.0*	Strenuous	1.5 days
Victoria Peak Trail	42.0*	Strenuous	4 days

*Round trip from CBWS Headquarters, walking time given
  Otherwise length is given of each trail from its beginning

CHAPTER 15

Trail Guides and Maps
Ernesto Saqui, Katherine M. Emmons, Dorothy Beveridge, James Beveridge, and Judy Lumb

This chapter describes the trails of the CBWS. The lengths are given as a round trip from the CBWS Headquarters. Difficulty of a trail is judged as "easy" if it is mostly level, "moderate" if there is some elevation change, and "strenuous" if the trail includes steep sections. The times are merely estimates because walking pace and time taken looking around or taking pictures varies tremendously.

Adequate footwear is needed when walking on the trails – no sandals or bare feet, please! Long-sleeved shirts, long pants, and insect repellent are recommended.

The Wildlife of Cockscomb Is Completely Protected! Please walk wisely with wildlife! Throughout the world, many species of wildlife face extinction because their habitats are being destroyed. Added to that is the severe exploitation of some species by humans. All forms of life are protected in the CBWS and visitors are not allowed to remove any plants or animals. Some visitors may be tempted to collect items to remember their time in the Cockscomb Basin. But even seeds, fruits, plants and butterflies are all protected and must remain where they are found. Instead, purchase a postcard or a book, or take some pictures. Please do not attempt to catch or interfere with any wildlife. This could hinder their basic functions, such as breeding or finding food. Likewise, species that you might find frightening or unpleasant are all important components of the Cockscomb Basin nature. Simply leave them alone!

CBWS Headquarters
We didn't feel lonely, because if you don't have music beside you, you don't need to worry. All the wonderful birds will just come and sing and you will feel merry.   —*Belizean student*

The Headquarters area holds much potential for nature study. You will be interested in the Visitor Center, of course, but there is plenty to see outside as well. Notice the vegetation and animal life around the Headquarters. Continued human disturbance in the immediate area around the Headquarters has made it quite different than the secondary forest growth surrounding it. However, the CBWS staff has to work continuously to hold back the vegetation.

A number of trees have been planted around the Headquarters area, including fruit trees, such as mango, soursop, and cashew. There is a mahogany tree that was planted by Britain's Prince Philip when he visited the CBWS in 1988 as the President of the World Wildlife Fund (see Chapter 2). Also seen is bucut, with its long leguminous pods, and tubroos or guanacaste, from which the Montezuma oropendolas call in the evening.

Leafcutter ants (wee wee ants) have created some magnificent highways across the ground and up various trees. They are fascinating to watch.

Army ants sometimes swarm like a single mass all over the ground, with an entourage of different birds in pursuit, eating up insects trying to escape from the ants. Normally, they only invade dwellings for a few hours, which afterwards are free of pests.

Butterflies are easy to find near the Headquarters. They often congregate around muddy puddles on the road. These puddles also attract frogs. After a rain, a blanket of eggs may be seen on the surface of a puddle. Soon they will hatch into tadpoles, visible only at night with flashlights.

Birds are everywhere. You can't avoid their morning chorus, so get up early and enjoy! Watch for flycatchers, seedeaters, blackbirds, and tanagers to name a few. Nests can be found in virtually every fruit tree during the dry season. Some are surprisingly accessible, so be careful. The evening is a good time to relax, sit and watch. The wide sky overhead is an excellent place to watch for other raptors, including hawks and eagles, as well as vultures.

From the helicopter pad or the campground, crested guans and toucans might be observed in the early morning. The low hoot-hoot of the blue-crowned motmot is often heard. This bird is much harder to see, but you might be rewarded with a glimpse of its colorful feathers on one of the trails. Maybe you will hear and see the laughing falcon, a beautiful bird with a human-sounding laugh.

Some of the jaguar sightings and signs have occurred right near the Headquarters. Large, noisy groups of visitors will keep them away, but if all is quiet, you may see tracks the next morning or hear them call at nightfall. Most visitors do not see a jaguar, but you may be the lucky one.

Armadillos have been spotted at the Headquarters, usually near the garbage pit. They venture forth after dark, and are disturbed by noise. Reptiles are very plentiful. Jesus Christ lizards and other smaller lizards are easily found.

Once I (Katherine Emmons) observed a harmless, but large, spotted rat snake, with a striking black and yellow pattern. It crawled above the ceiling of one of the cabins to look for resident prey. It flushed out several lizards in its search for a meal.

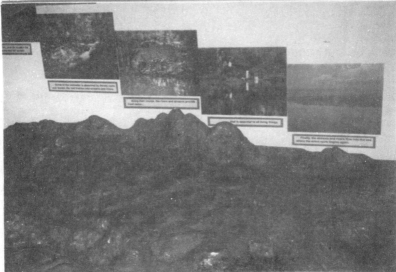

Above: *CBWS Visitor Center*
Below: *Model of the Cockscomb Basin in the Visitor Center*

The River Path

Length: <u>1.4 km</u>   Difficulty: <u>Easy</u>   Minimum Time: <u>30 min</u>

While going up the River Path you can stop along the way and listen to the different sounds that come from the different animals in the forest.   *–Belizean student*

The River Path is a pleasant, shady trail, broad enough for a fairly large group to pass comfortably. Because it leads to the Sanctuary's most popular bathing spot, it is a commonly traveled path. You can reach the river in about ten minutes, but take your time and look around.

Near the beginning of the trail are some plants that were introduced to the Cockscomb Basin by resident loggers. Most obvious are the large rubber trees. They are flourishing even though signs of the house have disappeared as the forest regenerates. **Nearby is a young negrito tree, which is native to the area and has medicinal properties.**

Picnic table next to South Stann Creek at the end of the River Path

Marker 1 originally marked a dead, but still standing ironwood tree that towered over the regenerating forest. It was a favorite perch for king vultures and many other birds. Plumbeous kites used it as a nesting site. In June of 1992 the old ironwood tree fell, so the trail guide was changed to refer to the fallen ironwood tree, which is rapidly decaying.

Notice the rather low height of much of the vegetation behind marker 2. This area was used by Maya families for milpa (slash and burn) agriculture and is in the process of regeneration. You can see remnants of domestic crops in the area, but the native vegetation is quickly taking advantage of the sunny area. Haul-back vines, heliconia, and trumpet trees (cecropia) take over first.

At the fork where the Curassow Trail goes off to the left, stop and look into the open area for birds. It is an excellent birding spot. Trogons, toucans, cotingas, jacamars and other spectacular birds are often seen at this trail intersection. Take the right fork to the River Path and notice that the vegetation begins to form a lovely canopy over the trail. Little light falls to the forest floor. As a result, this trail is more easily maintained than the trails that receive lots of sunlight where a green tangle is encouraged to grow. Every so often, one of the larger trees will fall, blocking the path and creating a gap with a sunny microclimate on the forest floor.

Stop for a moment and listen for sounds. Sometimes it will be silent, but you are likely to hear the rustle of a basilisk lizard, or the loud calling of brown jays or toucans. That momentary movement overhead may also be a squirrel or an iguana. The wildlife here is quick and elusive, but quiet observation reveals that you are definitely not alone!

If there has been a recent rain, look in the mud for tracks of peccary herds. A strong musky smell will tell you if they are actually nearby. Brocket deer (also called antelope) have similar tracks to peccary. The toes of deer tracks are somewhat sharper and they usually occur from only one or two animals because they do not travel in herds like the peccary (see Chapter 14).

Snakes can be spotted by the careful eye in the grass alongside the path. Snakes are generally very shy, and can usually feel the vibrations caused by your footsteps from some distance. Walk softly!

I (Katherine Emmons) once saw a small bird hopping madly into the middle of the path where the grass was short. Sure enough, it was being pursued by a speckled racer snake!

At The River

A close encounter with a river otter and a peaceful evening swim beneath the bribri trees watching the hummingbirds and toucans.
                                                              —U.S. visitor

South Stann Creek is an excellent place to cool off, but there is also a lot to see as well. Notice how the river ecosystem provides a different kind of wildlife habitat than the forest. The water, the forest, the riverbank, and the open space above the water surface allow for quite a diversity of life. The edge of the forest and the sunny area of the river overlap, resulting in a very dense growth of vegetation along the river banks. Trees that are found throughout the forest also grow on the riverbank, in addition to trees and plants that do best only in the riverine ecosystem. Their branches expand into the sunny gap over the river.

Lovely bribri trees shade the picnic table area, attracting a multitude of hummingbirds and nectar-eating insects, as well as bats at night. In the dry season you may see cicadas (also known as crickets or dry-weather crickets) emerging from their juvenile skins while hanging onto tree trunks and branches. The noise of the males is unmistakable and deafening.

Watch for signs of the river otters. Most commonly seen are slick mud slides on the river banks and droppings on top of rocks. The droppings are only obvious by their shape. Otherwise, they look like heaps of fish scales and broken crab shells.

Tadpoles can often be found where the water is shallow and slower-moving. Watch for tiny and medium-sized frogs and toads, often well-camouflaged in the reddish leaf litter of the small beach. A variety of fish can be observed, from tiny to huge. They are much easier to see with a diving mask, if one is available. In areas where a large amount of leaf litter has collected on the bottom, you can often find cichlids, fish that build nests and aggressively protect their eggs and hatchlings. You might also be able to identify them by their dark, striped markings.

Listen for the gurgling calls of the Montezuma oropendola. These birds usually build a nesting colony in large ceiba trees near the river. You may see dozens of hanging basket nests attended by adult birds flapping noisily back and forth.

The river area is a good place to watch other birds. Flycatchers are easy to observe, being less timid than other species. Look for nests in the trees overhanging the water.

Wearing shoes in the river is highly recommended. There are sharp rocks in many areas, and if your intention is to check out some of the more interesting things along the river, shoes are a must. Keep insect repellent at hand if you plan to spend time outside of the water. Mosquitoes and black flies are common near the river.

Self-Guided Nature Tour
Curassow and Rubber Tree Trails
Length: 2.2 km   Difficulty: Easy   Minimum Time: 1 hour

This self-guided nature tour is an excellent choice if you have time for a longer walk and also want to spend some time by the river because it also leads to the picnic table at the river. This guide is also available as a brochure for sale at the Visitor Center. Start down the River Path and take the left fork to the Curassow Trail.

1. This fallen ironwood tree (*Dialium guianense*) once emerged above the canopy before the forest was cleared for the timber camp and sawmill. Its dead branches and cavities were used by birds and bats for perching, roosting and nesting. Because ironwood is a very dense, hard wood, this log is slow to decompose.

The large, dark brown nest belongs to arboreal termites and is made from chewed wood. Termites are one of the main decomposers in the tropical forest, releasing the nutrients locked in the dead wood back to the soil to be used again.

2. This overgrown milpa (farm), an example of slash and burn subsistence agriculture, was part of a Mayan settlement abandoned in 1984. Various food plants including plantain, sugarcane, cassava and coco (elephant's ear) can still be seen. Without further disturbance this abandoned farm will become secondary forest, slowly returning to its former stature.

As you descend the steps, feel the transition to the shady, moist coolness provided by the forest. This creates a perfect environment for a rich variety of ferns and other shade-loving plants. Look carefully on your left for the large tree fern. Just past the bottom of the steps listen for the natural spring bubbling up on your right.

Notice the pretty stream on your left. This water is colder than the river water, because it has recently emerged from an underground spring. Although the fish here are smaller than in the river, otters (water dogs) have been seen fishing here. As soon as they see you, however, they make a quick and silent retreat.

3. This downed tree stump is evidence that the forest has been selectively logged, at first for mahogany (*Swietenia macrophylla*) and cedar (*Cedrela mexicana*), then later for secondary hardwoods like this nargusta (*Terminalia amazonia*) log. This stump is not completely dead and has grown some new shoots which may in time reach the canopy. Part of the log is also being returned to the soil through the decomposing action of fungi and insects. The rate of decomposition and nutrient recycling in the tropics may be up to 3-4 times faster than in northern, temperate forests.

272

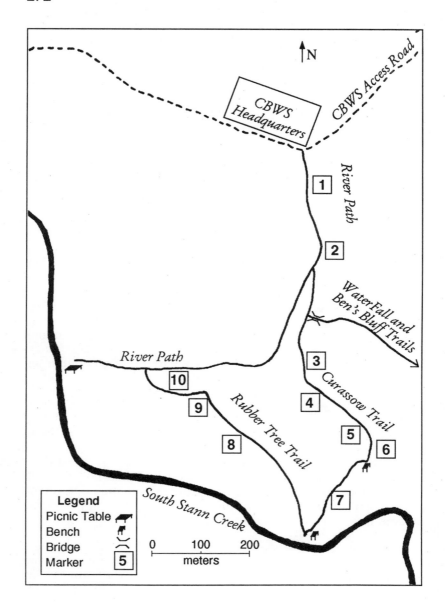

Map of the River Path, Rubber Tree Trail and Curassow Trail

4. The kaway tree (*Pterocarpus officinalis*) has large buttresses for support because its roots are shallow due to poor drainage and the concentration of soil nutrients close to the surface of the forest floor. The kaway produces thousands of small yellow flowers that are pollinated mainly by bees. The caterpillar of the magnificent blue morpho butterfly feeds off the leaves of the kaway. (An impressive kaway swamp can be seen on the Wari Loop.)

Notice the many epiphytes or air plants adorning the trunk of the kaway. Epiphytes are plants that grow on other plants for support or anchorage. They are especially adapted for obtaining their nutrients from rain water that trickles down the branches and trunk. The epiphytes at the top with the long strap-like leaves are bromeliads and are in the same family as the pineapple.

Continuing along the trail is a nice section of forest, with a variety of trees, vines, and other types of plants. This is a good place to observe the different forest layers and the decomposition on the moist forest floor. Many rainforest plants have shiny leaves with drip tips which quickly shed the water. Several trees are labeled here, including cohune palm, negrito, and mammee apple.

On your right you will see a small pond originating from the spring. This remains full during the dry season and provides a home to many small fish and aquatic insects. Look out for a mud turtle (*Kinosternon sp.*) hunting snails or fallen fruits.

As you walk further you will see a slow-moving stream on the left, wide enough to create a gap in the forest canopy. Here a lush variety of plants compete for sunlight.

Just past the handrail on your right observe the cactus-like plant with the long, spiny leaves. This is a bromeliad (*Bromelia pinguin*) that grows on the ground. The spines protect the plant from herbivores. After fruiting, the main stem dies, leaving behind small shoots which grow to mature plants.

5. Look about 5 m behind this marker for the strangler fig (*Ficus sp.*) roots engulfing the trunk of a kaway tree. Strangler figs begin as epiphytes, the seeds having been deposited by birds, bats or monkeys. They then send down clasping roots which form a network around the host tree. This eventually strangles the host tree until it dies and rots away, leaving the strangler fig standing as an independent tree.

6. The cohune palm (*Attalea cohune*) is an important component of this lowland wet forest and the largest of the Central American palms. Agouti (*Dasyprocta punctata,* local name: bush rabbit) manage to chew through the tough husk of the nuts to the coconut-like kernel inside. Many different animals also rest or nest in the fronds or cavities in rotting cohune trunks.

Local people use the fronds for roof thatching and extract oil from the kernel, which is used primarily in cooking and to heal dry skin and scalp. Charcoal made from the husk of these nuts was used during World War II to make filters for pilot's masks.

Enjoy a short rest on the bench by the creek and notice how thick the forest edge vegetation is on the opposite bank, as all of the plants compete for the bright sunlight in the opening. The long vine-like plants streaming down from the quamwood tree on your left are philodendrons, another common epiphyte in the lowland tropical forest.

7. The ceiba tree (*Ceiba pentandra*) is a forest giant reaching a height of 50 m and is found on forest margins and river sides. Like the kaway, the trunk is supported by large buttresses. Five to ten years may pass between flowerings, but one ceiba tree can produce up to 4,000 fruits, each containing 200 or more seeds. The flowers are pollinated primarily by bats but are also visited by hummingbirds, squirrels, bees, and other insects.

Kapok, the cotton-like fibers that carry the seeds away in the wind, have been used for stuffing life preservers, mattresses and cushions. The long, straight trunks are used for making dugout canoes. The word "ceiba" is thought to be an old Caribbean word for canoe. The ceiba is a sacred tree to the Maya.

Look on your left for the copal tree (*Protium copal*). This is also a sacred tree to the Maya. A resin is collected from the trunk and used as incense burned as a blessing.

When you reach the South Stann Creek overlook, the Curassow Trail merges with the Rubber Tree Trail. The river in front of you is South Stann Creek. It originates in the Cockscomb Basin and flows twelve miles to the sea, crossing the Southern Highway seven miles south of Maya Center.

The river supports a large fish population and other animals live in and near the river. The roots of the plants and trees along the river help to keep the hard rains from washing the shallow tropical soils into the river. What would happen if the trees and plants along the river were cut down?

This is a good place to spot large machaca fish. Machaca often feed on fruits and insects dropping from above so if you drop a stick into the water, they may swim over to check it out. This section of the river bed is wide, smooth, and sandy. The trail continues on the Rubber Tree Trail.

A few meters on your left is a slightly cleared space rapidly being reclaimed by the forest. It was the site of the acclimation cage where Harold's troop of black howler monkeys (*Alouatta pigra*) was

The intersection of the Curassow Trail and the Rubber Tree Trail

released in 1992. This was part of the reintroduction project (see Chapter 7). This site was chosen for the presence of many food trees. In addition, monkeys are reluctant to cross the nearby river, which makes locating and tracking them after their release much easier. Harold's troop still lives in this area. Look up in the tall trees for them.

One of their favorite fruits is the mammee apple (*Calocarpum mammosum*), so this cage was located near a young tree. It grows to 20 m and the wood is excellent for construction. However, because people also enjoy the fruit, the tree is rarely cut down. Nearby, cohune palms bear large bundles of nuts. Waris (white-lipped peccaries) chew the nuts and eat the inner husks. Large herds of waris pass through the forest when the cohune nuts are falling in December or January. You may see the trampled areas where they have foraged, or, perhaps hear the herd passing.

8. Notice the well-developed buttressed roots on this quamwood tree (*Schizolobium parahybum*). The quamwood is one of the most common tall trees of the Cockscomb Basin.

The quamwood drops its small, fine leaflets during the early dry season (February to March) and produces thousands of bright yellow flowers which attract huge numbers of bees and hummingbird pollinators. Each flower develops into a thin, black pod containing many seeds so that the total output of seeds is tremendous. Look for the flowers, leaves and seed pods on the forest floor. The quamwood is too soft to be used for lumber.

You are now entering a younger forest. This area was a farm abandoned about 5 years earlier than the one you saw at marker 2. Thus, the forest here is in a later stage of recovery.

9. The rubber tree (*Castilla elastica*) was once the main source of commercial rubber, but has now been replaced by man-made synthetics. The ancient Maya used the rubber for making balls for their games. Mayans today still use the rubber to make bags and for waterproofing garments.

10. In front of you is a patch of heliconia plants. These plants grow along streams, banks of rivers and other areas of bright sunlight. This is an indicator that this section of forest has been disturbed and is the process of regeneration. As the trees grow taller and shade increases, heliconia and other small sun-loving plants will become fewer.

Heliconias have striking red and yellow flowers. They are pollinated by hummingbirds. Their fruits are swallowed and the seeds dispersed by many other birds. The caterpillar of the owl butterfly, one of the largest in the world, feeds on the heliconia leaves. People use the leaves for coverings and for wrapping food.

On the trails and on the grounds of the Headquarters, look for bare trails which have been cleared by leafcutter ants, locally called wee wee. They transport freshly cut leaf pieces back to their underground nests which contain up to 5 million workers. They use the leaves to cultivate a fungus which they eat. Their large dirt-pile nests are hard to miss, and from them radiate highways in every direction. If you look closely at the ants you will see three sizes: large soldiers, medium workers, and tiny helpers, each with their own tasks.

The Rubber Tree Trail will now bring you to the River Path again. Turning left, it is only 100 meters to a picnic table by the river under the shade of bribri trees, a perfect place to have lunch and enjoy a refreshing swim. Turning right, it is a short walk up the grassy River Path to the CBWS Headquarters.

A River Float

Distance: <u>1 km</u>   Difficulty: <u>Easy</u>   Minimum Time: <u>1 hour</u>

Most of all, I liked the float down the river. At first I was scared but I got over it.   *–Belizean student*

The river float is a high point for many visitors. However, to ensure maximum safety and success, please consider the following:

Do not go if the river is high and swift.
Check with staff to see if it is safe, especially during the rainy season.
This activity is not recommended for children under 15 years of age unless they are good swimmers and are well-supervised.
Wearing shoes in the river is very important. The water can be low at times, and walking in shallow areas is a necessity.
Wearing long-sleeved shirts will protect you against insects.

Rent your tubes from the wardens and head to the River Overlook by way of the Victoria Peak Path and the Wari Loop. Carefully climb down the bank and hop on your tube. There is a lot to see on the river float. It is an excellent way to spot birds and an occasional mammal because you can keep very quiet while floating.

The vegetation forms a dense wall along the riverbank, its foliage providing cover for animals, and its fruits and flowers providing them with dinner. The early evening is a good time for a river float, because there is quite a lot of activity from birds and fish. During the early logging years, the timber resources of the area were floated down the river to the coast when the water was high.

Watch for kiskadees and other flycatchers swooping over the river. They sit on tree branches until they see a mosquito or other tasty morsel. Their nests are also often seen on tree branches over the river. Some even build nests hidden within driftwood clusters on temporary islands. This offers some safety from predators. Kingfishers are seen perching on nearby trees, or as they skim along, only inches from the river surface. They nest in holes in the muddy river bank. Herons and egrets can be spotted if you are quiet, but they will take off as you approach.

Hummingbirds of all shapes and sizes are easy to see on a river float. They are particularly attracted to the bribri blossoms that hang over the river and you can float right under them as they buzz about. Easily identified are the long-tailed hermit and the little hermit, but you may also spot a violet sabrewing or a rufous-tailed hummingbird.

As you float around the first bend, you will come to a shallow area. Even if the river is high enough to float on through, it is worth a stop to check the small sand beach on the left for jaguar, ocelot or otter tracks.

Be very careful a little farther on where most of the water runs to the left, and a little bit runs to the right. After a shallow section, the left fork becomes very swift and deep. Experienced floaters will probably enjoy this section, but others might become frightened. Pull up on the small beach to the right to look for tracks. This is also a good place to sit and watch the birds or perhaps even an otter. Toucans are often seen here.

About ten minutes into the float, you pass through a section with several large boulders. Can you see any otter droppings on the rocks? They look like heaps of fish scales and crab shells.

Beyond the boulders, look for a lovely strangler fig tree on the right. Its host tree, a cohune palm, is still living, and the crowns of both trees are visible. If you are lucky enough to be there when the strangler fig tree bears fruit in the Spring, hordes of large machaca fish wait below to swallow the fruits that drop. The small, sweet figs turn purple-black when they are ripe. They are also shaken down by feeding birds in the branches. You may see crested guans, chachalacas, toucans or olive-fronted parakeets that are also attracted to the fruits.

After the strangler fig, pay close attention to the river because it makes a fork. It is best to take the slow, shallow route on the right unless you have checked out the left fork already. It has a large tree branch that hangs low all the way across the water. At low water levels it is hard to get under and at higher levels the swift water may take you straight into the tree.

After that, you reach a lovely open section with more large boulders. Watch for the picnic table just beyond, it's time to get out! If you float farther, keep in mind you will have to walk back upriver, which can be quite difficult. It is not advisable if water is high.

South Stann Creek at the end of the river float

The Gibnut Loop and Tinamou Trail

Distance: <u>4.0 km</u>   Difficulty: <u>Moderate</u>   Minimum Time: <u>1 1/2 hours</u>

I finally found paradise...The colourful birds and butterflies and flowers. The proud hawk and gleaming insects! The scent of the forest, a feeling of peace.   *–Danish visitor*

The Gibnut Loop is a delightful relaxing walk that in part overlooks a pretty stream. Starting out by the Visitor Center, the trail is open and sunny. It is a good place to look for butterflies. The area is slowly regenerating after being cleared for milpa and logging.

A roadside hawk is often perched on a branch at the forest edge. He may call out a warning of your approach. Leaving the bright sun for the cool forest shade feels wonderful. As your eyes adjust, you may notice a gully through the trees on the left. Gullies like these are carved out during the rainy season, and often remain wet and muddy in the dry season. Blue-crowned motmots dig their burrows in the banks. Listen for their low "hoot hoot," especially at dawn and dusk. They are much harder to see under the forest cover because they sit very still.

As you descend the first set of steps, you may notice the red lady's lips flowers. The yellow part is actually the flower, and the seeds are bright blue. After the second set of steps there are beautiful buttress roots on the path. In wet times, they form small pools, with small fish. As they slowly dry out, the fish become stranded. You might also notice a nearby patch of *Spathiphyllum* plants, which are related to philodendrons. They have strongly scented white flowers.

The trail passes a wide, slow-moving section of the stream. In May of 1992 the first troop of translocated black howler monkeys, called Chuck's troop, was released here (see Chapter 7). The zoologists then returned to the Community Baboon Sanctuary for two more troops, released that year on the Tinamou and Rubber Tree Trails. The project continued for two more years, releasing a total of 62 monkeys.

Chuck's troop consisted of a male, two females, and an infant. The troop split up. The male wandered far out of the Sanctuary and was shot a year later. The two females joined two newly formed troops, one of which still occupies this area (as of May of 1995).

The small fruits of the carbonwood tree fall open on the trail, with a faint sweet smell and bright red insides. You may notice many trees on the Gibnut Loop marked with small, numbered disks. Please leave them there! These trees are part of a phenology study conducted by the CBWS staff. Every week or so, wardens take along charts and binoculars to determine the changes in leaves, flowers, and fruits. This type of study is important in determining food sources for the translocated monkeys. Trees like the wild custard apple, negrito and craboo are studied.

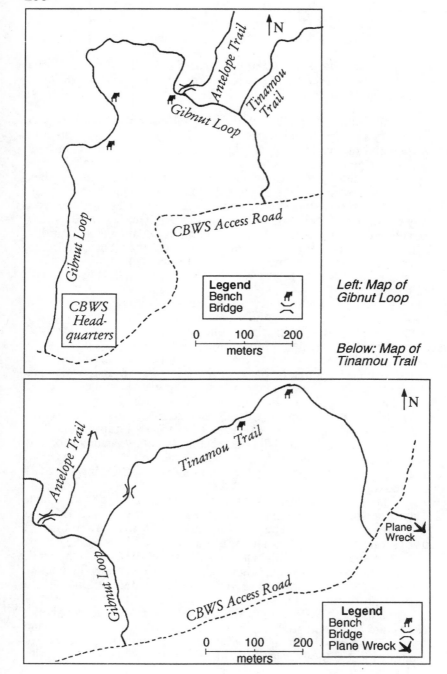

Legend
Bench
Bridge

0   100   200
meters

Left: Map of Gibnut Loop

Below: Map of Tinamou Trail

CBWS Access Road

CBWS Headquarters

Gibnut Loop

Antelope Trail

Tinamou Trail

N

Legend
Bench
Bridge
Plane Wreck

Plane Wreck

0   100   200
meters

The bridge at the intersection of the Antelope Trail and the Gibnut Loop

The trail continues along a lovely section of the stream. You will see examples of climbing philodendrons and trees with prop roots, along with a variety of other trees and shrubs that line the stream. Otters have been spotted in the stream, but whether you see one or not, take advantage of the picturesque places to stop and relax. Although it is hard to spot animal life in the forest, one can certainly sense living things all around when sitting quietly.

A very pleasant place to sit is on the bridge that connects the Gibnut Loop with the Antelope Trail. The bridge offers a beautiful view of the stream and surrounding vegetation. You may hear the repeated hooting of a ruddy ground-dove along with the sound of many other birds that may be difficult to see, perhaps an oriole or a woodcreeper. Any minute they may be drowned out by the loudest insects of all, the cicadas.

You will soon reach the entrance to the Tinamou Trail to the left. Continuing on the Gibnut Loop to the right will take you to the road and the CBWS Headquarters.

When the Tinamou Trail was cut, a nest of bright blue tinamou eggs was found. The great tinamou's shrill calls can be heard every evening in the CBWS. If you see a smallish, chicken-like bird running a few yards ahead of you along the trail, it is probably a slaty-breasted tinamou or a little tinamou.

The trail continues to follow the stream, at times along a sharp drop-off. You may spot various hummingbirds swooping in and out. You might see delicate, long white blossoms littering the path. The shape, color and sweet scent of these flowers attract nectar-drinking bats.

The great curassow eats fruits and seeds, and feeds wherever they can find food, whether it is on the ground, on low branches, or in the canopy. The curassows are more quiet than the crested guans and chachalacas and are thus less noticeable.

Eventually the trail comes out onto the CBWS Access Road. Your walk is not yet over. The road is an excellent place to spot jaguar tracks, provided there has not been too much traffic. These cats use the road and the maintained trails. Because parts of the road are dusty, it is one of the few good places to look for tracks when fresh mud is hard to find.

Do you see any long, brown and very fuzzy seed pods? These belong to the balsa tree. It is a fast-growing species often found in secondary forest. Plumbeous kites nest in a tree alongside the road. You may also come across a friendly snake or a troop of coatis. A typical dilemma at the CBWS, it is hard to decide whether to look up or down. While watching leafcutter ants on the ground, you may miss the king vulture overhead!

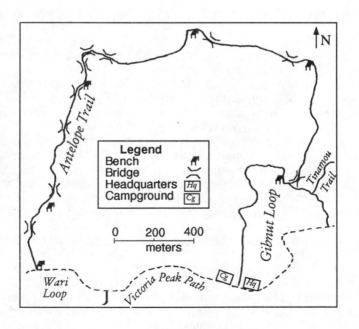

Map of Antelope Trail

The Antelope Trail
Length: <u>5. 5 km</u>   Difficulty: <u>Moderate</u>   Minimum time: <u>2 1/2 hours</u>

*The lovely stream will inspire artists and photographers.   It is also a
great place to cool off.*   *–South African visitor*

The Antelope Trail is named after the animal otherwise know as
the red brocket deer. Some sections of the trail are steep, but overall
the trail is not too difficult. However, a refreshing stop at the stream
will certainly make your hike worthwhile. It is best to start from the
Victoria Peak Path, because it can be hot coming back that way after
a long, tiring walk. Going this direction you return to the Headquarters by way of the shady Gibnut Loop.

The first part of the trail is relatively flat, and you walk among
some rather young trees, such as nargusta. The trees with little knobs
or spines on the trunk are perhaps young ceiba trees, or a tree
commonly called prickly yellow. Maybe you will spot a young,
spiny, climbing palm tree. This unusual plant (also known as the
basket tietie) can grow to be the longest plant in the forest and drapes
throughout the canopy. The rustling noise nearby may have been a
tayra (bush dog) or an iguana. A strong smell means it was probably
a peccary.

The mature cohune palm bears large clusters of small, stiff
flowers that are invaded (and pollinated) by bees – sometimes so
many bees that they cause flowers to rain down on top of your head!

Have you noticed the nests of the tree-dwelling termites? These
industrious creatures work fast to repair their nests whenever
damaged by their primary predator, the tamandua (antsbear). What
looks like an old nest that has fallen off a tree may be currently in
use. The termites simply vacate the damaged parts and seal them off
from the usable area.

You will cross several small streams before you come to a
larger stream, between two steep banks. There are some beautiful
emergent trees nearby, with large buttress roots. This stream is
lovely, and there are several small pools where you can cool off. One
can easily imagine a jaguar climbing on the mossy rocks for a drink.
A bit downstream from the trail is a large rocky overhang, a cool
place to sit and rest. The pools have crabs and a variety of fish,
including catfish. You may see small, voracious fish, called billums,
clustering around your shadow, hoping you will drop something
edible into the water. No matter how remote these little fish are, they
soon learn to expect food from you. This is because so much of their
diet (fruit, insects, and so on) drops from overhead. They will also
nibble on you!

Beyond the stream, there is a bit of a climb to the top of the next
hill. You will continue to see examples of prop roots, and lianas.
Lianas often start out growing like small trees until they find a host to

grow on. They look like a pale green stem with hardly any leaves, shooting up almost overnight, perhaps to take advantage of some transitory sunlight. Notice the roots that hang from the climbing philodendrons. They are extremely strong and flexible, and sometimes people collect them to use as rope. There is also a good chance you will come across a forest gap. It will be noticeable by the sun streaming through a hole in the canopy caused by a fallen tree. It will soon be filled with new growth, competing for sunlight. As along all the trails, there is a continuous carpet of leaf litter on the ground. However, it is usually not a thick carpet, because decomposition so quickly breaks down the leaves and allows their nutrients to be cycled back into the living plants of the forest.

The Antelope Trail is a good place to look for small birds, such as woodcreepers, thrushes and manakins, along with migratory species, such as warblers. Again, the birds are often easier to hear than to see. Many of them blend in very well with the forest surroundings, and others emerge as quick flashes of color. Woodpeckers are often heard drumming on the trunks of trees.

The log bridge marks the end of the Antelope Trail where it intersects with the Gibnut Loop. Either direction is about the same distance to the CBWS Headquarters.

Waterfall Trail

Length: 3.0 km   Difficulty: Strenuous   Minimum time: 1.2 hours

It is wonderful to go way to the top where the water is coming down.
It is as clear as a crystal, and you can bathe in the water if you wish.
—Belizean Student

If you have time, a hike to the waterfall is a must. It might be hard to get excited about the hot, steep walk, but think only of the cool reward that awaits you at the end. Take water and a snack, and leave some time for swimming and relaxing.

Starting on the Curassow trail, cross the bridge to the left after you reach the bottom of the steps. The forest contains small, slim trees and the trail is level and spongy. At night, this leaf litter becomes the byway of the elusive coral snake. You are not likely to see one of these beautiful (and deadly) creatures either in the day or night, but if you do, do not disturb it.

This trail is an excellent place to listen for the amazing sounds of the tiny red-capped manakin. The male makes a very loud snapping sound as a part of his courtship dance. Try to get a glimpse of him!

The trail passes the stream, and you see a signpost directing hikers to the left up Ben's Bluff. This is where the Waterfall Trail begins to climb. The original trail was quite steep, but a new trail with switch-backs was cut later. Please do not take short-cuts as this can hasten erosion and discourage the vegetation from growing. Proceed carefully because the slopes may be slippery. From the bench you have a very nice view of the steep creek bed. Make a careful descent to the falls. It is very slippery, so handrails have been installed to help your descent.

The six-meter falls and pool are a real treat! The water is much cooler than the river water and is quite refreshing after the hike. The waterfall pool has some deep places to avoid if you do not swim. A small path at the top of the railing leads to the top of the waterfall where there are small, pretty pools. Do not try to climb below the waterfall because it is too dangerous – steep, slippery and rocky.

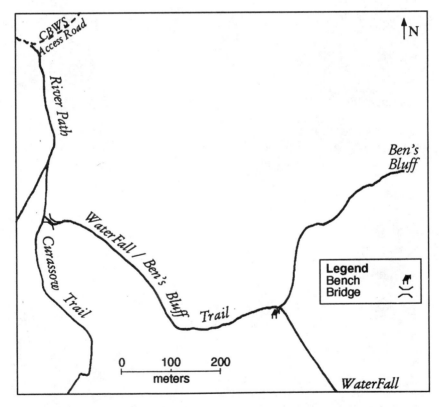

Map of the Waterfall and Ben's Bluff Trails
(Note: This map is not as accurate as the others because these trails have not been mapped in detail.)

Above: *The Waterfall*
Below: *The view from Ben's Bluff*

Ben's Bluff Trail

Length: <u>5.5 km</u>   Difficulty: <u>Strenuous</u>   Minimum time: 1.5 hour

I went to Ben's Bluff, which was very exciting. When I reached –
Wow! What a view! I could see the rainforest, which was green and
pretty.   *–Belizean Student*

Ben's Bluff is named after Ben Nottingham, who assisted Alan Rabinowitz in his studies of jaguars. They often climbed to the top of this hill to use hand-held antennas to locate the jaguars that had been captured and fitted with radio collars.

This is an excellent trail to examine the transition between the rainforest ecosystem and the pine forest ecosystem. From the top you see the surrounding hills and mountains, a visual reminder of why the area is called the Cockscomb Basin.

To start up Ben's Bluff, make a left off the Waterfall Trail and cross the stream. As you ascend, you will see pretty give-and-take palm trees with fan-like leaves. Climbing higher, you will notice the prehistoric-looking tree ferns. Tree ferns are not as strong as trees, so they don't make good hand-holds.

Luckily there are several benches on the way up. As you rest, you can thank the group of the Belize Youth Conservation Corps who first built these benches in 1991. As does everything in this forest, they rot rather quickly, and have to be replaced every few years.

On this climb, you might notice some bright red and black seeds that sometimes fall on the path. They are from some unseen legume overhead and are about the size of peas, larger than similar seeds that are often used to make necklaces.

When you notice a break in the canopy, you will have just passed through a narrow overlap zone between the broad-leaved rainforest and the pine forest ecosystems. In this narrow area, you will find species that belong to both systems. Beyond the overlap zone the air is drier, and the ridge is covered with a carpet of ferns, interspersed with shrubs and Caribbean pine, allowing for a relatively unobstructed view of the Basin. The trail is steep and rocky, but you are not yet done with your climb.

From the top you can look out on the entire Cockscomb Basin below, including the Headquarters area, the Outlier a bit to the right, and the Cockscomb Range with Victoria Peak in the distance. You can make out the path of the river by noticing the difference in vegetation along the Basin. If the quamwood is blooming, it is a beautiful sight with bright splotches of yellow throughout the Basin. There is a good chance that you will see vultures soaring below and other birds of prey (raptors).

The Wari Loop
Length: <u>3.7 km</u>   Difficulty: <u>Easy</u>   Minimum Time: <u>1.5 hours</u>

The kaway swamp on the Wari Loop is a very spiritual place, almost like a cathedral.   *— U.S. Visitor*

There are lots of mosquitoes on the Wari Loop, so be prepared for them. On your way to the Wari Loop turnoff, the Victoria Peak Path crosses two small streams and passes through a large stand of wild cane. Be careful of the sprouts. The tip is as sharp as a spear; you wouldn't want to fall on one. Once they sprout leaves, they are no longer dangerous. Here, the cane invades the old logging road which was passable by four-wheel drive until 1985. The CBWS wardens have to work hard to keep the path mowed.

This is an excellent place to look for butterflies, as they congregate around the flowers of sun-loving plants. Blue morpho butterflies are unmistakable when flying, but well-camouflaged when still. You might see a very fuzzy brown caterpillar feeding on a shrub along the path. Although soft and harmless-looking, these fuzzy hairs are capable of delivering quite a sting.

Turn off onto the Wari Loop and pass the River Overlook. As you continue, notice the dark shade offered by the forest. After a few more yards, there is an unmarked path that leads to the river. Nearby, under some shrubs, agouti burrows have been seen. A large tree on the bank has served as a shelter for a margay (tigercat). If one currently inhabits the tree, you might see its droppings nearby or in the hollow. From the riverbank, fish are easily spotted.

Back on the main path, look for disturbed leaf litter under the branches of shrubs. Peccaries hunt among them with their snouts for roots, seeds and fruits. If it is muddy, you may also spot their tracks.

Farther on the left, there is an oxbow pond that was once part of the river. During a flood, the river took a shortcut and carved out a new riverbed, leaving a few deep areas in the old river bed where water still collects. Boat-billed herons often nest here. Please be extremely quiet as you watch and do not disturb them. You may also spot other herons or egrets at the pond.

The Wari Loop is an excellent place to find jaguar tracks and other signs, such as scratch marks. When you pass a muddy spot, keep your eyes glued to the ground. You don't want to miss any jaguar tracks that might be there. If you see fresh scratch marks on trees, it means that a jaguar has been marking its territory, and you are standing in it!

A little farther on the left is another pond with beautiful water vines (water tietie), bromeliads, orchids and beautiful vines such as *Monstera* hanging on nearby trees. Look for frogs and turtles. If you are very lucky you might see a trogon sitting motionless on a branch.

Above: Bridge on Wari Loop
Below: Kaway swamp on Wari Loop

As the trail bends to the right, you continue straight just a few steps and find yourself in a beautiful kaway swamp. In the rainy season, it is favored by frogs and tapirs. These trees need a habitat that is periodically flooded. The swamp sometimes dries out at the end of the dry season, leaving watermarks on the buttress roots of the trees.

Gigantic water vines drape from one tree to another like a huge swing, about 25 cm in diameter. They may eventually drag several trees to the ground, forming a gap in the canopy and allowing light to reach new seedlings. These water vines are legumes and bear large, brown seed pods with hollows for several seeds. The seeds are beautifully smooth and dark brown, about one cm across. They are well-suited for a wet environment, because they float. This helps in their dispersal when the area is flooded. On the vines and tree trunks grow hundreds of epiphytes. Look for orchid flowers, bromeliads, and small creatures living among the epiphytes. You may see a blue morpho butterfly, an unforgettable sight.

Not far is a small stream, with a pleasant overlook from the bridge. Look out for the small but spiny pokenoboy palm. Never grab a tree without looking first, it might hurt! Notice the majestic quamwood trees above your head. They have large fern-like leaves with small pinnate leaflets. In February the forest blooms with their bright yellow flowers. Crested guans often forage in their crowns. After the flowers drop, flat tear-drop pods form, which are enjoyed by birds, including parrots and scarlet macaws. When you reach the open Victoria Peak Path, it is a 15-minute walk to the Headquarters.

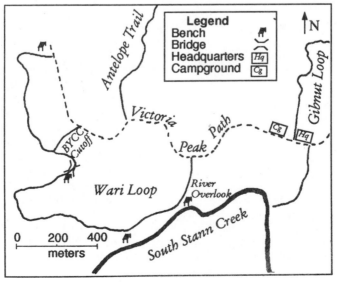

Map of Wari Loop

The Outlier as seen from Ben's Bluff

Outlier Trail

Length: <u>14 km</u> Difficulty: <u>Strenuous</u> Minimum Time: <u>10 hours</u>
(overnight recommended)

Compared to the mountains of Scotland, this is neither rugged nor high, but the tropical heat and humidity make it a hefty hike, and the view is awe-inspiring. — *Scottish Visitor*

There are three trails to high vantage points with excellent views of the Cockscomb Basin, Ben's Bluff (250 m), the Outlier (500 m), and Victoria Peak (1120 m). The Outlier Trail was constructed in April of 1995 by Raleigh International, a UK charity aimed at developing young people by involving them in conservation and community projects worldwide.

The trail is strenuous, and a guide is required for anyone wanting to make this climb. It is only advisable in dry weather, that is, from March through May. But this hard climb to the ridge of the northern rim of the Cockscomb Basin at 500 m is well worth the effort for those who wish to stand in awe at the splendid view over the whole of the Cockscomb Basin. It allows the opportunity to get off the beaten track into some of the most beautiful forest in the Cockscomb Basin.

From the CBWS Visitor Center, follow the Victoria Peak Path for 4 km. This trail was once a logging road. You will cross several recently constructed footbridges along the way.

After 4 km, a sign indicates a right turn to the Outlier. Follow this into the dense forest. The path is flat for approximately 1 km and then rises steeply, crossing several small streams. Yellow directional arrows mark the route.

A campsite is located approximately 2 km from the Victoria Peak Path turnoff. It is then a 45-minute climb to the viewpoint. The ridge has been cleared, offering a view both of the Cockscomb Basin and the northern slope of the Cockscomb Range.

Victoria Peak Trail
Length: <u>42 km</u>   Difficulty: <u>Strenuous</u>   Minimum Time: <u>4 days</u>

I was clinging to the rock face for dear life, but then I saw the little yellow flowers in the crevices. From the top, the rainforest stretches out as far as the eye can see with no signs of human habitation.
— *U. S. Visitor*

The Victoria Peak Trail leads to the second highest point in the country of Belize, a peak of 1120 m. This is a strenuous climb and you must hire a local guide. It is only advisable to climb Victoria Peak in dry weather (from March through May). While it is not a technical climb from a mountain climber's point of view, the heat, humidity and likelihood of rain even during dry weather make it difficult, even for those in good physical condition. A description is provided here to help the visitor decide if they want to hire a guide and take time to make this climb.

The first day's hike is relatively flat, following an old logging road. From the CBWS Headquarters follow the Victoria Peak Path on past the turnoff to the Outlier. The first primitive campsite is beside a beautiful river. Remember, these are not developed, level campsites, but merely places in the forest where it is feasible to pitch a tent.

On the second day the trail begins climbing. The steep up and down sections are quite strenuous like those on the Ben's Bluff Trail, except a whole day of it. If it happens to rain, the clay slopes become extremely slippery. The trail crosses many streams, some cascading. A small waterfall makes a lovely lunch site.

Although it is difficult to see through the dense forest, the guides will point out many things you might miss, such as scarlet macaws, king vultures, trogons, tapir tracks, or jaguar scratches on trees. Immense mahogany stumps are evidence of early logging operations. But during the second day the trail gets into primary forest, areas that the loggers never reached. This, in itself, is reason to take this hike. The campsite for the second night is in a glen at the base of Victoria Peak.

The third day is the climb up to Victoria Peak. The trail follows a dry streambed which is steep and rocky. The vegetation changes to elfin scrub as you climb above tree level.

The next section is a climb up a rock face with hand and foot holds in crevices of the rock to a level space. After this reprieve is another rock face, this one too steep to climb without assistance. There is a rope which the guides have secured and tested. For those brave enough to look around in the midst of this climb, there are flowers growing in the crevices in the rock and an excellent view of the valley below.

The trail then switches back and forth, climbing a steep slope with grass growing higher than 2 m. Another extremely steep ascent has a ladder made of tree branches and a rope for assistance. From the top of the ladder, the last ascent to the peak is around a boulder on the last outcrop, with tree roots for support.

The peak is covered in moss, a thick, deep moss with several different species, some coarse, some soft. On the established trail the moss is beaten down, but if you venture off the path, you could sink far down into the moss.

On a clear day, you can see all around, on all sides. You can see all the way to the ocean, over the whole Basin, and to the west and north, as well. There are no signs of human habitation, except for smoke from fires, since the dry season is the time that the fields are burned. You can see emergent trees towering out of the canopy. Whatever trees are in bloom are easily seen. This is how mahogany was found by loggers because the buff blossoms on the tall trees were obvious from any vantage point. It is extremely impressive because it is green, different shades of green, as far as you can see.

Tiger Fern Trail

The new Tiger Fern Trail and Campground were developed in 1996, too late to be included in these trail maps. The Trail starts from the south side of the CBWS Access Road a few minutes walk from the Headquarters. It begins level and stays that way for about a kilometer while crossing two creeks (or one creek twice). Then the trail becomes gradually steeper. Two benches provide rest breaks for the last half-kilometer climb to the top. The top is covered in tiger ferns with some pine and other trees, but not enough to spoil the view of the Cockscomb Basin and the Cockscomb Range, including Victoria Peak and the Outlier. It is three km from the start of the trail to the top, or six and a half km round trip from the Headquarters. Permission must be obtained for overnight use of the Tiger Fern Campground.

A Night Walk

Everything is different in the forest at night, the activity, the smells, the sounds. I loved turning off my flashlight and imagining the animals making all those splashes in the river.   — U.S. Visitor

The best reason for staying overnight in the CBWS is to take a night walk. The majority of the mammals in the CBWS are nocturnal, active at night. Of the cats, only the puma and jaguarundi are diurnal, active in the daytime. Jaguar, ocelot and margay all hunt at night. To improve one's chances of seeing a wild cat and experience this other dimension of the forest, night walks are highly recommended.

A fear of snakes is usually what keeps people from venturing out at night. To some extent it is justified because many snakes are active at night. But remember that snakes have no ambition to go out and bite people. When they sense you are near, most snakes will disappear quickly. It is a rare treat to get a close look at one. If you are vigilant and lucky, you may get a glimpse of a coral snake crossing the path ahead of you.

The only really dangerous snake is the fer-de-lance. Though it is not as poisonous as the coral snake, it is aggressive. If you see one, or any snake you cannot identify, do not molest it in any way. Do not poke at it, try to kill it, or throw anything at it. Aggressive snakes can move very fast and attack very quickly. Back off and give it some room. If the snake is blocking your way, choose another route.

Wear good, solid shoes with socks. Do not go with bare feet or sandals, please! Wear long pants and a long-sleeved shirt. Take extra flashlights and extra batteries for each flashlight. You don't have to use them all at once, but you don't want to get caught out in the jungle without a light.

Choose a trail you have been on before so you will be familiar with the terrain and major obstacles. One excellent route for a night walk is the River Path. For a longer walk, take the Curassow - Rubber Tree - River Path Loop. The Tinamou Trail, Gibnut Loop and Wari Loop are also good choices. Another option is to walk down the entrance road. The Antelope Trail is too long and the Waterfall and Ben's Bluff Trails are too steep for night hikes.

Any time of the night works well for a night walk. You can go out just before dusk and walk back in the dark; you can take the entire walk in the dark; or you can go out early in the morning and wait for dawn. Choose your route according to the conditions. On a bright, moonlit night, one of the trails under the canopy, such as the Rubber Tree Trail, Curassow Trail, Gibnut Loop or Wari Loop, might be a good choice. On a very dark, cloudy or moonless night you may want to stick to the River Path, Victoria Peak Path and Access Road with an opening above.

Walking to a spot by the river just before dusk, you can sit by the river side with your light off to listen and smell the forest. The River Overlook on the Wari Loop, or the picnic table on the River Path are good spots.

As dusk settles, the bird sounds gradually decrease and the bats come out. Insect sounds are continuous. Frogs sing intermittently most of the year. But in June, around the time of the first heavy rains, they come out in all their glory and the chorus is deafening (see Chapter 8). A gibnut may run under your feet. A peccary may be munching behind the bench. You may hear armadillos foraging in the forest.

While walking at night, hold your flashlight along the side of your face near your eyes. The eyes of most animals will reflect the light of your flashlight right back to your eyes. You cannot see this if your light is down at your side. You will notice the bright blue-green eye reflection of spiders. Even the smallest spiders have a noticeable reflection which can be seen as much as 15 meters away. Locate the spot of the reflection and walk directly to it. As you get closer you may no longer see the reflection, but you can usually find the spider if you remember where the reflection was.

The pauraque is a night bird that frequents open paths and the Headquarters area. It has an orange eyeshine. The bird has eyes on either side of its head, so you will generally see only one eye at a time. If you don't catch the eyeshine with your flashlight, they will appear like a brown rolled-up cecropia leaf until you get within a couple of meters. You might be startled as they fly up in front of you and then land further down the path to repeat the same scenario.

Listen for the kinkajou (night walker), especially from the Access Road. This nimble tree-dweller can be heard shaking the treetops as it searches for fruits. If you shine your light in its direction, you may see a light brown, almost catlike form and orange eyeshine. It will try to escape the glare by crashing through the branches to a more secluded spot from which it may scold you furiously. The kinkajou's voice sounds like a cross between a bark and sneeze.

Look also for porcupines. They are well-protected animals and fearful of bright flashlights. Their prehensile tail wraps around branches for stability. They have numerous spines sticking out from their black hair; and their noses are large and soft-looking.

The kaway swamp on the Wari Loop is a good place to see and hear the red-eyed tree frogs in June. You have to look closely at the green leaves to see the frogs, a little oval the same color as the leaf.

At the river or when crossing a stream you may come across numerous giant marine toads. They jump around sluggishly on the banks after sundown. They have a very dull eyeshine but are more easily spotted by their round, dumpy form. Unlike most forest animals, these toads make no effort to conceal themselves. Their skin contains a poisonous secretion that is very dangerous to most predators. On some nights they call loudly with a monotonous, motor-like sound that can be heard up and down the river, even at the CBWS Headquarters.

There other sounds you might hear. On the Wari Loop there are usually several herons, including the boat-billed and the tiger-heron. The snoring sound you hear there at night is the tiger-heron. During mating season (February and March), you might hear jaguars roar. They also sometimes roar as a territorial display at other times of the year. That sound must be distinguished from the howl of the baboon, the black howler monkey. Jaguars make a series of loud, hoarse coughs. The baboon howl is higher-pitched than the jaguar, but lower and more hoarse than you would expect from a monkey. The baboons howl as a territorial display any time of the day or night.

If you look very carefully, you may be able to see sleeping birds in the forest. They sleep with their heads tucked under their wings, extremely well-camouflaged, balls of green feathers blending into the forest background.

Maybe you will see the glow of two large cat eyes staring straight at you! Jaguars have a red eyeshine. Be careful not to overwhelm the cats with light. It does not take much light to see the reflection. They have been seen from vehicles on the Access Road, their eyes reflecting the headlights. The smaller ocelots and margays are nocturnal and have bright yellowish eyeshine. Pumas have a yellowish eyeshine, but they are more rarely seen than jaguars because they keep to the higher, drier pine ridges and are diurnal.

Bats are numerous in the CBWS, which is fortunate, because they are very beneficial. Insect-eating bats can often be seen at night in the CBWS Headquarters and other open areas as they help rid the air of mosquitoes and other insects. Other bat species eat nectar, fruit, pollen, blood, fish or small animals. You may be startled as they swoop close to you in the dark, but their sonar works well. They will not touch you or hurt you in any way.

Another variation on a night walk is to go out at 3 or 4 AM and watch the forest change as the dawn breaks. The tops of the hills on the Gibnut Loop are good places to sit for the dawn bird chorus. At first the only bird sounds you hear are the owls. There are two owls commonly heard in the CBWS, the ferruginous pygmy owl (*Glaucidium brasilianum*) and the mottled owl (*Ciccaba virgata*), neither of which make a typical "hooting" owl sound. The ferruginous pygmy owl has a short whistle repeated several times per second over and over again. The mottled owl has a mournful call, increasing in intensity and pitch and then dropping off quickly.

As it begins to get light, the owl sounds are replaced with a typical owl sound, a double "whoo whoo," made instead by the blue-crowned motmot (*Momotus momota*). Gradually other birds join the chorus, until the most raucous, the chachalacas (*Ortalis vetula*), sound the morning alarm about an hour after sunrise and a new day begins.

Mammal List
James Kamstra and Timothy J. McCarthy

The following list includes 63 species which have thus far been recorded from the Cockscomb Basin. The list should be considered preliminary because there are certainly more species, particularly bats and rodents. Large and medium-sized mammals are difficult enough to see, but the smaller species are more elusive and a challenge to identify. Unlike the more conspicuous birds, there is insufficient information to provide information on the abundance of each species.

Habitat Codes:
The habitat codes are given to indicate where a visitor might expect to see a particular mammal. In cases where this is not known specifically for Belize, habitats are assumed from information for other similar areas.

- F: Broad-leaved Forest
- S: Early Successional Shrub Thicket
- P: Pine Forest and Savanna
- R: Riparian Shrub Thicket
- A: Aquatic, Open Water of Creeks

Common Name	Scientific Name	Habitat
MARSUPIALS		
Common Opossum	*Didelphis marsupialis*	FSPR
Grey Four-eyed Opossum	*Philander opossum*	FS
Mexican Mouse Opossum	*Marmosa mexicana*	FS
Water Opossum	*Chironectes minimus*	RA
BATS		
Proboscis Bat	*Rhynchonycteris naso*	RA
Greater Fishing Bat	*Noctilio leporinus*	RA
Davy's Naked-backed Bat	*Pteronotus davyi*	F
Common Sword-nosed Bat	*Lonchorhina aurita*	F
Pale Spear-nosed Bat	*Phyllostomus discolor*	F
Fringe-lipped Bat	*Trachops cirrhosus*	F
Wooly False Vampire Bat	*Chrotopterus auritus*	F
Long-tongued Bat	*Glossophaga soricina*	F
Silky Short-tailed Bat	*Carollia brevicauda*	F
Seba's Short-tailed Bat	*Carollia perspicillata*	F
Little Yellow-shouldered Bat	*Sturnira lilium*	F
Common Tentmaking Bat	*Uroderma bilobatum*	F
Heller's Broad-nosed Bat	*Platyrrhinus helleri*	F
Jamaican Fruit-eating Bat	*Artibeus jamaicensis*	FS
Great Fruit-eating Bat	*Artibeus lituratus*	F
Pygmy Fruit-eating Bat	*Artibeus phaeotis*	F
Lowland Fruit-eating Bat	*Artibeus toltecus*	F
Watson's Fruit-eating Bat	*Artibeus watsoni*	F
Common Vampire Bat	*Desmodus rotundus*	FS

Common Name	Scientific Name	Habitat
BATS (*cont'd*)		
Funnel-eared Bat	*Natalus stramineus*	F
Spix's Disc-winged Bat	*Thyroptera tricolor*	F
Van Gelder's Bat	*Bauerus dubiaquercus*	F
Western Red Bat	*Lasiurus blossevillii*	F
Southern Yellow Bat	*Lasiurus ega*	F
Black Mastiff Bat	*Molossus rufus* (was *ater*)	F
EDENTATES		
Northern Tamandua	*Tamandua mexicana*	F
Nine-Banded Armadillo	*Dasypus novemcinctus*	FSR
PRIMATES		
Yucatan Black Howler Monkey	*Alouatta pigra*	F
Central American Spider Monkey	*Ateles geoffroyi*	F
RODENTS		
Deppe's Squirrel	*Sciurus deppei*	FS
Big-eared Climbing Rat	*Ototylomys phyllotis*	FS
Forest Spiny Pocket Mouse	*Heteromys desmarestianus*	FS
Hispid Pocket Gopher	*Orthogeomys hispidus*	S
Coues' Rice Rat	*Oryzomys couesi*	FSR
Alfaro's Rice Rat	*Oryzomys alfaroi*	F
Hispid Cotton Rat	*Sigmodon hispidus*	SR
Mexican Porcupine	*Coendou mexicanus*	F
Paca (Gibnut)	*Agouti paca*	FRA
Central American Agouti	*Dasyprocta punctata*	FSR
CARNIVORES		
Grey Fox	*Urocyon cinereoargenteus*	FSP
Cacomistle	*Bassariscus sumichrasti*	F
White-nosed Coati	*Nasua narica*	FSR
Kinkajou	*Potos flavus*	FR
Striped Hog-nosed Skunk	*Conepatus semistriatus*	FS
Tayra	*Eira barbara*	FSR
Neotropical River Otter	*Lutra longicaudis*	RA
Spotted Skunk	*Spilogale putorius*	S
Puma	*Puma concolor*	FSR
Jaguarundi	*Herpailurus yagouaroundi*	FSR
Ocelot	*Leopardus pardalis*	FSR
Margay	*Leopardus wiedii*	FSR
Jaguar	*Panthera onca*	FSR
PERISSODACTYLS and ARTIODACTYLS		
Baird's Tapir	*Tapirus bairdii*	FRA
White-lipped Peccary	*Tayassu pecari*	FSR
Collared Peccary	*Tayassu tajacu*	F
Red Brocket Deer	*Mazama americana*	FS
White-tailed Deer	*Odocoileus virginianus*	SP

Bird List
James Kamstra

The Cockscomb Basin provides habitat for most of the land bird species which could be expected in the southern half of Belize. A total of 296 species has been reported thus far but this list is not complete. To date, most of the bird observations come from the East Basin, particularly the vicinity of the Park Headquarters so the following checklist is most indicative of this area. Access into the higher elevations and the West Basin is more difficult and, therefore, the species and status of the birds there are less well known. The following codes accompany the checklist:

Abundance (A):
C - Common; species likely to be seen on more than 50% of visits to appropriate habitat, often abundant.
F - Fairly Common; species likely to be seen on 25 to 50% of visits to appropriate habitat.
U - Uncommon; species likely to be seen on 10 to 25% of visits to appropriate habitat.
R - Rare; species likely to be seen on less than 10% of visits to appropriate habitat, includes species only recorded once.

Status (S):
P - Permanent resident and probable breeder
S - Summer resident and probable breeder
W - Winter resident, temperate North American migrant
T - Transient, pass through in migration only
V - Visitor, non breeders which occasionally occur
? - Insufficient evidence to determine if P or V

Habitat (H):
F - Closed canopy forest, generally below 500 meters
E - Forest edge, interface between forest and shrub
S - Second growth shrub, former milpas and clearings
H - Highland forest, all habitats above 500 meters
P - Pineland or pine savanna on Cabbage Haul Ridge
R - Riparian floodplain thickets and dumb cane

Common Name	Scientific Name	A	S	H
Great Tinamou	*Tinamus major*	F	P	F
Little Tinamou	*Crypturellus soui*	R	P	F
Slaty-breasted Tinamou	*Crypturellus boucardi*	U	P	F
Least Grebe	*Tachybaptus dominicus*	R	P	A
Neotropic Cormorant	*Phalacrocorax olivaceus*	R	V	A
Anhinga	*Anhinga anhinga*	U	P	A
Magnificent Frigatebird	*Fregata magnificens*	R	V	Aerial
Little Blue Heron	*Egretta caerulea*	C	P	A
Snowy Egret	*Egretta thula*	U	V	A
Great Blue Heron	*Ardea herodias*	C	V	A
Great Egret	*Casmerodius albus*	U	V	A
Cattle Egret	*Bubulcus ibis*	F	V	SA
Green Heron	*Butorides virescens*	C	P	RA
Agami Heron (Chestnut-bellied)	*Agamia agami*	R	P	RA
Yellow-crowned Night Heron	*Nyctanassa violacea*	R	V	A
Bare-throated Tiger-Heron	*Tigrisoma mexicanum*	C	P	RA
Boat-billed Heron	*Cochlearius cochlearius*	U	P	RA
Wood Stork	*Mycteria americana*	U	V	RA
Muscovy Duck	*Cairina moschata*	R	V	A
Blue-winged Teal	*Anas discors*	R	W	A
Black Vulture	*Coragyps atratus*	F	P	FESP
Turkey Vulture	*Cathartes aura*	C	P	FESHP
King Vulture	*Sarcoramphus papa*	F	P	FESHP
Osprey	*Pandion haliaetus*	U	V	R
Grey-headed Kite	*Leptodon cayanensis*	R	P	FE
Hook-billed Kite	*Chondrohierax uncinatus*	R	P	FE
Swallow-tailed Kite	*Elanoides forficatus*	F	S	FHP
White-tailed Kite	*Elanus leucurus*	F	P	ESR
Snail Kite	*Rostrhamus sociabilis*	R	V	R
Double-toothed Kite	*Harpagas bidentatus*	R	P	FE
Plumbeous Kite	*Ictinia plumbea*	C	S	FESR
White Hawk	*Leucopternis albicollis*	F	P	FE
Common Black Hawk	*Buteogallus anthracinus*	R	P	E
Great Black Hawk	*Buteogallus urubitinga*	U	P	FE
Solitary Eagle	*Harpyhaliaetus solitarius*	R	P	FE
Grey Hawk	*Buteo nitidus*	C	P	ESR
Roadside Hawk	*Buteo magnirostris*	C	P	FESPR
Short-tailed Hawk	*Buteo brachyurus*	C	P	FESR
Red-tailed Hawk	*Buteo jamaicensis*	U	P	P
Black-and-white Hawk-Eagle	*Spizastur melanoleucus*	U	P	FEP
Black Hawk-Eagle	*Spizaetus tyrannus*	U	P	FE
Ornate Hawk-Eagle	*Spizaetus ornatus*	R	P	ER
Laughing Falcon	*Herpetotheres cachinnans*	C	P	FES
Barred Forest-Falcon	*Micrastur ruficollis*	R	P	F
Collared Forest-Falcon	*Micrastur semitorquatus*	U	P	F
American Kestrel	*Falco sparverius*	U	W	SP
Bat Falcon	*Falco rufigularis*	F	P	FER
Peregrine Falcon	*Falco peregrinus*	R	W	HR

Common Name	Scientific Name	A	S	H
Plain Chachalaca	*Ortalis vetula*	C	P	FESR
Crested Guan	*Penelope purpurascens*	F	P	FEHR
Great Curassow	*Crax rubra*	F	P	FH
Black-throated Bobwhite	*Colinus nigrogularis*	U	P	ES
Spotted Wood-Quail	*Odontophorus guttatus*	U	P	F
Limpkin	*Aramus guarauna*	R	V	RA
Ruddy Crake	*Laterallus ruber*	U	P	R
Grey-necked Wood-Rail	*Aramides cajanea*	F	P	RA
Sungrebe	*Heliornis fulica*	F	P	A
Solitary Sandpiper	*Tringa solitaria*	F	T	A
Spotted Sandpiper	*Actitis macularia*	C	W	A
Scaled Pigeon	*Columba speciosa*	F	P	FE
Pale-vented Pigeon	*Columba cayennensis*	C	P	FESPR
Short-billed Pigeon	*Columba nigrirostris*	F	P	FE
Ruddy Ground-Dove	*Columbina talpacoti*	C	P	ESR
Blue Ground-Dove	*Claravis pretiosa*	C	P	ESPR
White-tipped Dove	*Leptotila verreauxi*	R	P	FE
Grey-headed Dove	*Leptotila plumbeiceps*	F	P	F
Grey-chested Dove	*Leptotila cassini*	F	P	F
Ruddy Quail-Dove	*Geotrygon montana*	F	P	F
Scarlet Macaw	*Ara macao*	U	P	FER
Olive-throated Parakeet	*Aratinga astec*	C	P	ESR
Brown-hooded Parrot	*Pionopsitta haematotis*	R	P	E
White-crowned Parrot	*Pionus senilis*	C	P	FESHR
White-fronted Parrot	*Amazona albifrons*	U	P	F
Red-lored Parrot	*Amazona autumnalis*	C	P	FE
Mealy Parrot	*Amazona farinosa*	F	P	FH
Squirrel Cuckoo	*Piaya cayana*	C	P	FESR
Groove-billed Ani	*Crotophaga sulcirostris*	C	P	ESR
Variable Screech-Owl	*Otus atricapillus*	R	P	FH
Mottled Owl	*Ciccaba virgata*	C	P	FH
Black-and-white Owl	*Ciccaba nigrolineata*	R	P	F
Spectacled Owl	*Pulsatrix perspicillata*	R	P	F
Ferruginous Pygmy-Owl	*Glaucidium brasilianum*	F	P	ES
Least Pygmy-Owl	*Glaucidium minutissimum*	R	P	F
Striped Owl	*Asio clamator*	R	?	S
Common Nighthawk	*Chordeiles minor*	U	V	SR
Pauraque	*Nyctidromus albicollis*	C	P	FESRP
White-collared Swift	*Streptoprocne zonaris*	U	V	FH
Vaux's Swift	*Chaetura vauxi*	C	P	FESP
Lesser Swallow-tailed Swift	*Panyptila cayennensis*	U	P	FE
Band-tailed Barbthroat	*Threnetes ruckeri*	R	P	F
Long-tailed Hermit	*Phaethornis superciliosus*	C	P	FH
Little Hermit	*Phaethornis longuemareus*	C	P	FESHR
Scaly-breasted Hummingbird	*Phaeochroa cuvierii*	R	P	R
Wedge-tailed Sabrewing	*Campylopterus curvipennis*	U	P	FH
Violet Sabrewing	*Campylopterus hemileucurus*	F	P	FEH

Common Name	Scientific Name	A	S	H
White-necked Jacobin	*Florisuga mellivora*	C	P	SR
Brown Violet-ear	*Colibri delphinae*	R	?	H
Green-breasted Mango	*Anthracothorax prevostii*	F	P	ES
Fork-tailed Emerald	*Chlorostilbon canivetii*	F	P	ES
White-bellied Emerald	*Amazilia candida*	C	P	FESHR
Azure-crowned Hummingbird	*Amazilia cyanocephala*	F	P	P
Buff-bellied Hummingbird	*Amazilia yucatanensis*	U	P	EP
Rufous-tailed Hummingbird	*Amazilia tzacatl*	C	P	ESR
Stripe-tailed Hummingbird	*Eupherusa eximia*	?	P	H
Slaty-tailed Trogon	*Trogon massena*	F	P	FEH
Black-headed Trogon	*Trogon melanocephalus*	C	P	FER
Collared Trogon	*Trogon collaris*	R	P	FH
Violaceous Trogon	*Trogon violaceus*	C	P	FER
Ringed Kingfisher	*Ceryle torquata*	F	P	RA
Amazon Kingfisher	*Chloroceryle amazona*	C	P	RA
Green Kingfisher	*Chloroceryle americana*	C	P	RA
American Pygmy Kingfisher	*Chloroceryle aenea*	U	P	RA
Tody Motmot	*Hylomanes momotula*	F	P	H
Keel-billed Motmot	*Electron carinatum*	R	?	H
Blue-crowned Motmot	*Momotus momota*	C	P	FH
Rufous-tailed Jacamar	*Galbula ruficauda*	C	P	FE
White-necked Puffbird	*Notharchus macrorhynchos*	U	P	FE
White-whiskered Puffbird	*Malacoptila panamensis*	U	P	F
Emerald Toucanet	*Aulacorhynchus prasinus*	U	P	FEH
Collared Aracari	*Pteroglossus torquatus*	F	P	FER
Keel-billed Toucan	*Ramphastos sulfuratus*	F	P	FEH
Black-cheeked Woodpecker	*Melanerpes pucherani*	C	P	FE
Golden-fronted Woodpecker	*Melanerpes aurifrons*	C	P	ESPR
Smoky-brown Woodpecker	*Veniliornis fumigatus*	F	P	FE
Golden-olive Woodpecker	*Piculus rubiginosus*	C	P	ESPR
Chestnut-colored Woodpecker	*Celeus castaneus*	U	P	F
Lineated Woodpecker	*Dryocopus lineatus*	F	P	FER
Pale-billed Woodpecker	*Campephilus guatemalensis*	F	P	FE
Tawny-winged Woodcreeper	*Dendrocincla anabatina*	C	P	F
Ruddy Woodcreeper	*Dendrocincla homochroa*	F	P	FH
Olivaceous Woodcreeper	*Sittasomus griseicapillus*	F	P	F
Wedge-billed Woodcreeper	*Glyphorynchus spirurus*	F	P	F
Barred Woodcreeper	*Dendrocolaptes certhia*	R	P	F
Ivory-billed Woodcreeper	*Xiphorhynchus flavigaster*	C	P	FH
Streak-headed Woodcreeper	*Lepidocolaptes souleyetii*	F	P	F
Rufous-breasted Spinetail	*Synallaxis erythrothorax*	C	P	ESR
Buff-throated Foliage-gleaner	*Automolus ochrolaemus*	C	P	FH
Scaly-throated Leafscraper	*Sclerurus guatemalensis*	R	?	FS
Plain Xenops	*Xenops minutus*	F	P	F
Barred Antshrike	*Thamnophilus doliatus*	C	P	ESR

Common Name	Scientific Name	A	S	H
Plain Antvireo	*Dysithamnus mentalis*	F	P	FH
Dot-winged Antwren	*Microrhopias quixensis*	C	P	FER
Dusky Antbird	*Cercomacra tyrannina*	F	P	FE
Bare-crowned Antbird	*Gymnocichla nudiceps*	R	?	F
Black-faced Antthrush	*Formicarius analis*	F	P	F
Red-capped Manakin	*Pipra mentalis*	C	P	FEH
White-collared Manakin	*Manacus candei*	C	P	FE
Thrush-like Manakin	*Schiffornis turdinus*	F	P	F
Rufous Piha	*Lipaugus unirufus*	R	P	F
Lovely Cotinga	*Cotinga amabilis*	R	?	FE
Cinnamon Becard	*Pachyramphus cinnamomeus*	C	P	R
White-winged Becard	*Pachyramphus polychopterus*	R	P	ER
Rose-throated Becard	*Platypsaris aglaiae*	R	P	S
Masked Tityra	*Tityra semifasciata*	C	P	FEHR
Black-crowned Tityra	*Tityra inquisitor*	U	P	ER
Ochre-bellied Flycatcher	*Mionectes oleagineus*	F	P	F
Sepia-capped Flycatcher	*Leptopogon amaurocephalus*	R	P	E
Pileated Flycatcher	*Aechmolophus mexicanus*	C	P	ES
Slate-headed Tody-Flycatcher	*Todirostrum sylvia*	R	P	FE
Common Tody-Flycatcher	*Todirostrum cinereum*	C	P	ES
Yellow-bellied Tyrannulet	*Ornithion semiflavum*	R	P	E
Greenish Elaenia	*Myiopagis viridicata*	R	P	FE
Yellow-bellied Elaenia	*Elaenia flavogaster*	C	P	ESPR
Northern Bentbill	*Oncostoma cinereigulare*	C	P	FEH
Eye-ringed Flatbill	*Rhynchocyclus brevirostris*	R	P	H
Yellow-olive Flycatcher	*Tolmomyias sulphurescens*	U	P	FE
Stub-tailed Spadebill	*Platyrinchus cancrominus*	F	P	FH
Royal Flycatcher	*Onychorhynchus coronatus*	U	P	FER
Ruddy-tailed Flycatcher	*Terenotriccus erythrurus*	U	P	F
Sulphur-rumped Flycatcher	*Myiobius sulphureipygius*	C	P	F
Olive-sided Flycatcher	*Contopus borealis*	R	T	P
Tropical Pewee	*Contopus cinereus*	F	P	EP
Yellow-bellied Flycatcher	*Empidonax flaviventris*	C	W	FESR
Acadian Flycatcher	*Empidonax virescens*	U	W	E
Least Flycatcher	*Empidonax minimus*	F	W	E
Black Phoebe	*Sayornis nigricans*	F	P	R
Vermilion Flycatcher	*Pyrocephalus rubinus*	R	P	SP
Bright-rumped Attila	*Attila spadiceus*	F	P	FH
Rufous Mourner	*Rhytipterna holerythra*	U	P	F
Dusky-capped Flycatcher	*Myiarchus tuberculifer*	C	P	ESPR
Brown-crested Flycatcher	*Myiarchus tyrannulus*	C	P	ESPR
Tropical Kingbird	*Tyrannus melancholicus*	C	P	ESPR
Eastern Kingbird	*Tyrannus tyrannus*	C	T	ESR
Boat-billed Flycatcher	*Megarynchus pitangua*	U	P	E
Streaked Flycatcher	*Myiodynastes maculatus*	F	S	ESR
Sulphur-bellied Flycatcher	*Myiodynastes luteiventris*	F	S	ESR
Social Flycatcher	*Myiozetetes similis*	C	P	ESR
Piratic Flycatcher	*Legatus leucophaius*	C	S	ES
Great Kiskadee	*Pitangus sulphuratus*	C	P	ESPR

Common Name	Scientific Name	A	S	H
Tree Swallow	*Tachycineta bicolor*	U	W	S
Mangrove Swallow	*Tachycineta albilinea*	F	P	SR
Purple Martin	*Progne subis*	F	T	S
Grey-breasted Martin	*Progne chalybea*	C	S	
Northern Rough-winged Swallow	*Stelgidopteryx serripennis*	C	P	ESR
Barn Swallow	*Hirundo rustica*	C	T	SPR
Green Jay	*Cyanocorax yncas*	U	P	F
Brown Jay	*Psilorhinus morio*	C	P	FE
Band-backed Wren	*Campylorhynchus zonatus*	F	P	R
Spot-breasted Wren	*Thryothorus maculipectus*	C	P	FESR
House Wren	*Troglodytes aedon*	C	P	SR
White-bellied Wren	*Uropsila leucogastra*	R	P	E
White-breasted Wood-Wren	*Henicorhina leucosticta*	C	P	FH
Grey Catbird	*Dumetella carolinensis*	C	W	FESR
Slate-colored Solitaire	*Myadestes unicolor*	C	P	H
Swainson's Thrush	*Catharus ustulatus*	U	T	FE
Wood Thrush	*Hylocichla mustelina*	F	W	F
Clay-colored Robin	*Turdus grayi*	C	P	FESR
White-throated Thrush	*Turdus assimilis*	U	P	FH
Long-billed Gnatwren	*Ramphocaenus melanurus*	F	P	F
Tropical Gnatcatcher	*Polioptila plumbea*	U	P	FE
Cedar Waxwing	*Bombycilla cedrorum*	R	T	S
Green Shrike-Vireo	*Vireolanius pulchellus*	F	P	F
White-eyed Vireo	*Vireo griseus*	F	W	ES
Mangrove Vireo	*Vireo pallens*	R	P	S
Yellow-throated Vireo	*Vireo flavifrons*	R	W	R
Yellow-green Vireo	*Vireo flavoviridis*	C	S	FE
Tawny-crowned Greenlet	*Hylophilus ochraceiceps*	R	P	F
Lesser Greenlet	*Hylophilus decurtatus*	C	P	FEH
Bananaquit	*Coereba flaveola*	U	P	E
Blue-winged Warbler	*Vermivora pinus*	U	W	FE
Tennessee Warbler	*Vermivora peregrina*	F	W	FE
Northern Parula	*Parula americana*	R	W	FE
Yellow Warbler	*Dendroica petechia*	C	W	ES
Chestnut-sided Warbler	*Dendroica pensylvanica*	C	W	FE
Magnolia Warbler	*Dendroica magnolia*	C	W	FESR
Yellow-rumped Warbler	*Dendroica coronata*	F	W	ES
Black-throated Green Warbler	*Dendroica virens*	F	W	FE
Yellow-throated Warbler	*Dendroica dominica*	F	W	ESR
Grace's Warbler	*Dendroica graciae*	C	P	R
Palm Warbler	*Dendroica palmarum*	R	W	S
Bay-breasted Warbler	*Dendroica castanea*	F	T	F
Blackpoll Warbler	*Dendroica striata*	R	T	F
Black-and-white Warbler	*Mniotilta varia*	C	W	FE
American Redstart	*Setophaga ruticilla*	C	W	FEH

Common Name	Scientific Name	A	S	H
Prothonotary Warbler	*Protonotaria citrea*	F	T	R
Worm-eating Warbler	*Helmitheros vermivorus*	F	W	FEH
Swainson's Warbler	*Limnothlypis swainsonii*	R	W	F
Ovenbird	*Seiurus aurocapillus*	F	W	FS
Northern Waterthrush	*Seiurus noveboracensis*	F	W	FER
Louisiana Waterthrush	*Seiurus motacilla*	C	W	FER
Kentucky Warbler	*Oporornis formosus*	C	W	FE
Common Yellowthroat	*Geothlypis trichas*	C	W	SR
Grey-crowned Yellowthroat	*Geothlypis poliocephala*	U	P	P
Hooded Warbler	*Wilsonia citrina*	C	W	FE
Wilson's Warbler	*Wilsonia pusilla*	C	W	ES
Golden-crowned Warbler	*Basileuterus culicivorus*	R	P	H
Rufous-capped Warbler	*Basileuterus rufifrons*	U	P	P
Yellow-breasted Chat	*Icteria virens*	C	W	SR
Chestnut-headed Oropendola	*Zarhynchus wagleri*	R	P	R
Montezuma Oropendola	*Gymnostinops montezuma*	C	P	FESR
Yellow-billed Cacique	*Amblycercus holosericeus*	C	P	SR
Yellow-backed Oriole	*Icterus chrysater*	U	P	R
Yellow-tailed Oriole	*Icterus mesomelas*	C	P	ESR
Northern Oriole	*Icterus galbula*	C	W	ESR
Orchard Oriole	*Icterus spurius*	C	W	ESR
Black-cowled Oriole	*Icterus prosthemelas*	C	P	ESR
Melodious Blackbird	*Dives dives*	C	P	ESR
Great-tailed Grackle	*Cassidix mexicanus*	U	P	S
Bronzed Cowbird	*Molothrus aeneus*	C	P	ES
Giant Cowbird	*Scaphidura oryzivora*	F	P	SR
Common Bush-Tanager	*Chlorospingus ophthalmicus*	F	P	H
Grey-headed Tanager	*Eucometis penicillata*	U	P	FES
Black-throated Shrike-Tanager	*Lanio aurantius*	R	P	F
Red-crowned Ant-Tanager	*Habia rubica*	U	P	F
Red-throated Ant-Tanager	*Habia fuscicauda*	C	P	FEH
Hepatic Tanager	*Piranga flava*	C	P	P
Summer Tanager	*Piranga rubra*	U	W	FE
Scarlet Tanager	*Piranga olivacea*	R	T	F
White-winged Tanager	*Piranga leucoptera*	R	P	H
Crimson-collared Tanager	*Phlogothraupis sanguinolentus*	C	P	ESR
Scarlet-rumped Tanager	*Ramphocelus passerinii*	C	P	ESR
Blue-grey Tanager	*Thraupis episcopus*	C	P	FESR
Yellow-winged Tanager	*Thraupis abbas*	C	P	FESR
Scrub Euphonia	*Euphonia affinis*	R	P	E
Yellow-throated Euphonia	*Euphonia hirundinacea*	U	P	ES
Blue-hooded Euphonia	*Euphonia elegantissima*	R	?	F
Olive-backed Euphonia	*Euphonia gouldi*	C	P	FES
White-vented Euphonia	*Euphonia minuta*	R	?	H
Golden-hooded Tanager	*Tangara larvata*	C	P	FE
Green Honeycreeper	*Chlorophanes spiza*	F	P	FEH
Shining Honeycreeper	*Cyanerpes lucidus*	U	P	H
Red-legged Honeycreeper	*Cyanerpes cyaneus*	F	P	FE

Common Name	Scientific Name	A	S	H
Blue-black Grassquit	*Volatinia jacarina*	C	P	SR
Variable Seedeater	*Sporophila aurita*	C	P	SR
White-collared Seedeater	*Sporophila torqueola*	C	P	SPR
Thick-billed Seed-Finch	*Oryzoborus funereus*	F	P	SR
Dickcissel	*Spiza americana*	R	T	S
Rose-breasted Grosbeak	*Pheucticus ludovicianus*	F	W	FE
Black-faced Grosbeak	*Caryothraustes poliogaster*	C	P	FER
Black-headed Saltator	*Saltator atriceps*	C	P	FESR
Buff-throated Saltator	*Saltator maximus*	C	P	ESR
Greyish Saltator	*Saltator coerulescens*	C	P	ESR
Blue-black Grosbeak	*Cyanocompsa cyanoides*	F	P	FESR
Blue Grosbeak	*Guiraca caerulea*	F	T	ESR
Indigo Bunting	*Passerina cyanea*	C	W	ES
Painted Bunting	*Passerina ciris*	R	?	S
Rusty Sparrow	*Aimophila rufescens*	F	P	SP
Orange-billed Sparrow	*Arremon aurantiirostris*	C	P	FEH
Olive Sparrow	*Arremonops rufivirgatus*	R	P	S
Green-backed Sparrow	*Arremonops chloronotus*	F	P	FE

Amphibian and Reptile Lists
James Kamstra, Timothy McCarthy
and Jan Meerman

The following list is preliminary and includes only those species that have been positively identified within the CBWS. There are certainly many more species awaiting discovery. Many reptiles are elusive and hard to find. Some live only among epiphytes and in the upper canopy of the forest. Others are confined to higher elevations. We know little about the reptiles and amphibians of these areas in the CBWS. Similarly, the vast, remote West Basin remains largely unexplored.

There are no available field guides, which makes identification difficult. Some groups contain very similar species which can only be distinguished by technical characterization, such as frogs of the genus *Eleutherodactylus* and *Anolis* lizards. Many species, in fact, do not have recognized common names. Previous names are given in parentheses for species with updated nomenclature.

Habitat Codes:

The habitat codes are given to indicate where a visitor might expect to see a particular animal. In cases where this is not known specifically for Belize, habitats are assumed from information for other similar areas.

F - Broad-leaved Forest
S - Early Successional Shrub Thicket
P - Pine Forest and Savanna
R - Riparian Shrub Thicket
A - Aquatic, Open Water of Creeks

Common Name	Scientific Name	Habitat
AMPHIBIANS		
Caudata		
salamander	*Bolitoglossa mexicana*	RA
salamander	*Bolitoglossa rufescens*	RA
salamander	*Oedipina elongata*	RA
Anurans		
Marine Toad	*Bufo marinus*	SR
Gulf Coast Toad	*Bufo valliceps*	SRP
toad (newly discovered)	*Bufo campbelli*	SRP
Mexican Burrowing Toad	*Rhinophrynus dorsalis*	S
Maya Rain Frog	*Eleutherodactylus chac*	F
Lowland Rain Frog	*Eleutherodactylus rhodopsis*	F
Central American Rain Frog	*Eleutherodactylus rugulosus*	F
White-lipped Frog	*Leptodactylus labialis*	F
Red-eyed Tree Frog	*Agalychnis callidryas*	F
Variegated Tree Frog	*Hyla ebraccata*	F
Red-footed Tree Frog	*Hyla loquax*	F
Yellow Tree Frog	*Hyla microcephala*	FS
Cricket Tree Frog	*Hyla picta*	F
Stauffer's Tree Frog	*Scinax staufferi*	F
Mexican Tree Frog	*Smilisca baudinii*	FS
Blue-spotted Tree Frog	*Smilisca cyanosticta*	F
Narrowmouth Frog	*Gastrophryne elegans*	F
Glass Frog	*Hyalinobatrachium fleischmanni*	F
Sheep Frog	*Hypopachus variolosus*	F
Rio Grande Leopard Frog	*Rana berlandieri*	RA
Maya Mountain Frog	*Rana juliani (maculata)*	RA
Rainforest Frog	*Rana vaillanti (palmipes)*	RA
REPTILES		
Turtles - Testudines		
mud turtle	*Kinosternon acutum*	A
mud turtle	*Kinosternon leucostomum*	A
Black-bellied Turtle	*Rhinoclemys areolata*	A
Red-eared Slider	*Trachemys scripta (Pseudemys)*	A
Crocodilidans		
Morelet's Crocodile	*Crocodylus moreleti*	A
Lizards - Sauria		
Alligator lizard	*Celestus rozellae*	
Banded gecko	*Coleonyx elegans*	F
gecko	*Sphaerodactylus millepunctatus*	FS
anole	*Anolis capito*	F
anole	*Anolis lemurinus*	FS
anole	*Anolis sericeus*	F
anole	*Anolis tropidonotus*	F
anole	*Anolis uniformis*	FS

Common Name	**Scientific Name**	**Habitat**
Lizards - Sauria (cont.)		
Striped Basilisk	*Basiliscus vittatus*	FSRPA
Old Man Lizard	*Corytophanes cristatus*	F
Spiny-tailed Iguana	*Ctenosaura similis*	S
Green Iguana	*Iguana iguana*	RA
Casque-headed Iguana	*Laemanctus longipes*	A
Spiny Lizard	*Sceloporus chrysostictus*	FS
Sumichrast's Skink	*Eumeces sumichrasti*	F
Bronze Skink	*Mabuya unimarginata (brachypoda)*	F
Cherrie's Skink	*Sphenomorphus cherriei*	F
Central American Whiptail	*Ameiva festiva*	FS
Barred Whiptail	*Ameiva undulata*	FS
Yellow-spotted Night Lizard	*Lepidophyma flavimaculatum*	F
Snakes - Serpentes		
Boa constrictor	*Boa constrictor*	F
Crowned Snake	*Coniophanes bipunctatus*	F
Black-striped snake	*Coniophanes imperialis*	FSRPA
Black-tailed Indigo Snake	*Drymarchon corais*	FSRPA
Speckled Racer	*Drymobius margaritiferus*	SRP
Blunt-headed Tree Snake	*Imantodes cenchoa*	F
Tropical Kingsnake	*Lampropeltis triangulum*	F
Cat-eyed Snake	*Leptodeira septentrionalis*	F
Cat-eyed Snake	*Leptodeira frenata*	F
Green Tree Snake	*Leptophis ahaetulla*	F
Green-headed Tree Snake	*Leptophis mexicanus*	F
Coach Whip	*Masticophis mentovarius*	S
Red Coffee Snake	*Ninia sebae*	SR
Grey Vine Snake	*Oxybelis aeneus*	FS
Green Vine Snake	*Oxybelis fulgidus*	F
Imitacoral (no English name)	*Pliocercus elapoides*	
Colubrid Snake	*Pseustes poecilonotus*	F
Shovel-toothed snake	*Scaphiodontophis annulatus*	
Snail-eating Snake	*Sibon nebulata*	F
Spotted Rat Snake	*Spilotes pullatus*	FS
coral snake	*Micrurus hippocrepis*	F
coral snake	*Micrurus nigrocinctus*	FS
coral snake	*Micrurus diastema*	F
Fer-de-lance	*Bothrops asper*	FS
Jumping Viper	*Porthidium nummifer (Bothrops)*	FS

About the Contributors

Dorothy Beveridge has a Bachelor's degree in Early Childhood Education. She taught in North Carolina, Louisiana, California and Texas before moving to Belize in 1980. She is now a naturalized Belizean citizen and focuses on environmental education through volunteer activities and "Sea-ing is Belizing," a photography and guiding business she owns with her husband, Jim.

James Beveridge was born in Glasgow, Scotland, in 1942. By the time he left Britain at the age of 22, he was both a journeyman plumber and a scuba diver of first class rating and had been working professionally in both of those fields. He first visited Belize in 1969, but stayed only a few months before continuing south to the town of Leticia on the Amazon River. For two years he worked in the rainforest with tropical aquarium fish and snakes and acted as a guide for the scientific community.

In 1972, he returned to Belize and settled on Caye Caulker. Jim is now a naturalized Belizean and fulltime wildlife photographer and guide. He and his wife, Dorothy, own and operate "Sea-ing is Belizing" on Caye Caulker. He spends much of his time in the Cockscomb Basin Wildlife Sanctuary recording on film the widely varied wildlife of the rainforest.

Ed Boles has a Master's degree in Biology from the University of Southern Mississippi. He has been a Permanent Resident in Belize since 1980. He has conducted environmental assessments in connection with the Belize Center for Environmental Studies for a number of years and taught environmental field courses for the School of International Studies. He is currently a doctoral candidate in Environmental Science with a Watershed Focus at Jackson State University in Jackson, Mississippi. He is studying the Sibun River watershed in Belize for his doctoral research project.

Robin Brockett is a Conservation Affiliate of Zoo Atlanta and an Associate of Community Conservation Consultants. She is studying black howler monkey social behavior in the Community Baboon Sanctuary. For 11 years she worked as an animal keeper at the Bronx Zoo and Zoo Atlanta. She has training from the Art Institute of Atlanta and the Jersey Wildlife Preservation Trust. Having worked in animal rehabilitation in South America, she is in the process of developing a similar rehabilitation program in Belize.

Paula DeGiorgis was born and raised in California. She studied illustration at the Pasadena Art Center and now lives and works in Nevada City, California. She is best known for delicate textured watercolors in which she sensitively captures the idyllic moment.

Terry Lawson Dunn has a Bachelor's degree in wildlife science and a Master's degree in Environmental Communications. She started creating pen and ink drawings of tropical wildlife while working on bird research in Panama in 1986. Her intricate portraits of tropical birds have been shown in the Washington, D. C. area, where she works as an Educational Education Specialist for the World Wildlife Fund- U.S.

Katherine M. Emmons lived with her husband, Tony Abrahams, in the CBWS for four months in 1992 while she conducted environmental education research as part of her graduate studies with the University of California, Santa Barbara (Ph.D. 1994). This book originated out of her desire to share the magic of the Cockscomb Basin with local and foreign visitors alike. Her travels and work have taken her to many different countries. Most recently she has lived in Cape Town, in the "new" South Africa with her husband and son. She works as an Environmental Education Specialist.

Robert H. Horwich is Director of Community Conservation Consultants. He received his Ph.D. in 1967 from the University of Maryland and worked in a postdoctoral position in India with the Smithsonian Institute. He has studied primates in captivity and in the field in India and Central America since 1967. He has developed a successful model for reintroducing cranes into the wild and pioneered the reintroduction of the black howler monkey into the Cockscomb Basin. His work with community sanctuaries since 1984 led to the establishment of the Community Baboon Sanctuary in Belize. He continues to work on community conservation in Belize, Mexico, Russia, Vietnam and the United States.

James Kamstra resided in the Cockscomb Basin for four months in 1986, gathering data on flora, fauna, geography and history of the area which was then the Cockscomb Basin Forest Reserve. This served as his Master's thesis "An Ecological Survey of the Cockscomb Basin." He received his degree from York University, Toronto, Canada, the following year. James presently lives near Toronto where he is employed as a biologist for an environmental consulting firm. He returns to Belize periodically to guide ecotours.

Charles Koontz is a data analyst at the Wildlife Conservation Society's Scieince Resource Center. Since Charles retired from metallurgy and mechanical engineering in 1985, he has volunteered many hundreds of hours assisting wildlife scientists to visualize their data using specialized computer programs, many of which he wrote. He provided the maps and home range analysis for the project to reintroduce black howler monkeys into the CBWS. These maps were adapted for use as trail guides in Chapter 15.

Fred Koontz is Director of the Wildlife Conservation Society's Science Resource Center located in New York at the Bronx Zoo. The Center endeavors to apply new scientific methods and technological solutions to wildlife conservation problems. Fred received his Ph.D. degree in Zoology from the University of Maryland in 1984. He is the Project Director of the black howler monkey reintroduction to the CBWS.

Judy Lumb lives on Caye Caulker, Belize, and is currently the Editor of *Producciones de la Hamaca*. She earned a doctorate in microbiology from Stanford University and was on the faculty of Atlanta University for eighteen years until 1987 when she retired and moved to Belize. Since then she has done volunteer publication work for the Belize Audubon Society such as the layout of the quarterly newsletter. She has been involved in several projects supporting the CBWS and enjoys spending time there whenever possible.

Timothy McCarthy is based at The Carnegie Museum of Natural History, Pittsburgh, USA. He studies endemic species of montane small mammals in northwestern Ecuador, Lesser Antilles (Windward Islands), and northern Central America. He knows Belize best as he has lived and worked here over the past 22 years and remains at the service of the Belize Audubon Society, Department of Agriculture, Post Office, and other Belizean friends.

Jan Meerman was born in the Netherlands and came to Belize in 1989 to become manager of the Shipstern Nature Reserve and Butterfly Breeding Center in the Corozal district. In his spare time he started surveying the butterfly fauna of that area and later expanded his interests to other groups such as *Odonata*, amphibians, reptiles and plants. Together with his wife, Tineke Boomsma, he has also surveyed other areas of Belize, including the Cockscomb Basin Wildlife Sanctuary. After 5 years in the Shipstern Nature Reserve, he moved to the Cayo District and started "Belize Tropical Forest Studies," specializing in environmental impact assessments and biological surveys.

Linde Ostro was born in Bennington, Vermont, but raised in England. She returned to the United States to attend Haverford College where she was a history major. She worked at the Bronx Zoo in the Mammal Department from 1985 to 1994, during which time she earned her Master's degree from Fordham University. She is currently a doctoral candidate at Fordham University. In 1994-5, with her husband, Scott Silver, she spent 16 months in Belize doing her field work studying the black howler monkeys that have been translocated to the Cockscomb Basin Wildlife Sanctuary.

Amy Piel, originally from Wyoming, studied French and Art at the University of Wyoming. She plans to begin work next year on a. Bachelor of Fine Arts degree at the University of Montana. She is currently living and working in Yellowstone National Park.

Pedro Pixabaj graduated from Ecumenical College Sixth Form in May, 1995, with an Associate Degree in General Studies. He began working in the Black Howler Monkey Project in the CBWS in August, 1995. He also works with the phenology assessment and environmental education in the Sanctuary.

Emiliano Pop was born in San Antonio in the Toledo District of Belize and moved to Maya Center with his family where he was educated. He has been involved in the project to reintroduce black howler monkeys into the Cockscomb Basin Wildlife Sanctuary and is currently tracking the monkeys.

Ignacio Pop lived in San Antonio in the Toledo District of Belize until several families moved to Alabama and subsequently to Maya Center. When Alan Rabinowitz came to do his research, he and his family were living in Quam Bank, so they helped him in many ways and found a prominent place in the book. Ignacio and his son, Pedro, were the first wardens of the CBWS. Ignacio continues in that position today.

Osmany Salas has a BSc degree in Biology and Mathematics from Regis University in Denver, Colorado. Since 1990 he has been the Protected Areas Manager for the Belize Audubon Society.

Ernesto Saqui was born in San Antonio in the Toledo District of Belize. He completed primary school in his village and was attending high school in Punta Gorda when his family moved to the Stann Creek District, eventually settling in Maya Center. He became the first teacher in their new village, and then was given the opportunity to finish his education at Ecumenical College in

Dangriga. After four years as a trained teacher in Mango Creek, he became the Park Director of the Cockscomb Basin Wildlife Sanctuary in 1987, a position which he continues to hold. He has attended numerous training workshops, including a four-month internship in Wildlife Management at the Hawk Mountain Sanctuary in Kempton, Pennsylvania in 1989. In 1985 he was first elected as Maya Center Village Council Chairman and has been reelected ever since.

Hermelindo Saqui was born in San Antonio in the Toledo District of Belize and moved to Maya Center with his family. He was a warden in the Cockscomb Basin Wildlife Sanctuary and worked for three years tracking the reintroduced black howler monkeys.

Scott C. Silver was born and raised in New York City and earned the Bachelor's degree in Zoology at the State University of New York at Oswego. From 1984 - 1993 he worked at the Bronx Zoo in both the Mammals and Education Departments. He is now a doctoral candidate at Fordham University. He and his wife, Linde Ostro, first came to Belize on vacation in 1990. He assisted with the first translocation of the monkeys in 1992 and returned in 1994 with his wife for their doctoral fieldwork on "The Ecological Effects of Translocation of Black Howler Monkeys."

Contributor Index

Authors

Dorothy Beveridge 265-96
James Beveridge 151-75
Katherine M. Emmons 31, 35-68, 89-112, 125-49, 151-75, 177-86,
    187-246, 249-56, 265-96
Robert H. Horwich 69-80, 81-88, 89-112, 113-24
James Kamstra 1-7, 35-68, 125-49, 297-309
Fred Koontz 113-24
Judy Lumb 9-25, 35-68, 69-80, 89-112, 113-24, 249-56, 257-63, 265-96
Timothy McCarthy 89-112, 297-8, 307-9
Jan Meerman 177-86, 249-56, 307-9
Linde Ostro 113-24
Pedro Pixabaj 113-24
Emiliano Pop 113-24
Ignacio Pop 17-20
Ernesto Saqui 25-9, 113-24, 249-56, 257-63, 265-96
Hermelindo Saqui 113-24
Scott C. Silver 35-68, 113-24

Artists and Photographers

James Beveridge 4, 21(bottom), 49, 54, 66, 70, 72, 82, 84, 85, 87, 114,
    150-67, 171, 173, 251, 286(top), 289(top)
Ed Boles 102, 129, 140
Robin Brockett 61, 107
Paula DeGiorgis Cover Painting, 69, 80, 91, 180, 181
Terry Lawson Dunn 35, 68, 136, 142, 177(top), 186
Katherine M. Emmons 9, 33, 46, 47(top), 60, 64, 98, 103, 104, 128, 130,
    132, 134, 138, 139, 148, 151, 175, 177(bottom), 179, 189, 199, 201,
    204, 205, 207, 220, 223, 225, 246
Robert H. Horwich 81, 88, 109, 214
James Kamstra xiv, 2-3, 16(top), 34, 37, 38, 39, 43, 47(bottom), 168
Charles Koontz 121, 264, 272, 280, 282, 289, 290
Judy Lumb xiv, 1, 7, 8, 16(bottom), 21(top right), 23, 30, 44, 45, 52, 56,
    58, 59, 76, 116, 125, 149, 248, 249, 256-85, 289(bottom), 290, 296
Amy Piel 89, 92, 94, 95, 99, 101, 106, 112, 113, 124, 210
Osmany Salas 286(bottom), 291

Index

317

water tie-tie 63, 288
water vine 63, 288
Waterfall Trail 61, 121-4, 195, 284-7
watershed 197-8, 244
waterthrush, Louisiana 305
    northern 305
Watson's fruit-eating bat 297
Watt, Melanie 22
waxwing, cedar 304
wedge-billed woodcreeper 143, 302
wedge-tailed sabrewing 301
wee wee ants 179-80, 276, 282
West Basin 4-5, 14, 36, 38
Westby, Charles 11
western red bat 298
Westrom, Wendy 117
whipsnake, tropical 167, 308
whiptail, barred 309
    Central American 309
white hawk 132, 300
white mahogany 63
white maya 57
white-bellied emerald 138, 302
white-bellied wren 304
white-breasted wood-wren 304
white-collared manakin 144-5, 303
white-collared seedeater 306
white-collared swift 137, 301
white-crowned parrot 136, 301
white-eyed vireo 304
white-fronted parrot 301
white-lipped frog 308
white-lipped peccary 50, 106, 275, 298
white-necked jacobin 138, 302
white-necked puffbird 302
white-nosed coati 101, 298
white-tailed deer 108, 298
white-tailed kite 300
white-throated thrush 304
white-tipped dove 301
white-vented euphonia 305
white-whiskered puffbird 302
white-winged becard 145, 303
white-winged tanager 305
wild banana 48
wildlife 245
Wildlife Conservation Society 114
wildlife protection 27-31, 265
wildlife signs 258
Williams, Norris 26
Wilson, E. O. 177, 229
Wilson's warbler 305
Wilsonia citrina 305
Wilsonia pusilla 305
wishwilly 159, 308
wolfspiders 183
wood stork 300
wood thrush 304
wood-quail, spotted 301
wood-rail, grey-necked 126, 301
wood-warblers 147, 284, 304-5
wood-wren, white-breasted 304
woodcreeper, barred 302
    ivory-billed 143, 302
    olivaceous 143, 302

woodcreeper, ruddy 143, 302
    streak-headed 302
    tawny-winged 302
    wedge-billed 143, 302
woodcreepers 125, 143, 281, 284, 302
woodpecker, black-cheeked 143, 302
    chestnut-colored 143, 302
    golden-olive 143, 302
    lineated 143, 302
    pale-billed 143, 302
    smoky-brown 143, 302
woodpeckers 142, 302
wooly false vampire bat 91, 297
World Wildlife Fund 19, 22, 266
worm-eating warbler 305
wowla 164-6, 308
wren, band-backed 126, 304
    house 304
    spot-breasted 304
    white-bellied 304
wrens 304

X
xa'a yil ha' 9
Xenarthra 92, 298
xenops, plain 144, 302
Xenops minutus 144, 302
Xiphorhynchus flavigaster 143, 302
Xylopia frutescens 38

Y
yellow tree frog 153, 308
yellow warbler 304
yellow-backed oriole 148, 305
yellow-bellied elaenia 303
yellow-bellied flycatcher 127, 303
yellow-bellied turtle 174, 308
yellow-bellied tyrannulet 145, 303
yellow-billed cacique 147, 305
yellow-breasted chat 305
yellow-crowned night heron 300
yellow-green vireo 127, 304
yellow-olive flycatcher 145, 303
yellow-rumped warbler 304
yellow-spotted night lizard 162, 309
yellow-tailed oriole 148, 305
yellow-throated vireo 304
yellow-throated euphonia 305
yellow-throated warbler 304
yellow-winged tanager 149, 305
yellowjaw tommygoff 171, 308
yellowthroat, common 305
    grey-crowned 126, 147, 305
yemeri 38, 63
Yucatan black howler monkey 95-6, 298
Yucatan squirrel 97

Z
Zanthoxylum kellermani 38, 62, 283
Zarhynchus wagleri 305
zoos 31